TIP AND THE GIPPER

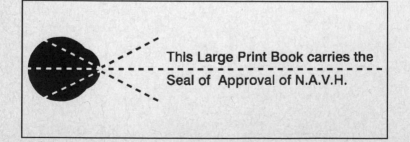

This Large Print Book carries the
Seal of Approval of N.A.V.H.

TIP AND THE GIPPER

WHEN POLITICS WORKED

CHRIS MATTHEWS

THORNDIKE PRESS
A part of Gale, Cengage Learning

GALE
CENGAGE Learning·

Detroit • New York • San Francisco • New Haven, Conn • Waterville, Maine • London

GALE
CENGAGE Learning®

LIBRARY OF CONGRESS CATALOGING-IN-PUBLICATION DATA

Matthews, Christopher, 1945–
    Tip and the Gipper : when politics worked / by Chris Matthews. — Large print edition.
        pages cm
    ISBN 978-1-4104-6416-3 (hardcover) — ISBN 1-4104-6416-4 (hardcover)
    1. United States—Politics and government—1981–1989. 2. Reagan, Ronald. 3. O'Neill, Tip. I. Title.
    E876.M375 2013
    973.927—dc23   2013034944

Published in 2013 by arrangement with Simon & Schuster, Inc.

Printed in Mexico
1 2 3 4 5 6 7 17 16 15 14 13

Dedicated to the memory of:
L. Kirk O'Donnell
and
Michael K. Deaver

CONTENTS

"There is nothing I love
as much as a good fight."
— FRANKLIN D. ROOSEVELT

PREFACE

Visitors to Washington are taken with its quiet grandeur. Just like they saw in the postcards, they witness the beauty of the Mall stretching from one horizon to the other. They see the Capitol itself up there on its hill, pay respects to the beloved Lincoln sitting high in his memorial, and gaze like children at the tall, clean obelisk honoring the city's namesake.

The truth is, no loud commerce or clanking industry disturbs the peace; no smokestacks darken the skies even in the distance. Tourists, generally speaking, are respectful rather than boisterous. Even the bureaucracy, busy along its daytime corridors, fails to shatter the stillness. Yet for all the statues and monuments loyally attesting to what's gone before, Washington is very much a living city.

And what makes it so is its jamboree of human voices engaged in discourse, debates, discussion, argument, compromise, leaks, gossip, criticism, and commentary, not to mention speechmaking. Undeniably the city's signature output, it's been this way since General Washington and Pierre L'Enfant together on horseback envisioned our new nation's capital in the late eighteenth century. It's a place where talking matters, and even more important, who's talking to whom.

Since the moment of its creation the city has been marked in every era by voices. Year in and year out, the questions they hurl into the air lie at the center of the American conversation, and this ritual of the voices is what animates our government.

And always there come the responding questions from the country: Shall the people hold sway? Will the winning faction deliver on its promises? Will the losing faction give way? Will a divided electorate see a spirit of compromise? These are the recurring quandaries that separate action from stalemate, a working democracy from one seized by dysfunction.

The framers of the American Constitution, who also made Washington the capital, established two great offices. One is the president of the United States; the other, the Speaker of the House of Representatives. The role of the first is to lead the country; the province of the Speaker, through custom and his prerogative to set the House agenda, is to control the government's purse strings. Not a dollar can be allocated that the Congress hasn't guaranteed by law or specifically appropriated.

This historic arrangement makes simple human bargaining a central task for the two leaders. The check-and-balance relationship between president and Speaker can either propel the government forward or not. Put plainly, they either talk, or they don't. When they join in alliance, the government rumbles ahead. When their interests collide, something's got to give. Either one side prevails, or a compromise is struck. Otherwise, the republic stalls.

This means that, for the Constitution to work, the two must be open to the larger picture, to resist base obstructionism, to accommodate differences for the common good. Historically, this coupling of president and Speaker has been a tricky one that encourages a choreography both quick-footed and wary.

I was witness, with eye and heart, to one of the most celebrated of these pairings. The time was the 1980s, the president was Ronald Reagan, and the Speaker was

Thomas P. O'Neill, Jr. Both were Irish-Americans. Both men were larger than life. The former was a California conservative Republican, elected in a landslide. He arrived in Washington to his very first job there, walking into the White House on Inauguration Day 1981. The latter was a New England liberal Democrat, a hardened, blooded Washington veteran who'd entered the House of Representatives in 1953 and had spent the twenty-eight years since finessing and cajoling his way to the top of the Hill.

The outsider and the insider: these two moved together in a remarkable, if sometimes rough, tandem. They argued mightily, each man belting out his separate, deeply cherished political philosophy — but then they would, both together, bow to the country's judgment. Decisions were made, action taken, outcomes achieved. They honored the voters, respected the other's role. Each liked to beat the other guy, not sabotage him.

During this period, government met its deadlines. Members of Congress listened and acted. Debates led to solutions. Shutdowns were averted. What needed to proceed did, and America's citizens were the beneficiaries.

Ronald Reagan and Tip O'Neill were definite political rivals. Just not always.

People in politics, like everyone else, like to talk about how different things were in the old days. They point to the relationship between President Reagan and Tip O'Neill — old-school guys, only two years apart in age, who were so different yet not, on some level, that different — whose commitment to comity came out of their shared integrity. They disagreed on the role of government, knew it, admitted it face-to-face. But they put concentrated effort into trying to get along even as they challenged each other. Why, we wonder, can't it be that way again?

Why won't our leaders work to accommodate each other, employing civility as they cooperate to accomplish goals in the country's best interests? Why must we continue to suffer their relentless gumming up of the works? What in our national character, in the ways we choose to deal with one another and respect different viewpoints, has changed so since the days of Reagan and O'Neill? How can we win back the faith that our republic is working?

Today we have government by tantrum. Rather than true debate, we get the daily threat of filibuster. Shutdowns are engineered as standard procedure. In place of hard-earned statecraft we witness new tricks of the trade. Presidents make "recess" appointments to end-run Senate consent. Tea Partyers in the House of Representatives act as if voting "Nay" constitutes twenty-first-century governance. Democrats in the Senate, for a while, refused to approve the annual budget — withholding consent to skip the embarrassment of admitting dire fiscal reality. Brinkmanship grabs today's headlines even as public faith dies a little with each disappointing eleventh-hour deal.

What's to be done? I truly believe it doesn't have to be this way. And the story I'm about to tell of these two extraordinary figures will show you why. My goal is to bring you the true account of what took place. Our country is less in need of a myth than a real-life account of one imperfect leader dealing with another. It serves no purpose in this time of habitual conflict to spin a tale of happy harmony; far better to illustrate how two very different figures managed to make politics work.

Ronald Reagan was dismissed by his enemies as a Hollywood lightweight, Tip O'Neill as a Tammany-style ward heeler. I refuse to add a third cartoon to those two. The credit for their civility goes not to their off-duty socializing and shared Irish stories:

it was their joint loyalty to American self-government. Tip's oldest son, an elected politician himself, put it best in a 2012 New York Times column: "What both men deplored more than each other's political philosophy was stalemate, and a country that was so polarized by ideology and party politics that it could not move forward. There were tough words and important disagreements . . . yet a stronger commitment to getting things done." They respected elections, accepted who had won, knew that duty came with office. It's all true.

I was there.

"Jody's a soldier."
Chief speechwriter Rick Hertzberg's final salute to Jimmy Carter's
finest warrior. When all was lost, we still had to face the dawn.

Chapter One:
Death of a Presidency

"Governor . . . there ain't
no *tonight* tonight."
— Jody Powell, President Carter's
press secretary, election eve 1980

When we switched from Air Force One to the presidential helicopter that election morning, I couldn't help thinking about the vanquished candidate sitting right there ahead of me in *Marine One.* He looked so rigid as to be frozen, or even, as it gruesomely occurred to me at the time, to be in the early stages of rigor mortis. Yet at that moment, he was still the president of the United States and so, despite everything, was being briefed by staff on matters unrelated to the situation he was now having to face. Couldn't such a business-as-usual exercise have at least been put off, if nothing else, for decency's sake? As I've often told people over the years, that helicopter ride into Plains was like being inside a giant bird, one that was dying.

As we headed low over the swirling grass, the reality of small-town Georgia suddenly came into view. Then a scratchy voice sounded over Secret Service chief Jerry Parr's walkie-talkie: "Dancer's on the ground." Mrs. Carter was there, waiting. Plains was where they were from, and it was where they would soon be headed back. On the ground, I walked past the train depot where, four years before, Carter had appeared on the platform to be applauded and cheered after winning the presidency. Passing the little station building, through the window I glimpsed two people alone in the room — Jimmy and Rosalynn. He'd asked to tell her himself. Just the two of them were now standing there. The long journey he'd convinced her to take with him was ending in defeat.

There were those in the Carter White House who believed that Ronald Reagan — a popular governor of California who'd made his name and fame originally in the movies, and later on TV — was the "best" Republican candidate our man could face in his reelection campaign. To them, Reagan seemed a handsome, likable lightweight, reliant on feel-good rhetoric and upbeat platitudes. However, by the fall of 1980, with the race in full swing, the Carter staffers saw the exorbitant price of this mistake.

For my part, I was about to experience from a punishing vantage point just how hard it was to beat Ronald Reagan.

It's not that there hadn't been warnings from those who'd previously made the mistake of underestimating him. Former California governor Pat Brown, denied a third State House term in 1966 by a Reagan landslide, had dropped in at the White House back in the spring specifically to pass on those lessons he'd learned the hard way. "You're going to say he's an actor and it won't work," Brown explained to Carter communications director Gerald Rafshoon. "That he's not really that smart and it won't work; that he's lazy and it won't work."

What he was describing with earned exasperation was the difficulty of getting any contempt, scorn, insult, or even past position to stick to Reagan. Under attack, the man was a master. However, having seen him lose the Republican nomination to Gerald Ford only four years earlier, we knew Ronald Reagan wasn't invincible. The trouble in the fall of 1980 was, he could well be something far worse: inevitable. The main asset any Republican candidate brought to this race for 1600 Pennsylvania Avenue was that he *wasn't* Jimmy Carter.

Reagan had already proved to be more than that. Beaten by George H. W. Bush in the Iowa Republican caucus in late January 1980, he rocketed back five weeks later with a decisive win in New Hampshire. There he not only disarmed the local voters but captivated the entire country when he sharply rebuked the moderator of the candidates' debate who'd asked to have Reagan's microphone switched off during a dispute. "I am paying for this microphone, Mr. Green," he reminded the fellow. Which was quite true — even if the man's name was Breen, not Green — since the Reagan campaign treasury was indeed footing the bill for the event.

It was the perfect moment for a man who'd picked and long perfectly played the role of a lifetime: the heroic citizen-politician. Yet his nifty retort up in New Hampshire also made for an homage to Reagan's own Hollywood past, appropriating brilliantly a line from Frank Capra's 1948 political drama, *State of the Union*. At the end of the movie, Spencer Tracy's character, vying for the Republican presidential nomination, must also fight for his right to speak. "Don't you shut me off, I'm paying for this broadcast," he threatens.

Still, despite such warnings as Pat Brown's, Carter staffers continued to pin their hopes on Reagan securing his party's nod. With his right-wing foreign policy, his old notions about making Social Security contributions "voluntary," and his early crusading against Medicare, Ronald Reagan appeared a more obviously vulnerable target than a serious contender like Bush or Gerald Ford (had he jumped into the fray). Looking back, I'd have to say certain Carter people were in a state of denial as we watched this guy keep on coming.

Reagan's superbly delivered quip, however, wasn't the only legacy of his New Hampshire victory. On the eve of that triumph he made the decision to reshape himself politically. Choosing a new campaign manager, conservative Irish-Catholic William J. Casey, who headed the OSS — the predecessor to the CIA — in Europe during World War II, he moved his base of operation off the West Coast. The man who spent his free time with the newly wealthy of Southern California was going gritty, forging a connection with the kinds of voters he'd not previously courted. Whatever roles Reagan had chosen to play in recent years, on and off the screen, he was now pushing further back into his life's repertoire.

It had been in 1940 that Reagan, then twenty-nine years old and only three years into his movie career, had been cast as George "the Gipper" Gipp in the film *Knute Rockne — All American.* It was the part of the stricken Notre Dame football hero whose famed deathbed words, "Win just one for the Gipper," would years later rally Notre Dame to a comeback victory. It now offered the presidential hopeful an evocative nickname. It would be one that spelled votes.

Forty years later, the surviving "Gipper" began aiming his campaign directly at those disaffected Democrats — the Irish and Italians and Polish-Americans, and other hardworking, proud, but frustrated citizens who just didn't "get" Jimmy Carter, who were furious at the humiliation of the Iranian hostage crisis, enraged at our flags being burned and trampled on by bearded militants from a place we didn't want to hear about — who were more than ready to hear his message.

Reinventing himself, Reagan was no longer the Hollywood guy, the hunk in swim trunks or jodhpurs. Instead, he'd morphed into if not quite an Irishman's Irishman then certainly a recognizable fellow ethnic. He was entitled, of course, being descended on his father's side from immigrants who'd left County Tipperary behind in the mid-nineteenth century. But it also amounted to more than that. Like the cowboy stars who *became* their characters — John Wayne, Roy Rogers, Gene Autry — Reagan would smoothly sand over where reality began and scripts left off. Now he wore the aura of a Notre Dame hero, though one who'd never actually attended Notre Dame, and became a beacon to its "subway alumni" across the country. They, plus millions of other folks just like them, soon would be known by quite a different name: "Reagan Democrats."

Along with the other Carter speechwriters, I watched Reagan dominate the Republican convention that summer. You couldn't help admiring a guy who would come up that summer with such a neatly confounding bait-and-switch as this: "The president lately has been saying that I am irresponsible. And you know, I'll admit to that if he'll confess he's responsible." What's the answer to that? You only dig yourself in deeper with every attempt.

And not only was Reagan, once anointed

his party's choice, putting the blame for the country's seemingly sorry state on the man in the White House — which is standard operating procedure for any opposition candidate — but there was something about his reach that struck me as truly audacious. What he seemed to be implying was that everything wrong in the world was now the fault of Jimmy Carter. His taking such an approach forced his rival, for his part, to defend absolutely everything voters didn't like — *absolutely everything* — beginning, not ending, with the humiliation of having our flag trampled on every night by scruffy, hateful Iranians.

Reagan had a mischievous way of sticking Carter with this burden of all things bad. "Can anyone look at the record of this administration and say, 'Well done'? Can anyone compare the state of our economy when the Carter administration took office with where we are today and say, 'Keep up the good work'? Can anyone look at our reduced standing in the world today and say, 'Let's have four more years of this'?" He was forcing voters to imagine themselves as cheerleaders for a gridiron squad that again and again kept fumbling the pigskin.

Throughout the summer, the polls remained too close to draw any conclusions.

26

Then, on Labor Day, came the first sign of real trouble. My wife, Kathleen — we'd gotten married that June — and I were spending that holiday Monday enjoying Georgetown. Toward evening we stopped by a Wisconsin Avenue college bar to check the news. I'd written Carter's big campaign kickoff speech, which he'd given earlier that day at a picnic he was attending down in Alabama. After he'd read my draft, he told me right there in the office — talk about an unusual occurrence! — how much he liked it, making me eager to see how it played on the networks. Suddenly on the TV screen above the bar appeared a tanned Ronald Reagan looking happy and relaxed, in his shirtsleeves. Standing, attractively windswept by the harbor breezes, the Statue of Liberty to his back, he spoke about our country and the hopes it stood for. His punch line was that the Democrats had betrayed those hopes.

"I'm here *because* it is the home of Democrats," he said in explaining his presence in Liberty State Park. "In this country," he went on confidently, "there are millions of Democrats who are just as unhappy with the way things are as all the rest of us." He was celebrating those millions of immigrants that New York's harbor has welcomed over

27

so many decades. "They didn't ask what this country could do for them, but what they could do to make this refuge the greatest home of freedom in history. . . . Today a president of the United States would have us believe that dream is over, or at least in need of change."

Ronald Reagan grasped the deep-running need shared by Americans to feel positive about their country and themselves. He himself believed completely in the brighter, shinier world of which he spoke, and his conviction was infectious. Jimmy Carter, a decent and honest man, had notoriously gone on national television the year before, offering a somber speech that faced the present and the future squarely but was barren of the blue skies Reagan now reminded Americans they had coming as their birthright.

Carter was never to live down the fallout from that speech, and with a reelection campaign looming on the horizon such a downbeat address had been far from strategic. Carter certainly had ample cause to share his concerns — about energy consumption, and each citizen's personal role in energy conservation — with his constituents. Yet he broached these subjects without suspecting how unpopular they would eventually make him, convinced that telling difficult truths would itself rouse the country to its time and its historic tasks. During that broadcast, now known as the "malaise speech," Jimmy Carter hadn't actually even used the word *malaise,* yet in speaking to the press, his pollster-advisor Patrick Caddell had framed the speech's themes that way, thus tarring Carter with its doleful stoicism.

Jimmy Carter was, it turns out, too much the smartest guy in a small town, a governor whose great virtue back in 1976 had been that he wasn't incumbent Gerald Ford and that he was untainted by proximity to Nixon, Watergate, or Washington. His current rival, also originally a small-town boy, and a two-term governor, appeared to be a figure out of a different solar system, and not only because he'd been a Hollywood star. The much-anticipated, long-awaited debate between the two, when it finally came, took place in the political eleventh hour, just a week before Election Day. It happened in Cleveland, and was a game-changer, though not to the incumbent's advantage.

By the next afternoon after that debate, traveling with the president I could assess the very visible lack of excitement at upstate

New York Democratic rallies. It amounted to negative reinforcement, telling me what I didn't want to know about the results. Next to Ronald Reagan, Jimmy Carter hadn't, with all his sincerity and earnestness, been able to seize a single advantage during the debate. There, at the Cleveland Convention Center, it had been Ronnie's evening from beginning to end. He'd been calm, confident, and even a bit condescending.

This time, the line of his that passed into history was the humorously reproachful "There you go again." Triggered by prim Carter statements characterizing Reagan's sometime stands on Social Security, Medicare, and the possibility of universal national health insurance, it said nothing and everything at the same time. Just four words, and it was all he needed to convey his message when it came to Carter's own problems. The challenger was putting the incumbent in his place, and the effect was devastating.

For Jimmy Carter, Iran had become a political wild card. When, at daybreak a year earlier, the American Embassy in Tehran had been stormed by militant students, with more than fifty diplomats and staff taken hostage, his calm handling of the crisis had initially brought strong public support. The effect, in this early period after the standoff began, was to make him invulnerable to the challenge to his renomination posed early on from the left by Senator Edward Kennedy. But as the months began turning into an entire year and the hostages remained in the control of their captors, the stagnant situation and the American powerlessness it came to symbolize became a reflection on Carter himself.

It was hard to argue otherwise. The fact is, the Iranian government had given its support to an act of war committed against the United States. According to the State Department, "any attack on an embassy is considered an attack on the country it represents." What could be clearer? For most Americans, the situation in Tehran was just one more example — along with rising OPEC oil prices and the then increasing domination of the American auto market by Japanese competition — of how our country was getting kicked around. But if there was an alternative to Carter's course it wasn't visible then and hasn't revealed itself since.

The final hope came in the early hours of Sunday morning, before the 1980 election. We had spent all Saturday campaigning in Texas, ending for the night in Chicago after a brief stopover in Milwaukee. Near midnight a local congressman had even convinced the president to make an appearance at a large Italian-American event, featuring sports heroes like Joe DiMaggio.

It was a short night. Around 2 a.m. I was awakened by a noise in the hall. Recognizing the clipped, military inflection of the Secret Service, I knew something was up. I heard someone say "Deacon," the president's code name. I called the Situation Room on my white "signal" phone. The woman who answered connected me quickly to the National Security Council staff. Then the good news: what I heard sounded like the hostages in Tehran were close to release. As I listened, it struck me the Ayatollah Khomeini's latest conditions were no more exacting than those we'd already said we could meet.

Once again, the same menacing wild card was back at the top of the deck. And, again, Jimmy Carter had no choice but to draw it. If he could manage to get the hostages out, he might still win reelection. If not, he probably couldn't. And everyone in the country understood that this was so.

Tragically for Carter, when later that Sunday the terms being demanded by Tehran became clear, the conditions that could determine his political fate, the news wasn't good. All along, the squabbling mullahs had thrown stumbling blocks in the way and now they were at it again. The hostages would not be getting out before Election Day. When President Carter went on television that night to release the news, I watched and heard victory escaping, literally, through the airwaves. What I wished at the time was that he'd have talked tougher, showing himself to be righteously furious at the Iranians for daring to mess with an American election. But I was only a speechwriter, not the man at the head of the country. His instincts of caution — pure Jimmy Carter, when you came right down to it — were clearly defensible for a president with the lives of captured citizens at risk. Yet I dreaded what the impact would be on Tuesday.

We awoke Monday, the final day before the election, to a speechwriters' crisis. The index cards containing Carter's election eve talking points — dictated to us by pollster Caddell and delivered, we thought, to the hallway outside press secretary Jody Powell's office, had not gotten to him. Hendrik "Rick" Hertzberg, the chief speechwriter, had to transcribe them from the backup copies on Air Force One after takeoff.

I could see the tension, exhaustion, and looming despair on the faces around me.

The major polls — Gallup and the *New York Times*/CBS — were too close to call. The one countervailing red flag — and it was bright crimson — was the fact that Lou Harris, who'd made his name polling presidential elections since he'd worked for Jack Kennedy's campaign back in 1960, had staked his reputation on Ronald Reagan as the winner.

At the first stop — in Akron, Ohio — Carter got out there and ramped up his attack on Reagan. First, he hit him for daring to quote Franklin Roosevelt; next, he belted him for saying "the New Deal was based on fascism." Then he bashed him for a whole laundry list, from opposing the minimum wage to failing to back "every single nuclear arms limitation agreement since the Second World War." After that, he swung at him for labeling Medicare "socialism and communism."

And once he'd gone this far, why not go all the way? So he did. He pronounced the campaign's "overriding issue" to be "peace and the control of nuclear weapons and preventing the spread of nuclear weapons to terrorist countries." The question facing the voter — he clearly implied — was peace or war. He was on one side, Carter made clear, while Ronald Reagan, his opponent, was on the other. The choice, for right-thinking voters, he implied, was an obvious one.

This was precisely what Caddell had advised against. The goal for Carter's last day of campaigning was to ignore Reagan and come across as "calm and presidential" in light of the latest news from Iran. Here was Carter making the explosive charge that his opponent's election would mean "war."

At this point I was listening to the president while standing in the shadow of Air Force One. Standing nearby was Steve Weisman, a *New York Times* reporter and a friend, who saw the pain cross my face. He wanted to know what was bothering me. Rick Hertzberg, alert to the possibility of a story developing in which a White House speechwriter is revealed as depressed by his boss's performance, pulled me aside. "Don't show your feelings like that," he cautioned.

Once the president returned to Air Force One, Jody Powell, his close aide of many years, gently pointed out that he might be overdoing it. "Some people seem to think you might have gone too heavy on Reagan," he pointed out. "I think they like it," Carter replied mildly. "It turns them on."

From Akron we flew to Granite City, then to East St. Louis and Springfield, Missouri.

35

After this we doubled back to Detroit. It had become clear that the only places where Carter was drawing an emotional reaction were African-American communities. I'll in fact never forget a previous appearance at a black church in northern New Jersey and the singing of "Amazing Grace." But now, at each stop, Carter simply did what every candidate before him had done when facing Reagan: he attacked him for being too far right, too in over his head for the big time, too extreme to be trusted with nuclear weapons. What else was there to do, even though we had been warned by Reagan's last electoral victim that these particular charges wouldn't work?

To our dismay, at least one network news program, CBS's, led that night with the one-year anniversary of the hostage-taking, not the next day's crucial election. Carter, receiving an update on the campaign coverage when he returned to the plane from the Detroit stop, was chiefly concerned not with the network accounts Rick replayed to him but with a piece of news his pollster had just given him. Out there in America, many voters were not even *aware,* despite all the drama of the weekend, that the hostages might soon be freed.

As we flew from Detroit to Portland,

across those vast stretches of seemingly unending plains and then abruptly over the Rockies, someone asked why we weren't stopping to campaign. "Because there's not a single state we're flying over that we have a chance of carrying," said domestic policy advisor David Rubenstein, voicing the awful truth.

When we got to Seattle, our last stop, Carter delivered his best speech of the campaign by far. I think it helped that we were in an airport hangar, which echoed his every word. With ten thousand people screaming, their voices resounding through the rafters, he was on fire. He had the rhythm; he had the audience. "How many of you believe we're going to whip the Republicans tomorrow?" Huge applause. "You don't know what it does to a man who's been campaigning since early this morning — I got up at five o'clock Washington time. When I asked Jody Powell, 'Where do we spend the night?' he said, 'Governor, this evening there ain't no *tonight* tonight.' "

Back on Air Force One, Carter joined us for drinks, a rare occurrence. He even invited the press up from the back of the cabin to join in. I couldn't help noticing that the back of his hand showed a mass of cuts made by the many rings and watches of the men and women in all those receiving lines. But it was all about to end. The next stop was to be Plains, Georgia, where Jimmy Carter would cast his own vote.

Then the news — dire and definite — came. While I sat with the press, worried that a few reporters were busily taking notes under the table during what was supposed to be an off-the-record chat with Carter, Jody and Rick went up to the front of the plane, to the president's cabin. The time was now 4 a.m. back in Washington. Three of his top advisors — Caddell, Chief of Staff Hamilton Jordan, and Jerry Rafshoon — were at the White House and had just minutes before received the latest poll results.

President Carter, Caddell told Jody, was going down by a landslide. All the neck-and-neck status, so recently reported, had been undone by the obstructionism of the factions in Tehran. After teasing us with the possibility of a settlement, the Iranians' demands seemed unchanged to the voters. We'd been taken for a ride again, one more time.

Carter was about to get the news. Returning to his cabin, he grinned when he first saw Jody and Rick. Still in an exuberant mood, still high from his thunderous Seattle reception, he had no way of suspecting the devastating news he was about to hear. "Is that Pat? Let me talk to him," he said. Then, with the phone at his ear, his face collapsed. I've often wondered if he knew in those closing days and hours that this was coming. Now it had.

Jody, seeing his boss of so many years in pain, now moved quickly and surely. He understood exactly what needed to be done and instructed Rick accordingly. "The presidency is gone," he told him somberly. "We want to try to keep from losing too much of the Senate and House." The mission now entrusted to Rick and me was to write a speech for Carter to use in Plains that would cool the country down, ease the hate, and attempt to limit Democratic losses. "Jody's a soldier," Rick said of the young Georgian who'd been with Carter from the start and now was guarding him to the end.

The memory of what transpired over the next several hours, as the plane headed southeast to Georgia, is indelible for me. There we were, a small band of defeated warriors huddled together in a snug, small room high above the American landscape, working resolutely to produce the words and phrases that would help make the best of a terrible situation.

Late that morning, back in Washington finally, I went out to cast my own vote. As I got to my polling station I remember there was a guy racing angrily into it. In my mind, whether it was true or not — maybe he was just having a bad morning — I saw him as one of the millions of irate citizens piling on, joining the massacre. His image burned itself into my mind's eye and became a sort of collector's item, a bit of unwanted memorabilia, from those last weeks of the campaign. Here was a voter, it seemed to me, so mad at Carter he intended to vote straight Republican with the intention of flushing the thirty-ninth president out of politics and out of his life once and for all.

That evening, I watched Carter show up ahead of time, well before he was expected, at the Sheraton Washington ballroom to concede defeat. It was the earliest concession speech by any American presidential candidate since 1904 and it would wind up costing several West Coast Democrats their seats. Stories would grow of people leaving the voting lines on word that the president had given up the fight. Nevertheless, I always assumed his hurry wasn't so much selfish on Carter's part as it was self-protective. He was exhausted. If he'd gotten any more exhausted, he wouldn't have been able to control his emotions, his very *self.*

The next morning, Kathleen and I woke up, had breakfast, got into our car, and began driving north toward Pennsylvania, with no particular destination in mind. What I didn't know then, as we hit the highway just to get away, was that the fierce battle I'd just witnessed, played out across the entire American landscape, was just a prelude.

Those two years with the Peace Corps in Swaziland changed my life. They got me off the academic track and into politics.

Chapter Two:
Starting Out

"Any schoolboy could see that man as a force must be measured by motion from a fixed point."
— Henry Adams,
The Education of Henry Adams

When you visit Capitol Hill as a tourist, the men and women working in the offices appear to have always belonged there. They make you think of soldiers manning a citadel: they're friendly but continually on guard. You're the outsider; they're the presiding officialdom; and the dividing line is clear. That's certainly how it struck me on long-ago high school trips to Washington.

It's different, though, once you become an insider. When you've passed through the gate and find yourself admitted to the inner sanctums, as I was in my mid-twenties, you never again refer to it as "the government." You realize all too quickly the distinct separateness of each congressional office, the jealousy with which each and every Senate staffer guards his or her position. You learn the same is true at the numerous executive agencies. You grasp this fast or you don't survive long.

I know, too, from experience that once you're inside Washington politics, in the thick of things, you have a far different sense of what goes on. You've discovered how the engine works because you're one of its parts. For the decade after returning home in 1971 from the Peace Corps in Africa, I was deeply involved with the day-to-day reality of the actual enterprise of governance. I worked as a staffer for a president and, before that, for a pair of senators — and was proud of the fact. Call that period of my life my apprenticeship. Those jobs taught and broadened me. The pace of the work was unrelenting; it absorbed me entirely.

My grandest political job — the inspiration for this book — was in every way a dream one. Even now I still have trouble believing how incredibly lucky I was. It was in 1981 that I was hired to be administrative assistant to the Speaker of the House, Thomas P. O'Neill, Jr. — better known as Tip — and soon found myself seated behind an imposing desk, suddenly more an insider in those marble hallways than I ever had fantasized.

Here's the story of how I got there.

In the late winter of 1971, I found myself returning to the United States after living and working for two years as a Peace Corps volunteer in the Kingdom of Swaziland. Turning down posts elsewhere, I'd been seized by the allure of Africa, jumping at the chance to engage actively there in economic development. It was the Vietnam era and I saw volunteering for the Peace Corps as a positive role I could take on for my country in the world. I'd majored in economics at Holy Cross, had gotten a full-ride scholarship to the University of North Carolina for graduate school, where I had spent the winter of 1967–68 as a devout supporter of antiwar presidential candidate Eugene McCarthy.

The notion of the Peace Corps appealed not only to my romantic idealism but my readiness to face a rite of passage. Who knows how these things are truly connected. My hunch is that the wild confidence I would now show — knocking on the doors of Capitol Hill offices where I knew no one — originated in that exhilarating period when I zipped around the back roads of southern Africa on a Suzuki 120, speaking my limited Zulu and trying to teach modern business methods to Swazi villagers at remote trading posts.

During a break from my job in Swaziland, I made my way, often hitchhiking, up through East Africa, with assorted adventures along the way. It was during a trip on the overnight Rhodesian Railways train from Lourenço Marques (now Maputo) in old Mozambique to Bulawayo that I stayed up enthralled by Ted Sorensen's memoir, *Kennedy*. I learned that he, at twenty-four, had been appointed, pretty much out of the blue in 1953, to be legislative assistant to the newly elected senator John F. Kennedy. Before this, the two hadn't really known each other, but JFK's hiring instincts proved impeccable. Sorensen, both as speechwriter and advisor, quickly revealed himself to be an indispensable player in his boss's sky-rocketing career.

It was heady stuff, reading such a thrilling firsthand account of faraway Washington and a young man's rise. On the other side of the world, I couldn't help wondering how I could manage to follow in his footsteps.

Along those lines I was greeted by a stroke of luck. A guy who had graduated before me from Holy Cross sent a letter describing his work for a United States senator in Washington. He told of being a "legislative assistant," the same title Sorensen held with Jack Kennedy. He included a giant detail that would give me confidence — he lacked a law degree. Suddenly a bar had been removed.

When I finished my Peace Corps tour and flew back to the United States there was snow on the ground. After a brief stop to see old friends down in Chapel Hill, I headed to Washington, D.C. There I began my quest for work in the Senate and House office buildings, and I had a ready answer for anyone asking what I wanted to be: "legislative assistant." It was the challenge I was daring myself to undertake. Yet, as I've said, I had no connections. All I possessed in the way of strategy was the notion of working my strengths. But what were they?

Since I'd just spent two years in Jack Kennedy's Peace Corps and, before that, had graduated from Holy Cross, the grand old Jesuit college in Worcester, Massachusetts, my first — I thought rather clever — idea was to make the rounds of the offices of every Irish-Catholic Democrat from the Northeast. Setting off earnestly, I spent a few weeks at this, focusing especially on members of the House Foreign Affairs

Committee. For a brief moment, I even had what looked to be the break of the century. A Foreign Affairs Committee member, an Irish-Catholic charmer, offered me a job at our first encounter. I was in! But then, a week later, to my disappointment, word from him reached me that "he couldn't work it out."

At first this was simply puzzling. But eventually I would learn that the FBI had been even more interested in him than I was, looking to get from him answers about reputed underworld connections. One concern was the body of a loan shark discovered in his basement. Call me a softy, but I thought then, and I think now, that he had wanted to spare me his emerging troubles.

With no other breaks coming my way, I can't say I wasn't getting discouraged, but I also wasn't giving up. Having worked my way through the Northeast Irish-Catholic congressional roster and finding no takers, I now showed up one afternoon in the offices of Senator Frank Moss, a Democrat from Utah. His administrative assistant — who would be called a "chief of staff" in today's Capitol Hill — made clear he liked me personally, as well as my Peace Corps experience, and not to mention my economics background. A former top aide to Senator Edward Kennedy and a devoted campaign lieutenant in Bobby Kennedy's 1968 presidential campaign, this fellow seemed to like my being Irish-Catholic as well as a Holy Cross grad from the Kennedys' home turf.

After setting me a task that served as a test, which I passed — it involved my explaining aspects of a murky tax law to an influential constituent — he came up with an offer of employment. My luck, it seemed, had turned. But the deal he came up with was far from what I'd envisioned. He explained that the only job he had available was that of a Capitol policeman. My face must have dropped. "It'll pay for the groceries," Moss's assistant assured me, recognizing my disappointment.

He was being practical, I realized, and it was, after all, a way in. So I said yes. The deal was, I'd spend the morning and early afternoon in the senator's office answering letters, frequently important ones. I was also given assignments to write brief speeches to be entered in the *Congressional Record.* Come mid-afternoon, I'd race over to the Capitol Building. After donning my uniform and buckling on my holster — I carried a Smith & Wesson .38 Police Special — I'd report for duty. My shift finished at eleven.

After three or four months doing this, I asked — insisted, really — to be made a full-time legislative assistant.

"It was Africa, wasn't it?" my County Antrim–born grandmom would later shrewdly observe, as she watched me adapt and begin my rise in the nation's capital. She knew, and, as I said, so did I.

I'd made the right decision. That brief period I spent working on the Capitol police force proved invaluable, giving me a perspective I'd not otherwise have known. I think that more so today, looking back. Most memorably, there were moments of absolute stillness, especially late in the evening, when the history of that extraordinary building was all mine. There were also encounters with colleagues I'll never forget. A fellow cop, a West Virginian named Leroy Taylor, one night posed me a question: "Chris," he said, "can you tell me why the little man loves his country?" As I wondered at the question itself, and why he was offering it, he explained it all with his answer. "Because it's all he's got," he said softly.

In truth, I wasn't alone having this gig early on my resume. Like Senate majority leader Harry Reid and the great Boston columnist Mike Barnicle, I'm proud to say I got my start as a Capitol cop. There were numerous duties: the ordinary ones like helping tourists find their way and standing guard on the West Front, but also the extraordinary ones like standing watch, as I did one day, outside the office containing the Pentagon Papers.

When, two years later, I left Senator Moss's employ, he had sound advice to offer, and I listened to what he said without truly absorbing it at the time. "Maybe you should dip a little deeper into these political waters." It was the surest kind of encouragement because it indicated the hopes he had for me. Later that year I was hired by Ralph Nader as one of four reporters covering Congress for the nonprofit Capitol Hill News Service, which he'd recently launched. It was my first time working as a journalist and one of the lessons I learned was that I liked investigating politicians a whole lot less than I honored their guts in running for office in the first place.

And, against the odds, running for office is just what I did myself after this. Here's how it came about: I'd just read a column by Hugh Sidey in *Time* magazine describing a young fellow, someone not so different from me who was running for Congress in the Philadelphia suburbs. It seemed to me that if this Republican in his twenties could confront the GOP machine out on his turf, there was no real reason I couldn't try to do the same against the old Democratic order on mine. Sure, it was a crazy long shot — Mr. Matthews Goes to Washington — but what you need to remember is that it was Watergate season back then and everywhere the political landscape was on the cusp of change. Maybe, just maybe, the voters in my home Philly district, where I'd grown up but where I knew nobody of political consequence, were ready for a dreamer like me.

In the end — and it wasn't a total shock — the incumbent Democrat won the primary. But my decision to run had risen out of a powerful impulse, and its effect on my life echoed powerfully for years to come. I received a rather respectable number of votes — 23 percent, and this showing was, I think, a decent performance given the circumstances: the fact that I was an unknown, knew no one myself of any influence, and had no money to spend. My campaign had been propelled almost entirely by the enthusiasm and energy of close to four hundred teenaged volunteers I'd personally recruited. The theme I ran on, "the high price of political corruption," was one to which they eagerly responded.

All these great kids simply signed on after hearing me give impassioned speeches in high schools around the district. (I still have the red, white, and blue spiral notebook I used to record their names and Election Day assignments.) Defeated, but proud of what I'd accomplished, I returned to Washington to find I was considered a veteran of the political wars.

Once back in D.C., I put in a brief stint working again for Frank Moss, who asked me now to write speeches for him. This was fine, as far as I was concerned — it was a lucky break. Next, Senator Moss took it upon himself to make an unexpected and even more generous gesture. Unbidden, he got on the phone to his old pal Senator Edmund Muskie of Maine, who'd just been named chairman of the new Senate Budget Committee, and convinced him to name me a key staffer.

Then, three years later, in 1977, came my biggest jump to date: from Capitol Hill to the White House. Richard Pettigrew, a former Speaker of the Florida House, had just been picked by Jimmy Carter to promote his plan to streamline the federal government. He now signed me on as a deputy. Carter had overseen a model reorganization when he was governor of Georgia, and it became a selling point in his presidential campaign that he would repeat the effort in Washington. My role at the President's Reorganization Project was similar to the one I'd had on the Senate Budget Committee, which meant I spent my creative energies helping to convince the American public to buy into what we were doing. The idea was to make government, if not smaller, then more efficient. Its crowning achievement was its successful reform of the federal civil service. It was considered at the time — and ever since — to be one of the administration's domestic triumphs.

After two years working hard in this job for the Carter administration, I'd made friends throughout the Old Executive Office Building. One of them, Rick Hertzberg, Carter's chief speechwriter, would one day in 1979 take me on his team. Though I was "no Ted Sorensen," Rick argued, I wrote fast and knew my politics. What made the case for me was a unique opportunity in the presidential speaking schedule. Jimmy Carter was set to address the National Conference of Catholic Charities. My draft won me the job.

So there I was, writing speeches for a president. It had actually taken only eight years, but much had happened and it seemed like a lot longer. The thought of doing this had once seized my imagination — and I've never forgotten the way it felt, traveling through the African night in that lonely train picturing my unknown future that lay so very far away.

President Reagan is about to make his historic declaration:
"Government is not the solution to our problem; government *is* the problem."

CHAPTER THREE:
STARRING RONALD REAGAN

"If you live in the river, you should make
friends with the crocodiles."
— INDIAN PROVERB

On November 4, 1980, Ronald Reagan was
elected president by a forty-four-state
landslide. With the excitement behind him
and the transition now under way, his focus
narrowed. Like any newly elected president
he now had to concentrate on his defining
purposes. Above all, he needed to win passage of the sweeping economic plan that
had anchored his platform. Among its bullet points: a 30 percent cut in individual
income tax rates accompanied by aggressive
slashes in domestic spending, this last to be
offset by new defense appropriations. While
concerned about the deficit, Reagan was
emphatic: he would be driven even more
forcefully by his vision of the military
buildup on which he'd set his Cold War-

rior's heart. To achieve such goals, he understood that he'd have to be able to count, and dependably so, on Democratic votes in the House of Representatives, the deliberative body in control of all budgetary decisions.

One thing was for certain, the mistakes of his predecessor provided a helpful blueprint — of what *not* to do. Jimmy Carter, a loner by temperament, had come to Washington detesting the city's cozy ways, resisting the dinners and other lures of its established hostesses, angering the old leadership by his aloofness. Ronald and Nancy Reagan, by contrast, had every intention of enjoying their new city even as he made it his mission to "deliver Washington" from its reigning ideology. His plan was to charm rivals and potential allies alike.

One powerful force at work in Reagan's favor would now be the survival instincts of those in the other party. Every election has twin results. First, the victor is decided. Next, a directional signal for going forward is sent. Not only had the Republicans captured the U.S. Senate, at the same time picking up thirty-three seats in the House, they'd also clearly intimated what was coming next. "Get out of the way of this guy!" was the unspoken message that now taunted

Democrats who'd held on to their seats; otherwise you might find yourself the next victim.

The plain facts backed up the implied threat, and so the sitting Democrats understood the wisdom of embracing caution when dealing with the White House. Top members of the House, after all, had gone down in defeat that November, including stalwarts like Ways and Means chairman Al Ullman of Oregon and John Brademas of Indiana, the majority whip. If such high-profile Democratic members, with substantial reelection coffers, could be beaten, who, then, was safe? Wasn't the shrewd move to ignore the leadership in Washington and look out for yourself back home? Wasn't it Tip himself who lived by that rule of survival?

Speaker Thomas P. "Tip" O'Neill, leader of the Democratic majority in the House was, by right and by duty, the responsible political officer. For half a century he'd forged a reputation for personal affability and partisan toughness. Yet the lesson learned in his first and only losing campaign — running for Cambridge City Council while still a Boston College senior — had never left him. On the eve of that defeat and while he was still smarting, a neighbor reproached him. Her complaint: he'd failed to "ask" her for her vote. It became axiomatic with him: don't take anyone for granted and pay the strictest attention to your own backyard.

From that moment on Tip O'Neill understood the extent to which voters' individual feelings matter, to be neglected only at a candidate's peril. In 1936, at the age of twenty-four, he was elected to the Massachusetts legislature, historically a Republican stronghold. For twelve years he endured the humiliations of minority status, but he'd finally had enough and set about putting together a statewide Democratic power network. Operating on the lesson he'd learned long ago from his father about the primacy of neighborhood concerns and personalities — "all politics is local" — he made it his watchword as he crisscrossed the commonwealth, recruiting candidates.

So it was in 1949, joined now by a majority of newly elected legislators, that the Tip-built coalition took control of the Massachusetts House. Still in his thirties, he became the state's first-ever Democratic Speaker. Four years later, when John F. Kennedy ran successfully for the Senate, Tip sought his seat in the U.S. House and won. Now it was 1980, nearly thirty years later, and his was the name to be reckoned with in Massachusetts political life. But, to his chagrin, he was forced to watch his home state — a Democratic bastion defended by his strong will, acquired savvy, and regular delivery of New Deal–grade pork barrel — go for Ronald Reagan.

But just days after Inauguration Day 1981, O'Neill had offered his hometown newspaper a benevolent view of the president-elect. "We find him very charismatic . . . and he's got a good political sense and he's got a lot of experience," he told the *Boston Globe.* ". . . Don't undersell him. He's a sharp fellow." He was also lucky, Tip pointed out — an attribute that counts for a lot everywhere, and most certainly in electoral politics.

Ever pragmatic, the Democrats' leader recognized the challenge now facing him. He also understood the stakes. At this moment the problem wasn't simply Reagan in the White House but the hard, inescapable fact of Republican control of the U.S. Senate. With another election just two years away, the Republicans might soon control both branches of Congress. The prospect of a grand realignment, Tip clearly understood, was exactly what the GOP was now relishing.

Having owned Capitol Hill with only two short breaks since the New Deal, the Democrats, with the advent of Ronald Reagan and those riding his coattails, had, as I've said, every reason to be uneasy. At a post-election press conference, Tip opted for a tone of pre-emptive diplomacy, referring to Reagan as "the admiral of the ship." The new president, he hoped, would be steering "the proper course" in "smooth" waters. The Speaker depicted his own party as having been hit by a "tidal wave." Still he rejected obstructionism. "We will cooperate in every way."

Reagan's opening move was to recruit a top-flight team of White House aides, a savvy group that included pragmatists and moderates. Illinois's Robert Michel, the Republican leader in the House, despite his seat on the other side of the aisle, had long been one of the Speaker's buddies. What Michel saw now was that the Speaker would regard favorably the efforts the new administration was making to assemble experienced players, however he might feel about their ultimate aims. "Tip is a very practical politician," was Michel's assessment as he took stock of the brand-new Washington landscape. He knew only too well the low regard in which Tip had held the previous president's people, having heard his frustrated private complaints about the tactics and attitudes of Carter's Georgia homeboys, above all political aide Hamilton Jordan — whom O'Neill had contemptuously rechristened "Hannibal Jerkin."

But while Tip's practicality was important, so was the fact that he counted himself, above all, a professional. He gave no sign of bearing any grudge at the incoming Republicans for the nastily personal TV ad they'd run against him. Chiefly financed by the National Republican Congressional Committee, it featured a Tip look-alike stranded in a black limo that had just run out of gas. Even worse than its poking fun at what O'Neill would himself refer to as his rough looks, the commercial portrayed him as arrogant and clueless. The on-screen "Tip" was a catered-to and spoiled Washington insider unable to recognize his tank was empty. When asked how he felt about this lampooning, the real Tip shrugged. "Water off a . . . ," he'd reply dismissively. He understood it was politics, where the opposition's duty was to hit hard enough so you could hear the smack.

Besides, this was not the time to look back. The election was a done deal. The present — and future — were all that counted. "I don't intend to allow my party to go down the drain," he vowed. He also made the prediction that the Democrats would bounce back in the first midterm election, still two years off. "We're going to gain seats," he insisted with gallant defiance, knowing full well the national political wind was gusting hard in the other direction.

At the other end of Pennsylvania Avenue, there was no need for such bravura. The Reagan production was rapidly getting under way. The president-elect was unusual in knowing his own weaknesses as well as being very aware of his strengths. Back in Hollywood, he'd had the benefit of a team: producer, director, screenwriter, costumer, etc., each of whom well understood his or her assignment. It was a familiar routine to him, having an expert on the set tell him where to stand and which camera to respect. He was accustomed to being told the plotline.

The first absolutely vital move he made, the significance of which can't be overestimated, was to hire James Addison Baker III, a Houston attorney and seasoned political advisor, as his chief of staff. Reagan cared more about getting it right than holding grudges. The fact that the much-admired

Baker had in the past strategized against him — working for Gerald Ford in the 1976 primaries and for George H. W. Bush in 1980 — was no lasting offense. He could find his way to accept a *pro* whom he saw as a fellow conservative. "I always throw my golf club in the direction I'm going," he'd say. Most important, Nancy Reagan, whose opinion counted for a great deal, agreed with her husband when it came to this crucial hire.

Though conservative in his beliefs, Jim Baker was comfortable in government and effective in politics. He now set to work with his boss's full confidence, having been given the authority to assemble a White House team. Choosing the aides who'd be dealing with Congress — half of which, remember, remained in Democratic hands — was an important part of this responsibility. Like David Gergen, appointed Reagan's communications director, the Princeton-educated Texan was evidence that the more centrist political lieutenants can be the most fearsome in battle; they're often cagier.

In Hollywood terms, you could call Baker the producer, the one taking larger-scale responsibility, the overall honcho. Michael Deaver, a close California friend of the Reagans and longtime GOP political operative named now as the White House deputy chief of staff, assumed the role of stage director. He was entrusted with choreographing Reagan's indelible turns, as he had done with that dazzling Labor Day appearance at the Statue of Liberty. The third key inside guy was Edwin Meese, a lawyer like Baker and, like Deaver, a Californian. He and Mike Deaver had worked closely together in the California State House during Reagan's two terms there. Arriving in Washington, Meese was given the title Counselor to the President for Policy, which allowed him to make sure the Reagan programs stayed on message.

This arrangement allowed the new president to concentrate on his essential dual roles: Ronald Reagan, keeper of the conservative faith, and Ronald Reagan, the performer. Relying on his aides to organize his presidential schedule and nail down the details, he would serve as the production's chief mastermind. He would also be the administration's leading man. He would *be* Ronald Reagan. He would *play* Ronald Reagan.

How perfectly Jim Baker understood the man and the operation he was running. He saw that an unwritten part of his job entailed keeping his boss focused on why he'd wanted to be president in the first place. Every cabdriver in D.C. would soon know what President Reagan stood for: to reduce taxes and government at home, and to defeat the Soviet Union abroad.

Reagan had been nursing grievances against the federal income tax ever since he'd been penalized back in the 1940s by what was then the high-end marginal rate of 90 percent. To avoid hitting that bracket, Reagan refused to make more than two movies annually. To Jim Baker he'd later explain, "Why should I have done a third picture — even if it was *Gone with the Wind*? What good would it have done me?" The star had never forgotten his outrage. As president, he was eager to start swinging the ax.

An across-the-board cut in marginal income tax rates was now President-elect Reagan's holy grail. To succeed in winning it would require a mix of ideological allegiance and political seduction. It was time for Ronald Reagan the political leader to cede the stage to Ronald Reagan the leading man. What he needed and wanted to do now was to start wooing Washington on its own terms. Unlike Jimmy Carter, here was a man who liked being liked and knew well how to work a room. Both had big grins —

but one was infectious while the other merely provided a too-easy target for editorial cartoonists. Carter, thoughtful and earnest, forever seemed the Sunday school teacher he actually was. Reagan, whom millions of Americans remembered nostalgically from his days hosting the popular *General Electric Theater* — and later, briefly, *Death Valley Days* — came off as a familiar, genial personality. He barely had to introduce himself to the country, since his face and voice were already in its mass consciousness.

He and Nancy first needed to introduce themselves to a much smaller group, social Washington. After all, as Nancy wisely saw, this was where they were going to live. As president and first lady, they soon were in demand and immediately began accepting invitations, seeking open channels into the local power culture. Not differentiating, really, between mandarin Republicans and mandarin Democrats, they early on attended a dinner given by publisher Katharine Graham, whose newspaper, the *Washington Post,* had overseen the ruthless cashiering of fellow Californian Richard Nixon. In the coming years, Kay Graham, the first lady of Washington society, and Nancy, the country's first lady, finding they liked each other, would lunch secretly. Used to having a circle of chums back in Los Angeles, the new first lady also formed other Washington friendships.

This was not Tip O'Neill's world, where the Reagans were beginning to circulate. His wife, Millie, whom he would salute for having "never changed," sought no part in the Washington whirl. She had stayed home in North Cambridge for much of his congressional career. Jim Baker, however, saw O'Neill as the highest-value target of the charm offensive. He was determined that the Reagan White House treat the Democratic Speaker with the respect he'd never received from the Carter gang. Baker believed that it was vital to keep communication lines open between the White House and the opposition as represented by the Speaker's office. For example, he thought it basic political wisdom to let Tip know what was coming, policywise, and to treat him properly, with the courtesy and respect he deserved — even when they disagreed. Baker knew that an important aspect of his job was to function as the White House's chief legislative strategist, and that meant he'd have to keep calibrating how to move these two heavyweights — Reagan and O'Neill — together.

Here's Baker's own version of how he saw it: "Like Jimmy Carter in 1976, Ronald Reagan had run as an outsider who criticized the Washington status quo. Unlike Carter, however, we made plans to extend an immediate olive branch to Congress." He later added, "I knew that President Reagan would have his hands full with a Democratic-controlled House that he had campaigned against vigorously. So it was even more essential to keep the lines of communications open and civil with Capitol Hill."

Like the man he served, Baker subscribed to the same goals, but it was his responsibility to do the careful planning. He knew what invitations to the White House were worth, whether the event was a breakfast for the GOP leadership or invitations extended to lucky members of Congress — Democrats included — to watch the Super Bowl with the president on the big screen in the White House family theater.

Baker, acting on Reagan's behalf, was right to fix Tip O'Neill squarely in his sights when it came to bestowing careful treatment. For one thing, you couldn't be trying to play the game of politics and fail to acknowledge the Speaker's essential Boston-Irish toughness, a part of Washington lore.

"I've known every speaker since World War II, including Sam Rayburn, one of the great ones," Nixon had recalled. "I would say that Tip O'Neill is certainly one of the ablest, but without question, he is the most ruthless and the most partisan speaker we have had in my lifetime. The only time he's bipartisan is when it will serve his partisan interest. He plays hardball. He doesn't know what softball is. So, under the circumstances, when I heard that he was taking over shaping the Democrats, I knew that we were in trouble." The veteran Bay State representative had, in fact, been the Democrat backrooming Nixon's impeachment.

Baker also knew about "Hannibal Jerkin." But it's likely he respected Tip for never criticizing Jimmy Carter himself personally, even as he wisecracked about Jordan. "We were particularly aware," he remembers, "of the imperative as a Republican administration dealing with a Democratic House, of finding a way to establish a relationship so we could deal. When we came in we had a 100-day plan. And that plan was to reduce the tax rates — the marginal tax rates — and get some spending cuts. We were going to focus with laser-like efficiency and intensity on getting that done. We knew from the time we first got there that none of this could happen if the Democratic House could not somehow be co-opted, be persuaded to vote for it."

For his part, Reagan, too, was well briefed on how shortsightedly Carter's aides had dealt with O'Neill and the Speaker's office. "He'd been aware of all that," Max Friedersdorf, Reagan's chief of congressional relations, told me, shaking his head. "They'd offended the Speaker from day one."

Exactly two weeks after Election Day, Ronald Reagan made a trip to the Hill, where he visited the Speaker in his office. According to Tip — in his memoir, *Man of the House* — they bonded in ways both expected and unexpected. "When President-elect Reagan came to my office in November of 1980, we two Irish-American pols got right down to business by swapping stories about the Notre Dame football team. I told Reagan how much I had enjoyed his Knute Rockne movie, and he graciously pointed out that his friend Pat O'Brien was the real star of that film."

In response, Reagan was able to share with his host their common New Deal roots. "He told me how, back in 1948, he and O'Brien had been part of Harry Truman's campaign train. O'Brien used to warm up the audiences, and Reagan would introduce the president. He took great delight in that story. . . . Before [he] left my office that day, I let him know that although we came from different parties, I looked forward to working with him. I reminded him that I had always been on good terms with the Republican leadership, and that despite our various disagreements in the House, we were always friends after six o'clock and on weekends.

"The president-elect seemed to like that formulation, and over the next six years he would often begin our telephone discussions by saying, 'Hello, Tip, is it after six o'clock?'

" 'Absolutely, Mr. President,' I would respond. Our watches must have been in sync, because even with our many intense political battles, we managed to maintain a pretty good friendship."

That first Reagan-O'Neill meeting contained only one discordant note. It came when Reagan reported to Tip how well he'd gotten along with the legislature as California governor. As O'Neill recalled it years later: "Reagan was proud that he, a Republican, had worked harmoniously with the Democratic state assembly. 'That was the minor leagues,' I said. 'You're in the big leagues now.'

"He seemed genuinely surprised to hear

that. Maybe he thought that Washington was just an extension of Sacramento." When the two walked out of the room together to confront the press, Tip promised not to turn up the heat for six months, adding that "we will work to turn America around and make the economy work."

"I echo what he said," Reagan was quick to agree. "We know, of course, that we're not going to accomplish anything without the cooperation of the House and the Senate. In other words, we're not going to just throw *surprises* up here at the Hill."

Obviously, the absence of actual issues — they talked neither policy nor politics — played a big part in the warmth of this first encounter. Push had not yet come to shove. It was simply about two pols of a shared generation finding themselves well able to like each other as people. This is despite the grand canyon of difference in their life experiences. "My father didn't get the world of Hollywood," Tom O'Neill told me decades later. "It was far different from the streets of North Cambridge."

Tip O'Neill and Ronald Reagan had yet to draw their weapons. Both were still looking for a way, if such a way still survived in the brutal arena of national politics, to fight without becoming enemies.

■ ■ ■

The day of Ronald Reagan's inauguration, January 20, 1981, was the warmest oath-taking day on record. Tip O'Neill, along with Senator Mark Hatfield of Oregon, was invited to join the president-elect and the outgoing Jimmy Carter on the ride up to Capitol Hill. Affable as always, Reagan attempted to break the ice with anecdotes from his Hollywood past. Carter, who had been up all night hoping for the hostages' return, smiled tightly but couldn't really follow the point of the stories. Later he'd ask his longtime media advisor Gerald Rafshoon, a man well acquainted with the movie biz, "Who's Jack Warner?"

Reagan's inauguration was the first set on the Capitol's West Front, overlooking the Mall, and the moment of his swearing-in was the signal, in Tehran, for the release of the hostages after 444 days. Timing is, indeed, everything. Another "long national nightmare" was over.

At a congressional lunch following the ceremony, in his toast President Reagan spoke of "the adversary relationships" that often are part of the constitutional territory that assures "checks and balances." But, he said, he hoped there'd be more cooperation than conflict. "I look forward to working with you on behalf of the people and that this partnership will continue." He and O'Neill both understood the delicate balance of power between them, one that would grow even more uncertain in the months to come. Though the Democrats controlled the House, dozens of their members were southern conservatives open to Reagan's embrace. Would their loyalties swing left or right?

But the headline-grabbing drama that had determined the election — the fate of the hostages in Tehran — was still playing out, right up until this very moment. After hearing for certain that the plane carrying the Americans was finally winging its way home, President Reagan announced to his congressional hosts: "With thanks to Almighty God, I have been given a tag line, the get-off line, that everyone wants for the end of a toast or a speech, or anything else. Some thirty minutes ago, the planes bearing our prisoners left Iranian airspace, and are now free of Iran. So we can all drink to this one: to all of us, together, doing what we all know we can do to make this country what it should be, what it can be, what it always has been."

Before leaving the Capitol, Reagan graciously obliged the Speaker's request that he put his now-presidential signature on a stack of commemorative stamped envelopes. As he did so, Reagan joked that he was counting a Democratic vote for each sheet he signed — which could have been a way of reminding the Speaker that his very ambitious plans for changing Washington and the country would mean poaching directly on Tip's terrain. The declaration he'd just made on the West Front — "Government is not the solution to our problem; government *is* the problem" — could not have been a starker rebuke. In hearing Reagan's words, how could O'Neill not have heard a denunciation of himself?

The new president meets the veteran Speaker:
two Irishmen of a different sort trying to figure each other out.

CHAPTER FOUR:
NEW KID ON THE BLOCK

"Civility is not a sign of weakness."
— JOHN F. KENNEDY
INAUGURAL ADDRESS

It was clear that Ronald Reagan respected Tip O'Neill both for his long career and for the high position he'd reached. O'Neill's failure to respond with equal regard — that crack about Sacramento being in the "minor leagues" — showed a genuine lapse of awareness. It's the wise gladiator, after all, who arrives at the arena prepared to face his rival's strengths. Ronald Reagan possessed numerous gifts, but one of the very greatest was the way, by simply being "Ronald Reagan," he continually induced foes to underestimate him. He would later tell biographer Lou Cannon how glad he'd been to see O'Neill fall into the old, familiar trap. But arriving back at the White House after his first trip to the Hill, Reagan couldn't help feeling galled. Even after he'd decisively trounced an incumbent American president, he had to hear his eight-year success in California being dismissed as Triple-A ball.

While Tip's quip welcoming him to the "big leagues" would continue to irritate the White House, it didn't bother the Speaker a bit. Meeting with journalists right after Reagan's visit to the Capitol, he made sure his sly put-down got into public circulation. After saying his guest had been taken aback by what he'd said, he added for good measure, "It won't be the last time he's surprised."

At the White House, Tip's chest-thumping didn't go down well. Even though the Speaker was the acknowledged Washington veteran of the two, he'd overstepped, the Reagan people felt, by rushing to emphasize his senior status in the pecking order.

Yet the Democrat's needling didn't mean the end to Reagan's campaign to win him over. Reagan was shrewder and more cunning than that. Soon after the inauguration, the O'Neills received an invitation to have dinner at the White House with the Reagans two weeks later. "Boy, am I in trouble," Tip laughed. "How am I going to fight with this guy?"

By January's end, the Reagan team was presented with a fifty-five-page plan of action. Prepared by pollster Richard Wirthlin and David Gergen, it came to be known simply as "The Black Book." It was intended as the administration's road map for the first hundred days, addressing the national mood as well as outlining action: "The first fundamental economic objective of the Reagan presidency must be to restore a sense of stability and confidence, to demonstrate that there is a steady hand at the helm." With this mission statement in hand, the president's staff understood exactly where they needed to position their man — not just as the anti-Carter but also as a serious leader fully ready to guide the ship of state. "The second fundamental economic objective of the Reagan presidency must be to convey a sense of hope, that there is a light at the end of the tunnel." As Jim Baker had already decided, the number-one priority was to be the economy: cutting taxes, cutting social programs. The implications for such proposals were serious and far-reaching.

It would fall to Tip O'Neill to play Horatius at the bridge.

For his part, Tip refused to believe in the reality of what others accepted as a populist-driven Reagan mandate; to him, the Democratic wipeout in November had been a repudiation of Carter pure and simple. In his opinion the GOP campaign promises were "so clearly preposterous" that any thinking person must reject them. Their inadequacy boiled down to a simple equation: "Surely everybody could see that you couldn't balance the budget, cut taxes, and increase defense spending all at the same time." But whether Tip's idea of the math's logic worked or not, Reagan was indeed planning a radical assault on the old liberal order.

In early February, the new president went on TV. No longer the candidate packed with promises, he was now the tough steward, explaining to the country the price of achieving the goals he had set. Like every president before him he was making the inevitable pivot from critic to manager.

I'm speaking to you tonight to give you a report on the state of the nation's economy. I regret to say that we're in the worst economic mess since the Great Depression.

Now, we've just had two years of back-to-back double-digit inflation — 13.3 percent in 1979, 12.4 percent in 1980.

The last time this happened was in World War I.

In 1960 mortgage interest rates averaged around six percent. They're two-and-a-half times as high now, 15.4 percent.

Let me try to put this in personal terms. Here is a dollar such as you earned, spent or saved in 1960. And here is a quarter, a dime and a penny — thirty-six cents. That's what this 1960 dollar is worth today.

To the Congress of the United States, I extend my hand in cooperation, and I believe we can go forward in a bipartisan manner. I've found a real willingness to cooperate on the part of Democrats and members of my own party.

We can leave our children with an unrepayable massive debt and a shattered economy, or we can leave them liberty in a land where every individual has the opportunity to be whatever God intended us to be. All it takes is a little common sense and recognition of our own ability. Together we can forge a new beginning for America.

So far, so good. In the *Washington Post* the next day, Lou Cannon, a career-long

Reagan-watcher, reported: "Last night, he was carefully conciliatory toward the opposition party, which still controls the U.S. House, as he has been most of the time since taking office." When it came to the opposition party's own response, Tip for the moment was as smooth as any diplomat. Asked by the *New York Times* his opinion of Reagan's maiden effort, Tip gave a thumbs-up. "He comes across beautifully," he said. "He's running high right now."

The day after this televised speech was Reagan's seventieth birthday. Included in a White House celebration to which a small group had been invited, Tip took a thoughtful gift, the flag that had flown from the Capitol on Inauguration Day.

Not long after this brief drop-in at 1600 Pennsylvania Avenue, Tip enjoyed another, to him unaccustomed, one. The occasion was that dinner party to which he'd been invited and was to bring Millie, his wife of forty years. Among the others on hand that evening in the White House private living quarters were Jim and Susan Baker, and also chief Hill liaison Max Friedersdorf and his wife. As soon as both the host and his guest of honor had put in their requests for "strong drinks" — this was Friedersdorf's observation — the two political leaders began swapping Irish stories. "Maybe Tip & I told too many," Reagan admitted later in his diary.

Parts of Tip's history fascinated his host. Like just about every other politician he'd met, the new president wanted the inside story on James Michael Curley, the legendary Boston mayor immortalized in the bestseller *The Last Hurrah*. Reagan, a fan of the 1958 movie version starring his pal Spencer Tracy, craved all the juicy details. Once Tip began launching into his colorful tales of the old days, listeners would be spellbound. "There are times when real life throws up characters who are more fantastic than any that are found in books," he liked to say. "When the good Lord made James Michael Curley, He broke the mold."

That night, however, it was a two-way street. For Ronald Reagan cast an equal spell over the Massachusetts congressman, as Tip would freely admit. The Irish anecdotes and jokes — Reagan was always well stocked with new ones — enhanced the sense of camaraderie as he kept the group well entertained. "He's a terrific storyteller, he's witty, and he's got an excellent sense of humor," pronounced the Speaker afterward. It had, according to Friedersdorf, been the president's own decision to invite the

O'Neills to be his and Nancy's first White House guests. That fact was of no little significance given the battle lines now being drawn.

The next morning Tip let the press know what an "enjoyable evening" he'd spent with the Reagans. "We didn't discuss politics." Nonetheless, it was obvious he didn't want anyone to think that one pleasant get-together might ever affect his principles. "We are not just going to let them tear asunder the government programs we have created," he said. "In the last thirty years middle America has been built up. When I was young there was rich and poor, and that was all. . . . My priority is to see that some people don't suffer for the good of others."

That afternoon the Speaker's schedule called for his return to the White House to attend a meeting about U.S.-Soviet trade policy. It was apparent both men still were feeling the goodwill of the previous evening. The topic now under discussion was the grain embargo put in place by Jimmy Carter the year before in response to the Soviet invasion of Afghanistan. But getting tough with the Soviets wound up punishing farmers here at home more than it harmed the Soviet Union, which simply went wheat-shopping elsewhere. Responding to the anger of the suffering midwestern agricultural states, Reagan had promised during his campaign to end the embargo.

At this point occurred one of those paradoxes of political life: Tip O'Neill and Ronald Reagan each held what would have normally been the other's position. The liberal Speaker, champion of relief for the little man, urged the hard-line anticommunist to beware of deciding the issue merely on the complaints from the farm states. Before making a concession, Reagan should demand a quid pro quo. "What are the Soviets giving us in return?"

"Tip had last word & it was a good one," Reagan jotted in his diary that night. "He told me I was Pres. and had to think of *all* the states. The gist was — was lifting the embargo good for the U.S. and our security vis a vis the Soviets?"

Here was a moment when Tip seemed as much advisor as adversary. And he'd been right when he'd told the *Times* that Reagan was riding high. Now the *Washington Post* reported that "by 77 to 17 percent, an overwhelming majority gives him positive marks on inspiring confidence in the White House." In other words, three-quarters of the American people — including a great many Democrats — were rooting for him.

O'Neill was perceptive enough to understand the country had a new leader that it wanted to believe in. After the tragedy of Dallas, after the quicksand of Vietnam, the scandal of Watergate, and the "malaise" of Jimmy Carter, it needed one. He realized how wrong it would be, even dangerous, to diminish such faith. Anyway, the most important job Tip had right now involved defense, not attack — at least for the moment.

He now needed to man his battle station on the Hill. From the bully pulpit of his regular daily press briefing, he stoutly warned that the Democratic House wasn't going to "rubber-stamp" whatever Reagan proposed. "I have been up here long enough," he stated, "to know that legislation in haste makes for a lot of waste." He was starting to signal the way he was going to deal with President Ronald Reagan.

Although not quite ready to take on Reagan mano a mano, Tip was slowly getting used to the new American political arena. "With a Republican in the White House and the House still controlled by the Democrats, I now assumed a new role — leader of the opposition," he'd later explain. "And with Jimmy Carter back in Georgia and Ted Kennedy now stuck in a Republican-controlled Senate, I also became the chief spokesman for the Democrats."

Two nights after the O'Neills had dined at the White House, Reagan presented his economic program to both houses of Congress. As custom dictated, the Speaker of the House introduced him. After Tip had performed these honors, the president fired his opening salvo. The size of the national debt, he said, was a looming danger.

"A few weeks ago, I called such a figure, a trillion dollars, incomprehensible, and I've been trying ever since to think of a way to illustrate how *big* a trillion really is. And the best I could come up with is that if you had a stack of thousand-dollar bills in your hand only four inches high, you'd be a millionaire. A trillion dollars would be a stack of thousand dollar bills sixty-seven miles high."

From there he moved on to the meat of his address, which dealt with why he had come to Washington, and called for a list of spending cuts that would come to include education, the arts, food stamps, and college loans, sparing only the military; now he threw down the gauntlet. "I would direct a question," he proposed, "to those who have indicated already an unwillingness to accept such a plan: have they an alternative which offers a greater chance of balancing the budget, reducing and eliminating inflation, stimulating the creation of jobs, and reducing the tax burden? And, if they haven't, are they suggesting we can continue on the present course without coming to a day of reckoning?"

It was a one-two punch: one, we have a big challenge here, and two, you Democrats don't have an answer to it, do you?

Watching the president deliver the address, as he sat behind him in the Speaker's chair, O'Neill could spot the difference between the enormous confidence Reagan had with a prepared script and his performance in meetings. For an old Washington hand like Tip, proficiency at the latter counted for much more. In the White House meetings they would now have regularly, he would watch Reagan and be fascinated by what seemed the president's near-total reliance on "3×5 cards" when discussing policy. Moreover, O'Neill said he had never sat down with a chief executive who so relied on cabinet officers to set out administration positions. What Tip had trouble understanding was how anyone so complete as a public personality could be so lacking in the substantive details of his chosen career.

What the Speaker failed to see was how

complete a self-creation Reagan really was, how anchored he was by a short list of basic beliefs, those concepts that both inspired and animated him. Not everything, it turns out, was contained in those index cards. It was a lesson Jim Baker had learned for himself soon after coming on board; he was astute enough to recognize early on how sharp Reagan could be when it came to matters both large and small as long as they linked to his core philosophy. "You want to talk to him about taxes or spending or the big stuff, the macro stuff. He can talk to you all day with no cards, no nothing."

As a committed Cold Warrior, Ronald Reagan would always be fully engaged when it came to the long struggle with the Soviet Union. Richard Allen, his newly named national security advisor, had once asked him to set forth his general view of U.S. policy with regard to Russia. Reagan's answer, given long before he would run for and win the presidency, could not have been more trenchant. "How about this? We win. They lose."

It's easy to see, if you know what you're looking for, that the differences between Tip O'Neill and Ronald Reagan were not personal but political. Their initial meetings show they would have gotten along smoothly had the moment in history been different. With all their differences in background, looks, and life experience, the fact is, they liked each other and would freely say so. But for all their Irish fellowship and bonhomie, something vitally important set the two apart, something too important ever to be ignored. Each was an idealist, yet each had settled on beliefs that stood fiercely opposed to the other's.

Now, on a very public stage, with enormous consequences that each understood differently, they were about to have it out.

Tip's guys.
Gary Hymel (*middle*) was the Speaker's AA, his key guy with both members and the press. Kirk O'Donnell (*right*), the Speaker's chief counsel, had the best day-to-day political mind I've come across. You wanted him in your corner. Thank God I had him in mine.

CHAPTER FIVE:
JOINING THE FIGHT

"I've learned that people only pay attention to what they discover for themselves."
— *PRETTY POISON,* 1968

As a politician Tip O'Neill beautifully fit the classic mold. He'd come of age and learned the rules in a legislative world where his man-to-man skills paid off. In all the time-honored ways, he kept his constituents back home satisfied while gaining friendship and respect among his peers down in Washington. In both worlds, he'd learned how to take care of himself. He knew how to wheel and deal, trade favors, and use his anger when necessary. Most of all he understood the advantages of having a trick or two up his sleeve.

In the first month after Reagan's inauguration, the president and Congress faced the nasty but predictable chore of having to raise the federal debt ceiling. It's a ritual requiring members to put their names *not* to new government spending but to the settling of old accounts. In other words, it mandates that a majority of the national legislators behave the way individual citizens must: you agree to pay your bills. While every recent president has had to regularly sign off on a hike in the debt ceiling, it had become over the years a regular occasion for partisan blame-pointing. In the previous year, 1980, not a single GOP House member had cast a vote agreeing to a raise in the ceiling, a partisan tactic well understood by O'Neill. It left the Democrats solely responsible for the higher national debt, and gave Republican candidates free rein to finger their Democratic rivals as out-of-control Washington spenders.

Now the situation was different: a Republican was in the White House. But no matter the reigning ideology, the buck stopped where it always had. Therefore, just like his much-mocked predecessor, Jimmy Carter, it was now Ronald Reagan's job to raise the debt ceiling. He couldn't do it without the Democrats, the majority party in the House of Representatives. Bottom line: there was no way for the new administration to accomplish the job without asking the Speaker to help round up the needed votes.

When Reagan's top lobbyist asked his support in getting the debt ceiling raised, the Massachusetts Democrat made a simple request. He wanted Max Friedersdorf to relay back to his boss precisely what the deal would be, which was that he, Tip O'Neill, wanted a personal note from the president to each and every Democratic member of the House asking for his or her support in the matter of raising the debt ceiling. Friedersdorf agreed on the spot and carried the message back to Reagan. The asked-for letters arrived the next day — all 243 of them.

It was a small, telling episode. Here was the Democratic congressional leader proposing a wholly pragmatic cease-fire. The debt-ceiling vote had offered each side a chance to discredit the other. O'Neill proposed avoiding harm to either party. Rather than have the House Democrats all vote "Nay," as he might have allowed, throwing a monkey wrench into Reagan's first-month agenda, the Speaker agreed to let as many as were necessary vote "Aye."

The sole condition he'd made stemmed from his desire to help protect the sitting members from their opponents' likely attacks come the next election. To accomplish this, he needed Ronald Reagan's cooperation. Looking to the future, if a Republican challenger were to slam one of O'Neill's Democrats for big spending, pointing to his vote to raise the debt ceiling as evidence, the note from Reagan would give him adequate cover. As an effective solution, it was an arrangement that worked, for both sides — and the republic moved on.

Dealing in such a way was Tip O'Neill's style, but change was not, and those who knew him understood this. He'd come to the House of Representatives in 1953 with a predecessor, the rich and handsome young war vet, John F. Kennedy, clearly a hard act to follow. From his many dealings with JFK over the subsequent years, Tip knew charisma firsthand. Certainly, too, his great hero Franklin Roosevelt had possessed an overabundance. These experiences, however, had not prepared him for what he now faced.

Tip now saw the response Reagan drew on February 18 at his first joint session of Congress. It was like nothing he'd ever witnessed. As tough and proud as he was, Tip must have glimpsed the shape of his future as he looked out into the historic chamber at all those familiar faces, many of whom he'd worked alongside, or in opposition to, for decades. Watching Reagan's effect on them, he could see both the appeal and, for him and his fellow Democrats, the menace.

When asked later about the seemingly mesmerized response to Reagan's appearance that night, O'Neill was candid. With the professionalism that anchored his political self, he told the press that the public reaction to the president's performance was "tremendously strong." He didn't stop there: "I don't know how many telegrams we've received. . . . The honeymoon is still on, no question about it."

As the weeks passed, O'Neill continued to feel the glare of Reagan's star power even if he chose not to admit it. Asked in early March if the new president's honeymoon was "wearing thin," he didn't take the bait. "We are not ready to play hardball yet," he said. Yet it was clear that the seeming ease with which the administration was getting out its message — with neither press nor public ready to break the spell — bothered him. "What I am curious of is the honeymoon with the *press*. I don't recall any president and a press having a honeymoon as this one." Soon, by the time only another week had passed, he was starting to acknowledge the challenge being put to him.

What he admitted, cautiously, was that the Democrats themselves, under his leadership, might bear some responsibility. "We haven't communicated well with the press," he said.

But still, it was a problem he understood how to address, at least on one level. The reporters covering the Hill were a known quantity. Faithfully, every day the Speaker would appear fifteen minutes before each House session in H210, his ceremonial office, and take their questions. He and they all understood the rules. There were no TV cameras present. For Tip, it was facing the world *beyond* H210 that threw him from his comfort zone.

"He was very persuasive with people individually or even in small groups but as a public speaker, it wasn't his strength," his daughter Susan told me. "And he knew that about himself, which is why he didn't like going on camera initially." Tip never minded admitting to his uneasy relationship with television; it was old news to him. "As you know," he'd joked to a group of journalists the year before, "I haven't won many campaigns based on my looks."

The career he'd made for himself, starting in Massachusetts, had been constructed in the age *before* television. Like Reagan, he'd grown up listening to the radio. But, unlike Reagan, his career hadn't begun in front of a microphone. Instead, he'd cut his teeth in person-to-person politics. Becoming over time a Capitol Hill insider, he'd ascended to the Speaker's chair through the potent mix of backroom popularity and cajolery. That was the way you did it, and he'd proved himself an adept maneuverer. The skill sets of the U.S. Congress were ones he'd observed throughout his career, matching and bettering them as needed.

The problem was, a different game was now afoot, and new talents were about to be asked of him. He'd be going up against a master of a medium, television. A few of the people around Tip recognized the problem and were in the market for a solution. One thing was for certain: he couldn't continue to hold back.

Early in 1981, I'd received a call from Martin Franks, whom I knew from the Democratic National Committee. He had an idea he wanted to discuss, one that would involve me. I was ready to listen. Back in the fall, I'd often counted on Marty to help with party background info on campaign speeches I was writing for Jimmy Carter. Now he'd moved on to a bigger job — executive director of the Democratic

Congressional Campaign Committee (DCCC) — and was thinking about the task before him in large terms. The Democrats had lost the White House and the Senate; the House now was their last redoubt. As the majority party there, they needed to be heard from; they needed to make noise, make it frequently, and make it *matter.*

After explaining this to me as background, all of which I well understood, Marty proceeded to get to exactly what was on his mind. The Speaker had been holding daily press conferences, regularly attended by those reporters whose congressional beats made them his captive audience. But the takeaway he tended to offer them was weak gruel: mostly just humdrum updates on the legislative schedule. It was a terrible sin of omission, Marty argued. Here was a stage Tip had all to himself every single working day, when Congress was in session, and yet it was an ongoing series of missed opportunities. Sure, he'd been doing it in exactly the same way ever since he'd first become Speaker four years earlier, and so had every Speaker before him. But why not think outside the box? Why not use those press conferences to get out the party's message, to *fight back,* to make *news?*

My role in this scheme, if Franks managed to talk me into it, was to sign on as communications director for the DCCC. There my chief mission would be to help Speaker of the House Tip O'Neill in his new role as party spokesman. What Marty was asking of me now was to meet with Congressman Tony Coelho, the young Californian who'd been elected to chair the campaign committee. He would be the House Democrat most responsible for getting Democrats to hold and strengthen the House majority in the 1982 elections.

I was skeptical. It's not that I doubted the potential of Marty and his boss Tony's Big Idea — but I wasn't sure I could manage to make it work. It seemed to me a man like Tip O'Neill would have a well-established operation that wouldn't readily admit strangers. Quite honestly, I also couldn't imagine him willingly taking assistance, let alone direction from someone not belonging to his handpicked inner circle. I'd grown up in Philadelphia and knew big-city pols; I knew they liked hiring people with deep-rooted connections and never wanted outsiders getting into their business. I'd assumed that Tip O'Neill was a proud captain who ran his ship the way he wanted to and wasn't willing to have an outsider, picked by Tony Coelho or anyone else, serving in his crew.

But what a challenge! It's always the challenge that gets me. And, of course, I saw the problem: it was Tip's image, clearly. He was the fellow — the symbol, really — whom the Reagan people had chosen to attack for the very reason that he *didn't* represent the new breed of post-Watergate Democrat. There was no confusing him with the party's Young Turks, those chosen in the elections of 1974 and 1976 who wanted to cut back on deficit spending, who wanted to skim down the size and bureaucracy of government, who wanted to modernize. In other words, he was hardly someone of my political generation. Nor was I of his.

Tip O'Neill was an old-school, street-corner figure, and a big spender to boot. How would I fit in with him? How would *he* fit with someone like me who hadn't inherited a New Deal attitude about government? Having grown up in a Republican family, I'd been drawn to the Democratic side by Eugene McCarthy and his anti–Vietnam War crusade in 1968. Then, as a Peace Corps trainee down in Louisiana, I'd cast my first presidential vote for Hubert Humphrey because of his civil rights leadership and, equally, because I liked his running mate, Edmund Muskie. The senator from Maine reminded me of McCarthy, and I saw him as a true reformer. This belief had been reinforced when, working on the Senate Budget Committee, I'd watched him working steadfastly to control the federal budget, controlling and bringing reason to government spending.

Yet even feeling strongly those concerns, I agreed to meet with Coelho. After the Californian and I had talked — I can't pinpoint the exact moment — I decided to go for it.

One thing I figured was that I'd be in for a dose of culture shock. I'd spent four years back in the 1960s at Holy Cross, and so had experienced New Englanders up close. But now it was 1981 and I'd just finished four years working alongside the Georgians who'd come up north with Jimmy Carter.

Once I'd signed on with Marty and Tony, my plan of action was to get myself well briefed by a couple of savvy guys about both the Speaker and his men. I needed to have a good idea beforehand of what sort of operation I was heading into. What was especially important was to get a snapshot of who my new colleagues were, how they fit into the pecking order of the O'Neill office, and how each interacted with Tip and with one other. It was critical to know what to expect before I took my place alongside the Speaker's team — which, like Reagan's, was a small, tight group.

What I learned is how much Tip relied on his closest aides when it came to the business of keeping Congress functioning. It was because these men had the Speaker's ear that other House members treated them with such respect and attention.

Here are the most important members of Tip's trusted associates, the ones I got the skinny on before meeting them. First, there was Kirk O'Donnell, chief counsel to the Speaker, who'd been, before he came to work for Tip, a highly effective top aide to Boston mayor Kevin White. It was Tip's son Christopher (known as "Kip") who'd encouraged his father to bring O'Donnell on board, looking to add to the staff the kind of political street smarts Kirk had in full. Kip also had wanted a skilled player who'd be able to see both the big and little picture. Most vitally, the son was looking for a person who'd protect his dad. Kirk had turned out to be a brilliant hire, going on to win the Speaker's highest accolade. He's "hard as a rock," Tip O'Neill would say of him approvingly. What impressed me, once I got to know him, was how fearless Kirk was, so absolutely sure of his position. Tip had to beg him to take the job. And Kirk was always willing to take on anyone who dared to confront him. That said, though, his reputation was always that of "a good guy" to have a beer with.

O'Donnell, I soon learned, was working in cahoots with Congressman Coelho when it came to bringing me in. Both believed the Speaker was poised to become a national figure far larger than any previous Capitol Hill leader. I should add that Kirk, older than his own years, was steeped in the ways of the bygone political world of Boston. Over the time we spent together he worked carefully to educate me with regard to the lore he held so dear, above all those political rules and maxims that had guided the previous generations. Most important, he made it very clear that there *are* rules and that they exist for good reason.

Gary Hymel, the Speaker's administrative assistant, was the most visible of O'Neill's top aides. His large desk, in the room right off the House chamber, adjoined the Speaker's ceremonial office, making him the front gatekeeper. A former newspaperman from New Orleans, he'd been a top aide for House majority leader Hale Boggs of Louisiana. Then, when the twin-engine plane carrying Boggs was tragically lost over

Alaska in 1972, Gary, with the agreement of the Boggs family, helped Tip, who'd been majority whip, to win election to become majority leader. In addition to handling the press, Gary was the Speaker's key liaison with southern members. Observing him in action, I could tell he was an extremely popular guy around the House.

Leo Diehl, who held the same highest-ranking title as Hymel, "Administrative Assistant," was another quintessential political operator. Elected to the Massachusetts legislature from an adjoining district in 1936, the same year as O'Neill, the two quickly became friends for life. Leo, who'd been crippled by polio as a boy, relied on crutches, refusing ever to resort to a wheelchair. He and Tip would, without the slightest embarrassment, sing old neighborhood songs — "Paddy McGinty's Goat" and "Nobody Knows What Happened to Mc-Carty" — on their way down those great corridors at night. Leo's desk was in the little anteroom to Tip's working office, hidden along the Capitol's East Front. From this well-placed spot he was entrusted by Tip to decide which lobbyists to let through the door, whom to hit up at fund-raising time, and what scores warranted settling. Leo and Millie O'Neill were the only ones who called the Speaker "Tom."

Ari Weiss, Tip's legislative whiz kid, came from a different generation and had a different set of skills. He somehow had the knack of knowing what was happening in the House each morning within minutes of arriving at his desk. It was uncanny. Because of this, the Speaker relied on him completely, always wanting Ari in the room and at his side whenever legislation was being discussed. Yet there was another, important fact to know about Ari, over and beyond his legislative radar, which was that he and Tip were rooted in a mutual past, despite the four-decade difference in their ages. "I knew his father and his mother," the Speaker liked to say, and this shared history was, for Tip, the coin of the realm.

The moment had now arrived for my first meeting with the man himself. It took place in his office on the East Front of the Capitol, secreted far away from visiting tourists. He was behind his desk and leaning toward me, his short-sleeved shirt showing off his huge forearms as I took my chair. He seemed to me at home in this world, *organic* to the place.

He was curious about me, and the feeling was obviously mutual. It's possible my notions before meeting him owed a lot to those caricatures I'd been recruited to help combat. With so many years intervening since then, it's hard to remember now at what moment my *imagined* Tip O'Neill suddenly merged with the real one. The one thing I will never forget is the "animal" aspect to him, something that dominated the space around him. If power is measured in physical presence, he projected it in strength. What sat before me was a bear of a man.

One thing that was clear from the start was that this national figure whose reputation I'd long known about regarded me as a professional. I'd arrived on his doorstep with advance billing that told him I could help fix his problem. If I'd been a golf pro— or a plumber, for that matter — he'd have treated me the same. Beyond that, what linked us right off the bat was the way his need matched up with my readiness to get to work. There were also the stakes that brought me there in the first place. What he and I both knew — and neither of us wanted to say, certainly not at this meeting, at least — was that if he didn't win this fight there wouldn't be another.

Given all this, I was relieved he felt no need for coyness. Looking me straight in the eye, he said, "Tell me what I'm doing wrong and what I'm doing right. Let's have a little conversation." After listening to what I had to say, he made an unforgettable declaration. "You know an old dog can learn new tricks," he pronounced. And, when I heard him say that, my sense of anticipation about what lay ahead, and what we might do together, kicked in. And guess what else? I saw how it would be a way to tap again into the fighting energy I'd felt back on Air Force One, writing speeches for President Carter.

It wasn't long before I was reporting for work. The pattern of my days now weirdly echoed that of a decade earlier when I'd split my time between Senator Moss's office by day and guarding the Capitol, armed and ready, by night. In the current era I would spend my mornings checking the national news and looking for ammo that Thomas P. O'Neill, Jr., the battling national Democrat, could fire at Ronald Reagan. I knew that O'Neill needed to get *larger,* to grab some top billing by injecting himself into the fast-moving news cycle.

Each day, too, I'd drop into Kirk O'Donnell's office to discuss with him the current agenda, specifically the topics to be covered at that morning's session in front of reporters. I soon began to produce short statements for Tip to use. They were designed to be what beat journalists call "news helper," colorful copy to liven up what they'd go back to their desks and file. My hope was that those covering Tip would be more likely to quote him if he delivered such lively zingers. That was the idea. But for a good many weeks, I'm sorry to admit, the Speaker decided to ignore any of the offerings I'd knocked out with such excitement.

After catching the Speaker's press conference each Tuesday through Thursday, which was usually over by noon, I'd walk over to the headquarters of the DCCC on nearby North Capitol Street to tackle whatever was waiting for me there. If on the Speaker's team I was playing defense, here I was on offense.

At the DCCC one of the ideas I came up with was the creation of the Congressional News Service, a made-for-the-occasion periodical whose only purpose was to stir up trouble for incumbent GOP House members. The contents of any "edition" consisted solely of customized news items featuring Republican members of Congress that would then be mailed to their local newspapers and TV and radio stations. It was modeled after Nader's Capitol Hill News Service, where I'd once worked, but the content we now assembled was specifically focused on Republicans. It consisted of embarrassing items that normally went unmentioned in official constituent newsletters, for example, how much this member or that had enthusiastically enjoyed that year's Paris Air Show. To keep it legit, each edition, with its official-looking banner, included a credit line at the bottom of the page clearly reading "Democratic Congressional Campaign Committee." That said, I'll be the first to admit the size of the typeface required not just excellent eyesight but a weary editor's alertness.

I remember one punchy Congressional News Service headline I particularly enjoyed. It read, COYNE CAN'T COUNT! The member in this case was James K. Coyne III — a freshman Republican from Bucks County, Pennsylvania, who may not even have remembered the legislation involved until the Congressional News Service reminded him. The best I can recall, it derided the Republican doctrine that cutting taxes and raising defense spending would somehow avoid higher deficits. But any sins the opposition committed, however obscure, were rightly fair game, as far as I was concerned, and so I'd write up the stories I liked and send them out. Later, after a newspaper in Congressman Coyne's district had used our item, I received a clipping of it attached to an appreciative note from the Democrat whom Coyne had beaten the year before. *Keep up the good work* was the message.

What I was doing was partisan politics at its most basic, nothing on a very high level but definitely a lot of fun. The goal was to hit back effectively at the same dozens of House Republicans, for the purposes of 1982, who'd managed to KO House Democrats in 1980. We were targeting not only the usual swing districts but also some historically Democratic ones that had been carried by Reagan.

Yet our fear remained that Ronald Reagan would do such a bang-up job as president that he'd sweep those same Republicans right back in a second time. Not only would he protect them, he'd *entrench* them.

In early March, Tip O'Neill made a fateful decision. Believing as he did that the American people make only one national decision politically, whom to elect president of the United States, it was an inevitable one. He decided, in his words, to "give Reagan his schedule." He was going to allow the White House's fiscal agenda — all the spending and tax cuts — to be debated and voted upon in the House by August 1. There would be no procedural games, no foot-dragging. The voters wanted Ronald Reagan, so now they would get him, and in sufficient time to judge the results by the 1982 congressional elections.

This decision, which won for Tip a personal thank-you call from the president, was actually a strategic withdrawal. "I was convinced that if the Democrats were perceived as stalling in the midst of a national economic crisis, there would be hell to pay in the midterm elections," he said. If Reagan got his program and it failed to produce positive results, the Democrats would be rewarded at the polls.

Tip knew that he had little leeway. The situation facing him in the House was far worse even than it appeared on paper. Over the past decades, with only the brief exceptions of the early New Deal and the Great Society, the Congress had been ruled by a conservative alliance of Republicans and southern Democrats, two factions sharing common ground when it came to increased national defense spending or opposition to social legislation. Meeting with the Democratic Conservative Forum, a group composed of southern Democrats, Reagan now found himself surprised but delighted to hear that their own list of proposed spending cuts topped his by $10 billion. "You've made my day," he told them, thrilled.

As they were assembling their forces and their ammunition, it was critical that Reagan and his shotgun guard, Jim Baker, avoid any missteps. When Senate Republicans surprised the White House with their plan to "freeze" Social Security benefits, denying retirees their expected cost-of-living adjustments, the Reagan team quickly stomped it to death. They knew better than to touch what Kirk O'Donnell had christened the "third rail" of American politics.

The Reagan team, in fact, was smart enough to steer clear of *anything* at all that might stall its momentum. It knew that the spring and summer of its inaugural year was the once-in-a-presidency moment to launch the administration's program on its way. The Senate Budget Committee, where I'd worked under Edmund Muskie, was now in Republican control and moving fast, to the chagrin of liberal Democrats, on Reagan's cuts. As the last days of March drew on, the committee was swinging into action on the White House plan. "We have undone thirty years of social legislation in three days," New York's senator Daniel Patrick Moynihan remarked blackly.

The Democrats, looking around, believed

that the country's affections for Ronald Reagan could not possibly grow deeper. The sole consolation they could offer themselves was that all honeymoons, especially the political sort, come to an end.

President Reagan in range of John Hinckley. Fortunately for us all, the Secret Service's Jerry Paar was closest when the bullets flew. He had Reagan crouched and covered in a speeding car within seconds, and at George Washington University Hospital in just under three minutes.

CHAPTER SIX:
THE LORD IS MY SHEPHERD

"I do not know that in our time we have seen such a display. It makes us proud of our president."
— SENATOR DANIEL PATRICK MOYNIHAN

As a White House speechwriter, I'd known Jerry Parr up close: he'd been the head Secret Service agent responsible for protecting the president. Parr had come to the White House during Carter's presidency, having earlier served both at home and abroad. On that sad November morning when Carter had flown south to cast his vote in Plains, Jerry was there with us on *Marine One*. On the inaugural platform he'd been the fellow positioned, first, in back of Carter, and, once the torch was passed, behind Carter's successor, Ronald Reagan, sworn in as the fortieth president of the United States.

The young Jerry Parr had set his heart on

becoming a Secret Service agent from an early age. When he was nine he'd talked his dad into taking him to the movie *Code of the Secret Service,* whose hero, Lieutenant Brass Bancroft, a dashing agent and ace pilot, was played by a busy young actor, Ronald Reagan. This was Reagan's fourteenth movie after only two years in Hollywood, and he would appear as Brass Bancroft four times altogether. According to the buildup, Brass and his fellow agents were required to be "dauntless in the face of danger" and "fearless in the face of death." Hoping to keep audiences hooked on the series, publicists at Warner Bros. came up with the idea of starting a Brass Bancroft fan club, which they called the "Junior Secret Service Club." Anyone joining it would receive a membership card signed by Ronald Reagan. The nine-year-old Jerry Parr had been so enthusiastic about *Code of the Secret Service* he went back to see it again and again.

In 1962, at the age of thirty-two, after stints with the air force and a public utility company in Florida and then earning a previously deferred college degree, Parr fulfilled his boyhood dream of becoming a Secret Service agent. After being accepted into the program, he found himself to be the oldest trainee in his class. Over the following years, Parr served diligently, rose through the ranks, and finally was put in charge of presidential protection — as head of the Secret Service White House detail — in 1979.

Inspired so many years before by Ronald Reagan, in ways that wound up giving shape to his life, Jerry Parr, a little over four decades later, now was about to return the favor.

History often produces strange parallels. In March 1981, another moviegoer, twenty-five-year-old John Hinckley, would also reveal himself to have been greatly influenced by a film, and to be equally motivated to act out what he'd seen on the big screen. A depressed college dropout, whose wealthy family was in the oil business, Hinckley seemed to fail at everything he tried. Repeatedly viewing Martin Scorsese's grimly violent *Taxi Driver* — released originally in 1976 — he became obsessed with one of its stars, Jodie Foster. She'd memorably played a preteen prostitute in the movie, but by the time of Ronald Reagan's election she'd entered college and was a freshman at Yale. Determined to make Foster notice him, Hinckley first moved to New Haven, writing and phoning her repeatedly. But when his attentions proved entirely unwanted, he began to envision impressing her by the magnitude of an extreme act he would plan and commit.

Since a central plotline of *Taxi Driver* had been the determination of a loner — Travis Bickle, played by Robert De Niro — to assassinate a politician, this was the course Hinckley decided upon in his quest to prove to Foster his devotion. After leaving New Haven, Hinckley first fixed on the idea of shooting Jimmy Carter and, following him to Nashville, back in early October, wound up arrested instead on a concealed weapons charge. After paying a fine of $62.50, he was released.

On March 30, 1981, at two thirty in the afternoon, a lunch being given by the National Conference of the Building and Construction Trades Department of the AFL-CIO in the International Ballroom of the Washington Hilton was just ending. The event's speaker had been Ronald Reagan, who'd launched into his speech at 2:03 p.m. Among the topics were the deficit, his tax-cutting agenda, his determination to reduce federal regulations, and the intensive military buildup he planned. He also told the audience, "I hope you'll forgive me if I point with some pride to the fact that I'm the first President of the United States to hold a lifetime membership in an AFL-CIO union" — which in his case was the Screen Actors Guild.

As soon as he'd finished speaking, Reagan left the building by the side exit on T Street to approach the waiting presidential motorcade — where, nearby, John Hinckley was lying in wait. Raising a .22-caliber revolver, he fired six shots. One hit James Brady, the president's press secretary. Another wounded D.C. police officer Thomas Delahanty. A third struck Secret Service agent Timothy McCarthy. Although Hinckley missed hitting President Reagan directly, one of the bullets ricocheted off the presidential limousine and entered President Reagan's lung, lodging approximately an inch from his heart.

Following the Secret Service rule of "cover and evacuate," Jerry Parr, who'd been standing right behind Reagan, grabbed him and shoved him onto the backseat of the waiting limo, then jumped on top of him. "Let's get out of here," he yelled to the driver. "Haul ass!"

Here's Reagan's account from his journal of those harrowing moments:

My day to address the Bldg. & Const.
Trades Nat. Conf. A.F.L.C.I.O. at the Hilton Ballroom — 2 P.M. Speech not riotously
received — still it was successful. Left the
hotel at the usual side entrance and
headed for the car — suddenly there was
a burst of gun fire from the left. SS Agent
pushed me onto the floor of the car &
jumped on top. I felt a blow in my upper
back that was unbelievably painful. I was
sure he'd broken my rib. The car took off.
I sat up on the edge of the seat almost
paralyzed by pain. Then I began coughing
up blood which made both of us think —
yes I had broken a rib & it had punctured
a lung. He switched orders from W.H. to
Geo. Wash. U. Hosp.

Here's White House detail chief Parr's statement to the FBI:

We were, I suppose, three or four feet
from the limousine when I heard what
sounded like firecrackers or a small caliber
weapon. I heard one shot. There was a
short interval then three or four other
shots. My reaction was instantly to shove
the President forward into the limousine.
    . . . at Dupont Circle he started spitting
up this blood — profuse amounts of red,

bright red, frothy blood. And I thought, "Well, what would cause that? Maybe landing on top of him cracked a rib. Maybe I punctured a rib."

We really were moving quite rapidly at that time. The president said, "I'm having trouble breathing and I think I cut the inside of my mouth."

Suddenly Agent Parr noticed an alarming change in the injured man's condition: Reagan's lips were turning blue. From his training, Parr knew this indicated bleeding in the lung. Recognizing the perilous situation, he knew it would waste precious time continuing on to the White House. "I think we should go to the hospital," Parr told the president.

"Okay," Reagan agreed. Though he'd recoiled at hearing the gunshots at the Hilton, he hadn't even realized at first he'd been hit, and was obviously in shock, though alert. And so Parr directed the driver now to change course and turn west, making for George Washington University Hospital.

Barely three minutes after leaving the Hilton, the speeding motorcade screeched to a halt in front of the emergency room doors. "This is the president!" yelled Parr. It was a magnificent execution of duty. There's almost no question that Jerry Parr's quick thinking was what saved his wounded companion's life.

The rest of the performance upon their arrival was pure Reagan. Despite the high stakes and the very clear danger, it took a veteran showman to understand so beautifully the role he now needed to play, knowing that the front-row audience would be his country. He was determined to walk through the doors of the hospital under his own strength. More remarkably, even now he stopped to chat with people standing outside the building. But Reagan's determination could carry him only through the hospital doors. Twenty feet inside, Paar saw his eyes suddenly roll back in his head and he collapsed. He and another agent caught him before he reached the floor. Despite the brio he exhibited, the president had lost 50 percent of his blood supply through internal bleeding and now would require a surgeon's skills to extract the unexploded slug resting precariously near his heart.

"Honey, I forgot to duck," he confessed sheepishly upon spying his distraught wife, Nancy, who'd been rushed to his side. No one minded that he'd taken this one from Jack Dempsey, who'd said the same thing after losing the 1926 heavyweight title to

Gene Tunney. He then topped it with his quip to the medical team about to operate on him. "I hope you're all Republicans," he said before succumbing to the anesthesia.

Within a week of the attempt on his life, President Ronald Reagan seemed to be going about the business of running the country, issuing new proposals on such issues as air quality and auto safety regulations. That at least is the story the public was getting. The truth was far scarier. The country's leader was in far worse condition — a reality Jim Baker and the others around him decided should be kept from the American people and the world.

This alone became a challenge. Baker learned that Senator Strom Thurmond, the aging Dixiecrat-turned-Republican, had talked his way past hospital officials into Reagan's presence. This had infuriated Nancy Reagan, which prompted Baker to assign Max Friedersdorf to take charge 24/7 of keeping the president from being disturbed.

"Jim called me with the story," Friedersdorf reported. "Told me to get over to the hospital and stay in the president's room and make sure no one, despite any credentials or rank, got into the sickroom."

Jim Baker, ever strategic, had ruled that the first representative of official Washington to visit the convalescing president would be the leader of the opposition. Eventually, after several days, once Reagan was able to start receiving approved company, the first person to be admitted to his bedside was Tip O'Neill.

"I was in the room on my chair where Baker had posted me," is how Friedersdorf remembers it. When the Speaker came in, "he nodded my way and walked over to the bed and grasped both the president's hands, and said 'God bless you, Mr. President.'

"The president still seemed groggy . . . with lots of tubes and needles running in and out of his body. But when he saw Tip, he lit up and gave the Speaker a big smile, and said 'Thanks for coming, Tip.' Then, still holding one of the president's hands, the Speaker got down on his knees and said he would like to offer a prayer for the president, choosing the Twenty-third Psalm. 'The Lord is my shepherd; I shall not want. He maketh me to lie down in green pastures . . .' " It seemed clear to Friedersdorf, witnessing the encounter, that Reagan, though weak, was paying attention. "He recited part of the prayer with the Speaker in almost a whisper."

Once they'd finished, the Speaker let go of the president's hand, stood up, and bent to kiss him on the forehead. " 'I'd better be going,' he told the patient. 'I don't want to tire you out.' " During this privileged visit to GW Hospital, Tip saw firsthand the reality of Reagan's condition. Like the rest of the country, he'd been led to believe the president was experiencing a robust recovery. Instead he found himself kneeling within inches of a seventy-year-old man lying there in great pain.

The Speaker had been asked by the White House not to comment on the president's condition. "I suspect that in the first day or two after the shooting he was probably closer to death than most of us realized," he later said. "If he hadn't been so strong and hardy, it could have been all over."

The week before the shooting Reagan and Nancy had spent the evening at Ford's Theatre. The benefit was for a cause important to Millie O'Neill, its chairwoman. The two couples sat together in the first row. Captured on videotape taken that night, the president and the Speaker can be seen laughing and enjoying themselves while a juggler-comedian performs with antic precision on the stage, his long knives whirling barely an arm's length away in front of them. I can remember Tip talking in the office about his uneasiness at those knives flying so close.

Yet Reagan had glimpsed a shadow there in Ford's Theatre. "I looked up at the presidential box above the stage where Abe Lincoln had been sitting the night he was shot and felt a curious sensation. . . . I thought that even with all the Secret Service protection we now had, it was probably still possible for someone who had enough determination to get close enough to a president to shoot him." Tip O'Neill, who'd greeted Reagan at the street door that night, would say later that he, too, actually had had the same thought, undoubtedly inspired by the historic surroundings and suddenly realizing how vulnerable Reagan — as president — was.

Ronald Reagan had dodged death, but only narrowly. He would return to the White House the same but different, changed by this close brush with his own mortality. The causes that had mattered so deeply to him in the past now became his life's abiding purpose.

"A lot of the people you have under contract
don't know a football from a cantaloupe," actor Pat O'Brien
told producer Jack Warner. "This guy does."

CHAPTER SEVEN:
RONALD REAGAN'S JOURNEY

"Go West, young man."
— HORACE GREELEY

Tip O'Neill viewed Ronald Reagan as a man who'd gotten ahead in life by virtue of the enviable gifts — good looks, athleticism, a voice made for the broadcast booth or the cowboy movie — bestowed on him at birth. What bugged the Speaker so much about the former California governor and movie star was the belief that handsome guys like his new rival had to have had it easy, and being handsome *and* having it easy was an affront to those who weren't and didn't.

Yet in life, just as in the movies, the illusion is everything. When you're seeing the finished, glossy production, as Tip was, you're not rooting around for the discarded scenes. As any student of Ronald Wilson Reagan's origins knows, the script for the future president's story threw plenty of obstacles in his way early on.

He'd come into the world in Tampico, Illinois, a hamlet around one hundred miles west of Chicago. Over the next seven years the Reagans moved five times in Illinois, including a stint in Chicago itself, but eventually returned to Tampico, where they lived above the local variety store until young Ron — nicknamed "Dutch" ("he looks like a fat Little Dutchman," his father said of the newborn) — was nine. Now they moved again, to the much larger town of Dixon. His father, Jack, a salesman, proved a not so able provider, and keeping two growing boys fed was often a struggle for Nelle, his mother. Neil Reagan, Reagan's older brother and only sibling, remembered being sent out for a ten-cent soup bone; it would have to stretch through an entire week of dinners. In ways like this Nelle Reagan continually put her natural optimism to work for her, a trait she'd pass on to her second son.

The family situation wasn't helped by the fact that Jack Reagan drank too much, suffering — and forcing his wife and children to suffer — from what his younger son would term "the Irish curse." Reagan would write, painfully, of having returned home one afternoon to the sight of his father sprawled out on the front porch, a spectacle for the neighbors to see, judge, and share. And yet the difficulties of his home life didn't prevent Dutch Reagan from playing varsity football his last two years — though passionately determined, he'd been too small until then — and being popular enough to be elected Dixon High student body president when he was a senior. He was also president of the Dramatic Club.

As he entered his late teens, Reagan looked past his family and its difficulties to begin taking charge of the future he wanted for himself, a path that would test both his ambition and his ingenuity. Setting out to convince Eureka College to help with the costs of his education — it was 1928, the year before the Great Depression began — he did the job so well they wound up offering a scholarship fully covering his tuition as well as half his board. To pay for the difference he worked as a "hasher," serving meals, first for a fraternity, later at a girls' dorm.

When he first headed west after graduating from college — his majors had been economics and sociology — he made it only as far as another midwestern hub, Davenport, Iowa, just across the Illinois border. There he landed a slot as a sportscaster in a budding medium open to newcomers: radio. After Davenport, once he'd gained experience behind the microphone, he struck out and headed due west again, making it this time just a bit farther into Iowa, to a station in Des Moines.

Then, finally, he was ready for the biggest western leap of all: California. In 1937, five years after saying good-bye to Illinois, it was now "goodbye sports . . . hello Hollywood!" for the twenty-six-year-old Reagan. It made perfect sense.

Nancy Reagan, who knew her husband better than anyone, later succinctly explained to me: he couldn't get *stuck* out there in middle America. She understood her future husband's youthful yearnings to escape because she'd once experienced them herself. A native New Yorker, she'd moved to Chicago at the age of eight when her divorced mother remarried. Returning after her four years at Smith College, she, too, managed to escape and never come back. They were two of a kind — the kind that didn't stay put until they got where they were meant to be.

It was a moment of manifest destiny: Ronald Reagan proceeding *all the way* west for the first time. He'd gone as a radio sportscaster, sent to Los Angeles to report on spring training. But the chance to take a Warner Bros. screen test trumped his original purpose, to keep an eye on the Chicago Cubs, warming up for the season on Catalina Island.

As they say in politics, you *make* your breaks. In Los Angeles, he spotted a poster advertising the evening's entertainment in the Biltmore Hotel's ballroom. One performer was a singer he knew from Des Moines. He sent a note inviting her to dinner between shows. This led to her offering to introduce him to her agent, who in turn proved able to arrange a screen test for the young radio announcer. It was a break that led to a two-hundred-dollar-a-week, seven-year Warner Bros. contract that Reagan quickly signed, agreeing with the stipulation that he be billed as Ronald, not "Dutch," Reagan, the name he'd been going by. He was on his way.

Reagan's first film saw him playing a radio reporter, the very job he'd just left behind. *Love Is on the Air* was a B picture shot and released quickly as the second half of a double feature. The reviews in the trades were approving, "likeable" being the basic verdict — and, of course, they weren't wrong. It would prove to be his lifelong signature quality. Over the next few years,

Ronald Reagan, working regularly, turned up — more than once, as I've said — as Brass Bancroft the Secret Service agent. He appeared as a military cadet in the 1938 comedy *Brother Rat* with Jane Wyman, whom he'd soon make his first wife, and as an army private in *Sergeant Murphy* (1938), the title character of which was a horse. In a change of pace, he was a pleasure-loving playboy in the Bette Davis picture *Dark Victory* (1939). His big break arrived in 1940, the year *Knute Rockne — All American* was released.

On the Warner lot, Reagan had become pals with Pat O'Brien, one of the most prolific stars of the era and the leader of Hollywood's "Irish mafia," a group that included James Cagney, Spencer Tracy, and others. Each day at lunch in the Warner Bros. commissary O'Brien would hold court, surrounded by his buddies, and before long he invited Reagan to join the gang.

When O'Brien won the part of famed Notre Dame coach Knute Rockne in a highly anticipated upcoming biopic, he soon learned from Reagan how eager he was to be in it, and that he'd grown up worshipping both Rockne and George Gipp, the young football player who'd died in 1920 just days after leading his team to victory. The young Reagan had been so taken with the Gipp story that he'd once even started writing a screenplay of his own. To press his case at Warner Bros., he brought in his college yearbook, which showed him on the playing field. In an effort to help, O'Brien made sure the studio bosses knew the young contract actor was the real deal. "This is a helluva important role. A lot of the people you have under contract don't know a football from a cantaloupe. This guy does," O'Brien told Jack Warner.

In a further effort to help, O'Brien interceded with producer Hal Wallis on behalf of his younger friend. Finding Wallis initially reluctant, he then extended himself in an even larger gesture, offering to read Rockne's lines for the screen test Reagan needed to ace in order to win the part. It all helped. When *Knute Rockne — All American* premiered in South Bend, Indiana, home of the University of Notre Dame, a quarter million fans greeted the cast. The Gipper role would prove a turning point in Ronald Reagan's career.

Reagan's next career peak — the role he himself considered his best — was *Kings Row,* in which he played, as he often did in those years, the hero's best friend. Opening in early 1942, just months after Pearl Harbor, *Kings Row* established its claim on filmic immortality by virtue of a simple five-word question: "Where's the rest of me?" It's what Reagan's character, Drake McHugh, demands to know after waking from surgery to discover both his legs amputated by a sadistic doctor. Reagan would go on to make the famous line the title of his 1965 autobiography.

Measured by box office, though, the most important movie for the future president was a film released in 1942, *Desperate Journey.* It reteamed him with Errol Flynn. Two years earlier they'd appeared together in *Santa Fe Trail,* in a thrilling wartime tale directed by Michael Curtiz, best known today for *Casablanca. Desperate Journey* follows the perilous path through Nazi Germany of an RAF bomber crew shot down and trying, against enormous odds, to escape. It was the number-two-grossing film of the year, second only to the enormously loved *Mrs. Miniver.*

Yet by the time *Kings Row* and *Desperate Journey* opened, they were showing to a country that was not the same as when the movies were filmed. On December 8, 1941, the day after Pearl Harbor was attacked, Franklin D. Roosevelt went before Congress to ask it to declare the United States officially at war. If America was at war, so was Hollywood. The movie industry, an important one for national morale, became a critical part of the war effort.

The month before he'd moved to Los Angeles from Des Moines, Reagan had joined the Army Enlisted Reserve. Arriving in Hollywood, he was appointed second lieutenant in the cavalry. With the United States now in the war, he was ordered to active duty — it was April 1942, two months after *Kings Row* had opened in theaters. His eyesight — he suffered from astigmatism — kept him from assignment to a combat unit.

Transferring from the cavalry to the Army Air Corps, the actor was sent first to a public relations unit and then to the just-created First Motion Picture Unit. Never before had a military unit been made up completely of movie professionals dedicated to putting all their skills, talent, and imagination into training and propaganda films. It was this unit, based in Culver City in the former Hal Roach Studios (once home to Laurel and Hardy, among other comedy greats, and now dubbed Fort Roach), to which Ronald Reagan would be attached for most of the rest of the war. In 1943, a twenty-two-minute film he'd narrated, *Be-*

yond the Line of Duty, won the Oscar for "Best Short Subject." Though he both appeared in and voiced-over numerous movies, he was also the unit's personnel officer, and at the end of his active duty in 1945, when he returned to civilian life, he held the rank of captain.

Wars leave no one they've touched the same. Though he'd spent the years of World War II far from the front, making films in Culver City and Burbank, Ronald Reagan had served honorably. He'd contributed exactly as the U.S. government had called upon him to do. Yet not only did the postwar landscape he confronted now look and seem different; so did he.

One of those who apparently saw him in a new — and unflattering — light was his wife of eight years, Jane Wyman. They'd married in 1940, two years after shooting *Brother Rat* together. She'd become a Warner contract player in 1936 at nineteen, having appeared, though often as an uncredited chorus girl, in thirty or so pictures by the time they started dating. A native Missourian, she, too, had gotten her showbiz start in radio, as a singer. She'd also been twice married by the time she walked down the aisle with Reagan.

But by 1948, when they divorced, she was

the bigger star of the two. She'd been nominated for the Academy Award for Best Actress in 1946, for *The Yearling,* and in 1948 won it for *Johnny Belinda.* Given the couple's high profile, the Hollywood gossip mills went to town avidly recycling all the cruel remarks she'd allegedly made about her spouse and the father of her two children. For his part, Reagan seemed to be in denial and still deeply devoted to his marriage.

Wyman was said to have confided in a friend one night at a cocktail party: "Don't ask Ronnie what time it is because he will tell you how a watch is made." As far as she was concerned, her soon-to-be ex-husband number three was "America's number one goody two shoes." She on the other hand had recently taken a lover — Lew Ayres, her *Johnny Belinda* costar. Her cruelest line may well have been delivered to Reagan face-to-face when he returned home one day from work: "You bore me," she said. "Leave!"

Long before his divorce from Wyman, and even their marriage itself, Reagan had developed an obsessive passion of his own: politics. By his own account, it had begun back in 1928, the year he entered Eureka

College. There, he and his fellow students, angered by the administration's decision to eliminate a number of courses — which also meant laying off the professors who taught them — decided to call a strike. Such a protest would shut down the campus. But the stand was worth making, the student leaders felt, and, despite his freshman status, Dutch Reagan was the one picked, at the meeting of the entire student body, to make the motion to strike.

Here's how he recalled the impact the speech had on the audience, but most of all on him: "When I came to actually presenting the motion . . . they came to their feet with a roar — even the faculty members present voted by acclamation. It was heady wine. Hell, with two more lines, I could have had them riding through 'every Middlesex village and farm' — without horses yet."

When it came to Hollywood actors, the truth was there was something about Ronald Reagan that set him apart. Soon after he'd arrived on the Warner lot a decade earlier, colleagues noticed he paid as much attention to actual news headlines as the ones in *Daily Variety*. Robert Cummings, his *Kings Row* costar, recalled Reagan holding forth frequently on the set. "All the cast used to sit around waiting for the cameramen to light the scene — sometimes it was long, tedious hours, because almost all of the entire outdoor scenes were shot indoors. So we'd listen to Ronnie talk about foreign affairs and the economy and things like that. . . . Whether he knew what he was doing at the time or not, I don't know — it wasn't a lecture — but he took the center of the stage."

Ron Reagan, the president's son — by his second wife, Nancy, whom Ronald married in 1952 — later would describe his father as having had two selves. One, he wrote, was the "public" Reagan who "wanted and needed acclaim and recognition" but would "disavow ambition." Alongside this visible Reagan, he believed, existed another "private" one, within whom the drive to get ahead "burned with a cold but steady flame." According to the younger Reagan, the Ronald Reagan whom the world assumed it knew "could not have existed without the Ronald Reagan he rarely let anyone see." In the years following World War II, as Reagan faced setbacks, that hidden, private self seems to have been the main engine of the changes and choices he faced and made. It was also the part of Ronald Reagan that was deeply driven by his political thinking.

In the late 1940s, he realized he wasn't being considered for parts that would have been offered to him after *Kings Row* and *Desperate Journey* — that is, if he hadn't spent those World War II years in uniform. The world had moved on, other handsome newcomers were arriving, and audience tastes were changing.

It's not that he had *no* work in front of the cameras during this period. He shot a few B pictures every year, including the much-remembered *Bedtime for Bonzo* (1951). It's that the gleam of Ronald Reagan, movie star, had lost much of its previous luster. The charmed existence that Tip O'Neill imagined was his rival's lifelong birthright was nowhere to be seen. Though Reagan had gotten out of Illinois just as he'd always meant to, had gone on to appear on movie posters and had his name lit brightly on marquees, his career now looked to be headed downward. What remained to him were the grit and resilience — an integral part of his secret self — that adversaries would continue to underestimate at their peril.

Offscreen, Reagan's marriage in 1952 to Nancy Davis — a young actress ten years his junior — was the best evidence that fortune could still favor him. Their union was the stuff of fan magazines: she'd dated Clark Gable, and William Holden was best man at their wedding. But it was Nancy's rock-solid devotion to her husband and belief in him that made her exactly the soul mate he needed. "My life really began when I married my husband," she often said. The same, most certainly, could be said for Ronald Reagan.

Politically, Reagan was evolving. While Nancy's own loyalties were influenced by her stepfather Loyal Davis's staunch Republicanism, his new son-in-law — who'd voted for FDR, supported the New Deal, campaigned for Harry Truman, and, more than that, had backed Helen Gahagan Douglas in her California Senate race against Richard Nixon — would remain a registered Democrat for another decade.

In 1937 Reagan had joined the Screen Actors Guild shortly after arriving in Hollywood. He'd gone onto its board as an alternate in 1941. Then, after the war, he resumed his involvement (serving at one point as an alternate for Boris Karloff). In 1946 he became vice president, and the next year, the guild's president. SAG was then involved in a bitter dispute with a craft union coalition, the Conference of Studio

Unions (CSU), whose hard-left leadership wanted its support. Ugly violence had broken out at the Warner Bros. gates between strikers and those wanting to cross the CSU picket lines. In the weeks that followed, Reagan became a persuasive SAG voice against continuing to honor those picket lines, and many fellow union members began falling in step behind him. Threatened by anonymous phone calls, he began carrying a .32 pistol. His rousing speech to the SAG membership now produced a stunning return-to-work vote: 2,748 to 509. The studio bosses also applauded his position. "Ronnie Reagan has turned out to be a tower of strength," declared Jack Warner, "not only for the actors but for the whole industry."

Reagan would go on to serve as SAG president for a total of seven terms. Despite his long-held ambition to act and to be thought well of as an actor, he was proving a natural at this real-life role he liked to call the "citizen-politician." Those who want to dismiss Ronald Reagan merely as a good-looking guy inspired to enter politics as his screen career started fading should take a moment to consider the heartfelt eloquence of testimony he gave in the fall of 1947, seven months after being elected president of the Screen Actors Guild. His audience: the House Committee on Un-American Activities (HUAC). The issue: communist influence in the movie industry.

Like many other Hollywood liberals of his era, Reagan walked a middle line between the arch anticommunists and those more tolerantly inclined. While acknowledging that the Communist Party undoubtedly wished to exploit Hollywood as a propaganda tool in any way it could, he vehemently objected to the idea that they were getting away with it. When asked by Robert Stripling, HUAC's chief investigator, "What steps should be taken to rid the motion picture industry of any communist influences?" here was Reagan's reply:

Well, sir, ninety-nine percent of us are pretty well aware of what is going on, and I think, within the bounds of our democratic rights and never once stepping over the rights given us by democracy, we have done a pretty good job in our business of keeping those people's activities curtailed. After all, we must recognize them at present as a political party. On that basis we have exposed their lies when we came across them, we have opposed their propaganda, and I can certainly testify that in the case of the Screen Actors Guild we have been eminently successful in preventing them from, with their usual tactics, trying to run a majority of an organization with a well-organized minority.

In opposing those people, the best thing to do is make democracy work. In the Screen Actors Guild we make it work by insuring everyone a vote and by keeping everyone informed. I believe that, as Thomas Jefferson put it, if all the American people know all of the facts they will never make a mistake. Whether or not the Party should be outlawed, that is a matter for the government to decide. As a citizen, I would hesitate to see any political party outlawed on the basis of its political ideology. We have spent a hundred and seventy years in this country on the basis that democracy is strong enough to stand up and fight against the inroads of any ideology. However, if it is proven that an organization is an agent of a foreign power, or in any way not a legitimate political party — and I think the government is capable of proving that — then that is another matter. I happen to be very proud of the industry in which I work. I happen to be very proud of the way in which we conducted the fight. I do not believe the Communists have ever at any time been able to use the motion picture screen as a sounding board for their philosophy or ideology.

It's a statement that, delivered with respectful courtesy and a genial forthrightness, neatly claims its own ground. Ronald Reagan was taking a stand proclaiming full faith in democracy — and, along with it, his belief in the American people's good judgment. It comes off without even a lurking shadow of partisanship or of politics as we normally think of them. Here was a man who'd been student body president in high school, who went on to deliver what he considered his maiden crowd-stirring political speech when just a college freshman. Sitting up there on Capitol Hill in 1947, responding to the House committee's questions, he was no amateur. Acting had been the detour, as would become increasingly clear.

By 1954, that detour was offering precarious turns in the road. His agent, Lew Wasserman, had gotten him a two-week stand as emcee of a Las Vegas revue act. It had him cracking Irish jokes and playing straight man to the other performers. "It's a long way down for Reagan from his box-office glory of 11 years ago," ran a cruel

151

item in the trade press.

Now came Wasserman to the rescue. Within weeks Reagan began his eight-year tenure presenting *General Electric Theater;* he was the half-hour anthology broadcast's first and only continuing host. It would prove a huge career opportunity for him. Airing on Sundays at 9 p.m., EST, the GE-sponsored program featured a wide range of stars: James Dean, Jack Benny, Natalie Wood, Lee Marvin, Sammy Davis, Jr. Over the eight years it ran, the weekly guests represented a virtual *Who's Who* of mid-twentieth-century show business. *GE Theater* was the way Americans growing up in the 1950s — Bill Clinton and me, to name just two — got to know and like Ronald Reagan.

And not only did he welcome us to *GE* every Sunday; Reagan also went to the road on its behalf. Traveling to hundreds of cities and towns by train, he became the company's representative both to the outside world and to itself. A typical day might include a local press conference, a Chamber of Commerce lunch, and a civic association evening banquet, with a high school or college campus appearance in between, as well as sessions with General Electric employees in their offices and on their factory floors. "I am seen by more people in one week than I am in a full year in movie theaters," is how Reagan chose to frame his remarkable new visibility. As of 1958 he was one of the most recognized figures in the country — not as an actor in a role but as Ronald Reagan himself.

Despite having been the public face of General Electric to millions of Americans — personally greeting and meeting, it's estimated, at least a quarter of a million of them as he continuously toured — the relationship ended abruptly in 1962. What they had once seen as positive about Reagan's rhetoric — his call to arms against big government at home and communism abroad — may have been viewed by corporate execs as impolitic. The larger factor was ratings. *GE Theater,* at one time the third highest rated show on all of television, was now fighting a long battle with *Bonanza* for its time slot.

In 1964 Ronald Reagan emerged fully into the open as a leader of the new conservative wing of the Republican Party. What brought him this increased prominence was a stirring stump speech he was tirelessly giving out on the Republican circuit in support of Senator Barry Goldwater, the Arizonan who was then the GOP presidential candidate.

Called "A Time for Choosing," the Goldwater campaign paid to have it nationally televised the week before Election Day.

Social Security, he said, "is not insurance but is a welfare program and Social Security dues are a tax for the general use of the government." Proclaiming that the country had "a rendezvous with destiny," Reagan preached his beliefs with a fervor that had slowly but steadily been building deep inside him. "We'll preserve for our children this, the last best hope of man on earth, or we'll sentence them to take the last step into a thousand years of darkness." It was a speech he'd been polishing for years, and he meant it all, every single word and thought.

When Reagan ran for governor of California two years later and won a monumental victory, beating incumbent governor Edmund G. "Pat" Brown by a million votes, he had turned himself into a singular political force to be reckoned with. Yet Democrats across the country, especially in Washington, would continue to question his legitimacy as a rising star — one with a bigger future than he'd ever had as a Warner contract player. They saw him more as a strictly California phenomenon, a West Coast punch line who'd never play beyond Sacramento.

Ignoring the million votes, they preferred to believe Ronald Reagan to be simply a good-looking, good-natured fellow who'd gotten his career from a screen test. Yet the signs indicating a different scenario had been there early on, as they are for most politicians — for anyone looking to see. Those who end up running for office can rarely hide the ambition in their youth.

His critics were ignoring a more basic fact. To denigrate Reagan's profession — dismissing him as a fellow who'd played against a chimp or shilled for lightbulbs — was to miss a very big and obvious truth: people *like* actors and are fascinated by them. Pat Brown, a man whom voters had failed ever to be fascinated by, actually appeared in a televised campaign ad in which he's seen warning a group of schoolchildren against the dangerous world represented by his opponent, the movie star. "I'm running against an actor . . . and you know who shot Lincoln, don'tcha?" It's even more peculiar an attack if you consider the number of California voters connected to the movie business.

In reality, the political Ronald Reagan was playing a role he'd created himself: the outsider as representative of all the decent, honest people fed up with standard-issue politicians. "As a politician, he would always have you believe that he was a reluctant candidate — he became a governor, then president, only because people insisted they needed him," his son Ron Reagan observed.

When accused of being poorly equipped by professional background to run the huge state of California, Reagan had blown off his detractors with one of those pronouncements he specialized in. "The man who *has* the job," he countered, "has more experience than anybody. That's why I'm running."

The way Reagan came to perfect the role of citizen-politician can be seen at the climax of the speech he gave accepting the 1980 Republican presidential nomination. Just as he was about to leave the convention podium that July night in 1980, he appeared to go through a slight moment of indecision. "I have thought of something," he said, briefly pausing, "that is not part of my speech and I'm worried over whether I should do it." It was a brilliant moment of stagecraft. His listeners waited, curious. Now they were actively in the scene along with him, the audience that could not see the script on the card in front of him.

"Can we doubt," he then asked, his voice

ringing with purpose, "that only a Divine Providence placed this land, this island of freedom, here as a refuge for all those people in the world who yearn to breathe freely: Jews and Christians enduring persecution behind the Iron Curtain, the boat people of Southeast Asia, of Cuba and Haiti, the victims of drought and famine in Africa, the freedom fighters of Afghanistan, and our own countrymen held in savage captivity.

"I'll confess," he went on, "that I've been a little afraid to suggest what I'm going to suggest — I'm more afraid not to — that we begin our crusade joined together in a moment of silent prayer."

It was a moment, too, of transformation for Reagan. No longer the actor and foregoing the role of politician, he was now one of the people daring to speak against "them," those who would challenge the right to pray at such a moment.

Ronald Reagan, not yet elected president, had gotten to precisely where he wanted to be in life.

His concluding words: "God bless America."

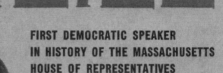

THOMAS P.
O'NEILL JR.

**FIRST DEMOCRATIC SPEAKER
IN HISTORY OF THE MASSACHUSETTS
HOUSE OF REPRESENTATIVES**

HE'S A LEADER!

HE'S A DOER!

HE FOLLOWS THRU!

HE'S YOUR MAN FOR
CONGRESS

Thomas P. "Tip" O'Neill, Jr., won fifty electoral contests in his long career.
In 1952 he took John F. Kennedy's seat in the U.S. House.

CHAPTER EIGHT:
THE RISE OF TIP O'NEILL

"All politics is local."
— THOMAS P. O'NEILL, SR.

Unlike Ronald Reagan, Tip O'Neill never faced poverty. When he was tapped for the annual "Horatio Alger Award," the Speaker turned down the honor. "I'm not eligible," the proud Irish-American told me to tell the association presenting it. "I wasn't born poor."

His father, Thomas Philip O'Neill, Sr., was the superintendent of sewers in the city of Cambridge, Massachusetts, responsible for 150 miles of municipal sewer lines. Powerful enough to be nicknamed "the Governor" in the neighborhoods, he commanded an army of employees, which meant a ready supply of patronage always at his disposal. If you did your chores for the local Democratic Party, that entitled you to a "snow button." If you showed up wearing it the next time snow fell, you could be assured of a paying job clearing the streets. If you didn't have the button, you were out in the cold.

Thomas Jr., his second son, though never without the comforts of a home, quickly learned how unfair life can be — and in profound ways. He was only nine months old when his mother died of tuberculosis. Without a wife to care for his three children — the O'Neill brood included an older brother and sister, William and Mary Rose — the father often needed to fob off the baby, especially, on relatives. Young O'Neill remembered being "passed from aunt to aunt," and, as he was to recall, "it wasn't a happy time." The sadness didn't end there. When his father married again, his home life failed to brighten. While he never voiced complaints about his stepmother, for young Tip her entry into the family quite clearly made for disappointed hopes.

But unlike Reagan, who, though popular and a joiner, was always alone in a crowd, O'Neill found warmth in his friends, and they in him. Unlike his future rival, Tip, when young, ran with a gang. In the company of his usual crowd of North Cambridge boys, he hung out daily at a storefront known as Barry's Corner. Among the

O'Neill pals of that era were "Red" Fitzgerald, "Frogsy" Broussard, "Moose" O'Connell, and others known by similarly colorful nicknames.

Tip's own lifelong moniker derived from a nineteenth-century left fielder who'd played for the old St. Louis Browns, James Edward "Tip" O'Neill. The original "Tip" had nearly a .500 batting average, inflated by the rule back then of counting walks as hits. O'Neill would earn those many walks by tipping off one pitch after another until the pitcher couldn't avoid missing the plate or throwing an easy one to hit. Obviously, among his gifts was simple, brute patience, a quality that comes in handy, especially in politics, where waiting your turn is more often than not the safest route to the top.

The kids at Barry's Corner were townies and early in life instinctively understood the truth of what that meant. A little more than two miles down Massachusetts Avenue stood Harvard University, a citadel of privilege and prestige that could not have been further away had it been on the moon. Accepting the hard divide between town and gown, Tip O'Neill and his gang recognized their place in the scheme of things. That didn't mean they liked it.

Many decades later the future Speaker

would still be smarting from the humiliation he'd felt the summer he was a chubby fourteen-year-old with a job cutting grass and trimming hedges in Harvard Yard. "Up off your ass, O'Neill," he recalled his crabby boss frequently yelling at him. "Off your ass!" He was warning the local kid he wasn't going to get away with performing his job sitting down. He was supposed to be clipping away on his knees. The fellow seemed intent on putting the North Cambridge boy down, making *sure* he knew his place — and, not surprisingly, Tip took it personally. Would such an employer have talked to a Harvard student that way? Then again, would a Harvard student have been out there with his shears in the sweltering sun?

The fact that Tip realized the divide separating his world from the other didn't mean the sharp reality of it didn't rankle. As F. Scott Fitzgerald well knew — *The Great Gatsby* had been published just two years earlier — the most powerful aspirations arise from rejection, fueling the dreams of those born on the wrong side looking in. Here's Tip's own version of the classic outsider tale, a very specific memory of that summer when he was fourteen and working in a part of his hometown where he didn't belong:

On a beautiful June day, as I was going about my daily grind, the class of 1927 gathered in a huge canvas tent to celebrate commencement. Inside, I could see hundreds of young men standing around in their white linen suits, laughing and talking. They were also drinking champagne, which was illegal in 1927 because of Prohibition. I remember that scene like it was yesterday, and I can still feel the anger I felt then, almost sixty years ago, as I write these words. It was the illegal champagne that really annoyed me. Who the hell do these people think they are, I said to myself, that the law means nothing to them? On that commencement day at Harvard, as I watched those privileged, confident Ivy League Yankees who had everything handed to them in life, I made a resolution. Someday, I vowed, I would work to make sure my own people could go to places like Harvard, where they could avail themselves of the same opportunities that these young college men took for granted.

If Ronald Reagan's political course had been set, when he was a middle-aged man, in late 1940s Hollywood, by his distaste for the hard-left labor factions' tactics as they struck the Hollywood studios, and also by his righteous indignation at the hefty bite the federal income tax took from his film earnings, Tip O'Neill's epiphany had come when much younger. And it had lodged in him in a way that would create a different path. Taking a clear-eyed look at the landscape close to home, the teenaged Tip had viewed political power through a very different prism. His goal, he decided early in life, would be to stand against those who defended social and economic injustice.

A year later the still-adolescent Tip was engaged in politics as a volunteer, knocking on doors and handing out campaign literature for New York Democratic governor Al Smith. The first Catholic to be nominated to run for president, Smith was a man of the people, one whose working-class origins always informed his outlook. As a representative in the New York State Assembly, Smith had drawn national attention early in his career when he spoke out forcefully for workplace safety after the infamous 1911 Triangle Shirtwaist Factory fire. Thus, when he led fellow Democrats in the fight against Herbert Hoover to gain the White House in 1928, Tip was a natural foot soldier for the cause. Though it turned out to be a lost one, it gave the eager young man a taste of the valiant, idealistic battles he hoped one day to wage.

Unlike his brother William, who'd left the environs of Boston for Holy Cross in central Massachusetts, Tip attended Boston College as a day student. It was one of those moments in life when a fortunate break more resembles a disadvantage, but for Tip O'Neill staying close to home made a lasting, enriching difference. By not following Bill to Worcester, he remained a neighborhood guy, never losing touch with his childhood buddies, the crew at Barry's Corner. As a "day hop," coming and going from classes across the Charles River, he was able to maintain his local identity and popularity. By staying regular in his habits, surroundings, and friends, he was able to sink his roots even deeper into the community where his paternal grandfather, Patrick O'Neill, had first settled seventy years earlier.

We've seen how the young Ronald Reagan chafed under what seemed to him the petty tyrannies and claustrophobic scale of small-town Illinois life. Tip O'Neill, on the other hand, was a man at home, and at one, with his native environment. Cambridge was where he'd been born, where he'd grown up, and where he intended to make his mark. He couldn't wait to get into politics on his own behalf.

While he was still a senior at BC, Tip ran unsuccessfully for the Cambridge City Council. What this meant in the short term was severe disappointment when he failed to win the seat. But for the long haul that first struggle Tip waged in the public eye left him indisputably wiser. Two maxims he heard at this time were to remain lifelong souvenirs of his maiden, losing race. The first was a signal — and, eventually for Tip, a signature — piece of advice imparted to him by his dad. According to Thomas Sr., his boy had stumbled for a simple reason: he'd failed to focus sufficiently on his own North Cambridge turf. "All politics is local," the father pronounced firmly. It was less a reproach than a fact of life, a truth he'd expected his son instinctively to understand.

According to him, what Tip should have done, rather than spreading himself thin canvassing the entire district, trying to convince strangers of his worth, was first to lock in decisively the loyalty of supporters closer to home. Then, after that was accomplished, he could be free to head farther afield. "Local" meant his own natural constituency, comprising those citizens nearest

166

in both geography and affinity, already well disposed to him and to his family, not needing to be sold on his value. The ideas, and ideals, embodied in the word *local* were to form his core philosophy when it came to political behavior.

The second lesson Tip absorbed was the result of a scolding he received the day before the election from a certain Mrs. Elizabeth O'Brien, who lived across the street from the O'Neills and was far from satisfied with the way the "Governor's boy" had comported himself during the campaign. She explained she was going to vote for him *even though he'd never personally come to her seeking support.* "Tom, let me tell you something: people *like* to be *asked,*" she informed him, surprised, as his father had been, at his ignorance. Happily, Tip was a quick learner and didn't need to hear either of these adages a second time.

In 1934 Tip was given a thrilling opportunity, one offered for purely local reasons. Marguerite "Missy" LeHand, who'd grown up not far from the O'Neill family and knew them, had been private secretary to Franklin Roosevelt since 1920. A year after she'd gone to work for the then — and ultimately unsuccessful — vice presidential candidate, FDR suffered the polio attack that left him paralyzed, unable to walk.

Despite this enormous handicap, he achieved what can only be called an extraordinary political comeback over the next decade, even though his enemies and rivals had regarded him as definitively sidelined. In 1932 Roosevelt ran for the presidency and won. Now Tip, thanks to Miss LeHand, who knew of the young man's political interests and ambitions, and that he'd campaigned for FDR as he had for Al Smith, found himself invited to Washington to meet her boss. When he got to the White House and was ushered into his hero's presence, he was stunned to see him seated in a wheelchair. "I was so shocked that my chin just about hit my chest," he later wrote.

Tip felt honor-bound to keep the president's secret. It was an early political confidence, of the highest order, but Tip perceived it also as a matter of personal respect on his part. The meeting, along with the trust the president had placed in him, left an indelible impression and contributed significantly to the formation of his ongoing political loyalties.

In 1936, having absorbed the earlier lessons of defeat, Thomas P. "Tip" O'Neill, Jr., was elected to the Massachusetts state legislature. He was twenty-three and, already at that early age, in exactly the place he was meant to be. That he entered politics and would make his life there certainly came as no surprise to one of the nuns who'd once taught him. She later told an interviewer: "Tom was never much of a student. But he was always popular and a leader even then. He led the boys' debating team and always won. Tom could talk you deaf, dumb and blind."

From the beginning, Tip based his political service on the primary needs of the citizens around him, whose lives he understood. Better still, he understood the dignity of those lives, and believed in that dignity. As a result, jobs, for him, were an all-important factor of the human equation, and, as such, the responsibility of an elected public servant. There was never any question in his mind that government could — and should — put people to work. He'd seen the connection between the two clearly ever since he'd spotted his first snow button. Winter created the jobs: government made sure the right people got them.

Starting in the 1920s and 1930s, New England was increasingly losing ground when it came to holding on to large-scale employers. The once widespread and prosperous regional textile industry had moved to cheaper territory below the Mason-Dixon Line, followed there by the shoe factories. A campaign slogan of "work and wages" was incentive enough to compel worried voters to back any Democratic candidate promising them. Yet Tip O'Neill, the freshman state representative from Cambridge, as concerned about jobs as he possibly could be, was also now revealing a concern for issues beyond the parochial ones that had guided him there in the first place.

One of these new concerns he now weighed in on was the importance of fighting any encroachment against our civil liberties. In his first months at the State House, young O'Neill made his name — for better or worse, you'd have to say — by siding with those casting votes to repeal a law mandating a loyalty oath for teachers. A politician taking this side of the argument would be seen in some precincts merely as an alert civil libertarian, while in others such a suspect position would not only elicit scorn but also likely draw the all-purpose epithet *communist.* Confident of the rightness of his position, however, Tip was willing to suffer the townie contempt at the same time as he earned the approval of his old nemeses, the Harvard Square types. At the next election, he won by an even larger margin.

In 1941, Tip married Mildred Ann Miller, a Somerville girl and high school classmate whose father was a streetcar operator, and whisked his bride off to New York for their honeymoon. He'd timed the wedding to occur on a particular weekday, one he considered special but for reasons having nothing to do with connubial love and everything to do with what was happening in New York the very next night. Tip would take his new wife of just twenty-four hours to the Polo Grounds to see Billy Conn fight Joe Louis in front of a crowd of fifty-four thousand people, a contest that's now the stuff of legend. In the thirteenth round, "The Pittsburgh Kid" had the champion on points, but then foolishly went for a knockout. It was he who got kayoed, instead. Afterward Conn famously quipped to a reporter, "What's the use of being Irish if you can't be thick?" Resuming their honeymoon, Tip and Millie headed the next day for Atlantic City.

Over the next five years Tip worked earnestly at his job, making his way up the Democratic ladder in the state legislature, storing up credit in the party as he did so. The universe in which he labored each day was an orderly one, with set rules, based on a code of behavior understood and agreed upon by all: you served your time in lower offices, worked your way "through the chairs" to head up a committee, knowing that you could, if fortune looked favorably, rise beyond the normal ranks to a privileged position such as a seat in the U.S. Congress. Still, everyone realized that such rewards could never come your way until you'd "worked your way up through the vineyards."

Then, in 1946, the year after World War II had ended, a wild card suddenly appeared on the horizon, changing the political game not just for Cambridge but eventually for Massachusetts as well. And, later, the country, too. This newcomer knew little of how Tip O'Neill's world was supposed to work and certainly had never heard of — nor was in need of — a snow button. What he possessed was a dazzlingly heroic war record and a father, one of the richest men in the country, anxious to sell it to the voters. If he didn't fit in politically, well, that was a truth he was aware of from the get-go. Jack Kennedy understood better than anyone to what extent he came on the scene as a carpetbagger. "I had never lived very much in the district," he dictated into a tape recorder fifteen years later, in what appears

172

to have been the beginnings of a memoir, ". . . and on top of that I had gone to Harvard, not a particularly popular institution at that time in the 11th Congressional District."

In the way such matters normally were taken care of, Tip had the seat earmarked for a pal of his, another Cambridge street-corner guy, Mike Neville. He, like Tip, was a wait-your-turn good soldier — and, now, his time seemingly had come. Neville looked to be a shoo-in, especially once the experienced pols had taken a good look at the new kid on the block. "By the time I met Jack Kennedy, I couldn't believe this skinny, pasty-looking kid was a candidate for anything," Tip remembered thinking, and so had simply dismissed the Kennedy scion's chances.

By this time a skilled veteran of the Massachusetts political wars, with a good sense of what would play on his home turf and what wouldn't, he simply didn't, or couldn't, see the obvious: that is, the pure magic of John F. Kennedy. Instead, he put his belief in the system he knew, ignoring the evidence of change squarely facing him. In fact, the opinion of other observers, then and now, has held that the handsome, charming young Kennedy could have beaten

Mike Neville even without all the money his father spent to ensure his triumph.

The sweeping Kennedy victory, however, did nothing to interfere with O'Neill's own ambitions. In 1948, Tip saw the potential for a Massachusetts-wide canvass to recruit young war heroes and other attractive veterans to run for the state legislature and, recognizing this, he organized the effort, which was successful. It made for an historic coup, with the Democrats achieving a majority of seats and Tip himself elected, at the age of thirty-seven, as the first Democratic and first Roman Catholic Speaker in the history of the commonwealth.

Four years later, in 1952, with Kennedy claiming his right to move up to the U.S. Senate — he would defeat the Republican incumbent, the effortlessly upper-class Henry Cabot Lodge, Jr. — Tip O'Neill himself had ambitions for the House seat vacated by Jack, which he won after a tough primary fight. For decades afterward he would publicly pay glowing tribute to the man he'd succeeded, even though, privately, he was slow to admire the younger man's political skills. The truth was, he had little choice, given the Kennedy family's influence in both Boston and the state, and so could only bridle at the role he found himself forced to play, not being entirely his own man and having to do their bidding as needed. He would spend decades regretting the slighting words the Kennedys had given him to say about the much-respected Lodge in an election-eve radio broadcast. And to add insult to that indignity, even after he'd done their dirty work, he heard from trustworthy sources that Bobby Kennedy, one of the two younger brothers, was considering a run against him, looking at Jack's onetime seat as family property. Furious, Tip promised Jack that if his kid brother decided to pursue such a challenge it would be "the dirtiest campaign you ever saw."

Jack Kennedy did do one favor for Tip. It came as a piece of cagey advice. In early 1953, just as the country was getting used to calling General Dwight D. Eisenhower "President," and he himself was moving across Capitol Hill to his Senate office, Kennedy told O'Neill, now a member of the House freshman class, to "be nice to John McCormack." McCormack had been second only to Sam Rayburn in the Democratic leadership since before the war. Clear to him were Tip's institutional ambitions. Jack figured that once Tip found his footing and acclimated himself to the House, ingratiating himself with McCormack, who'd been elected from Massachusetts to the House of Representatives in 1928, was the surest route for O'Neill to reach leadership himself.

Tip soon became a dedicated member of what was known on Capitol Hill as the "Tuesday to Thursday club." Though it was a tiring commute, it was the option he, along with a group of colleagues from Massachusetts, chose. They'd carpool down to the capital on Mondays, returning on Thursday evenings. Only rarely would he ever spend four entire weekdays in Washington, preferring instead to enjoy as much time at home with his family as could be managed. To make up for his regular absences, Tip would make breakfast and school lunches for the kids — he and Millie had five children: two daughters and three sons — on Friday and Monday so that Millie could sleep later.

During his Capitol Hill working days O'Neill led a bachelor's existence, rooming with another freshman member of the Massachusetts delegation, Edward Boland from Springfield. They were a definite odd couple: the short, quiet Boland, the large, ebullient O'Neill. The only things the two men kept in their apartment refrigerator were orange juice — which Boland would hand-squeeze — diet soda, beer, and cigars. For Tip, the evening ritual was dinner out, usually followed by late-night card games. On one evening he'd meet his pals at the University Club, on another at the Army-Navy.

All this time, O'Neill was counting the cards, and not just there on the table. He never stopped making friends — in both parties — recognizing the importance of keeping track of who was where and knowing how to connect the dots. That way, he'd have the high cards and the flushes when he needed them. "Incidentally, I'm absolutely convinced," he would say, "that one of the secrets behind my eventual rise to power is that I ate in restaurants every night with my friends and colleagues from the House." Hanging out in just the way he so skillfully — and genuinely — did over the years forged many a friendship, including across-the-aisle loyalties. These last came in particularly handy whenever a fellow member found himself in a situation where his ethics were being called into question. "I don't want to see any man go to jail," Tip would say.

The practical results of his tireless networking, and also the lasting bonds he forged, formed the plus side of the lifestyle adopted by Tip in Washington. But there was a negative aspect, too: the pastimes he favored meant that his regular intake of rich food, alcohol, and cigar smoke, plus the late nights, continually offered a very real threat to Tip's weight and overall health. It wasn't hard to see. Yet, as he would point out, there were just three ways to spend those Tuesday-to-Thursdays: either drinking, chasing women, or playing cards. "Some fellas like women. Some fellas like booze. Other fellas like cards. Cards keep you out of trouble." He'd made his choice and stuck with it, and it gave him a bon vivant's view of the city. "Many a morning I've seen that flag flying up there at dawn," he once told me as we drove up Independence Avenue with the Capitol in full view.

One fellow with whom Tip had occasionally played cards was Vice President Richard Nixon. "Not a bad guy," he'd say to me years later. In his 1987 memoir, *Man of the House,* he described Nixon as "bright and gregarious." The only problem with him, according to Tip, was that Nixon talked too much during the poker games. Still, they were amicable enough that Nixon felt able to ask the Democrat for help during the 1960 presidential race. One week he passed on word to Tip that he hoped he might meet him at the game early so they could talk. When O'Neill obliged, Nixon made his pitch. Jack Kennedy, he said, wasn't going to make it through the primaries; Lyndon Johnson was sure to be the Democratic candidate. Therefore, he felt it was all right if he asked O'Neill for the name of a young gung ho campaign operative. O'Neill, agreeing that this was fair, came up with one recommendation, who happened to be Senator Leverett Saltonstall's administrative assistant. His name: Charles Colson, later a key figure in the Watergate scandal.

Besides running for and winning reelection every two years, thus amassing seniority as the 1950s turned into the 1960s, O'Neill was able to use that institutional advantage for the folks back home. From his position on the Rules Committee, and later in the House leadership, along with his close friendship with Eddie Boland and Silvio Conte, also from Massachusetts, on the Appropriations Committee, O'Neill played a central role in Boston's latter-day economic development. He won federal money for Boston College and other universities, for medical research for the Massachusetts General Hospital, for new transit systems like the Silver Line in the Seaport district, and, finally, for the greatest public works project of them all, the Central Artery, best known as the "Big Dig."

Tip's political tactics, seasoned by years of effectiveness, were frequently of the hardball sort. When he needed to be tough, he never hesitated to hit, and hit where it hurt. His formidability showed itself most memorably in late 1963, just after Jack Kennedy's funeral, when President Lyndon Johnson announced he was closing the Boston Navy Yard, not only one of the region's most significant employers but also a symbolic one. The larger-than-life Texan in the White House, himself no political sissy and a man whose wrath (and revenge) was always to be feared, then went even further, adding insult to the injury. At the behest of top aide Joe Califano, an alumnus, he agreed to give the commencement address that year at Holy Cross rather than at Tip's alma mater, Boston College — completely ignoring the Speaker's invitation several months earlier — and this was, for certain, a swipe too many. Only when O'Neill used his position on the Rules Committee to keep the vital Johnson bills from reaching the House floor did the angry president, boxed in and not liking it one bit, finally relent. The Navy Yard remained open.

However, with his stance on the increasingly polarizing issue of the Vietnam War O'Neill offered his boldest challenge to the Johnson White House. Tip's children, especially Susan — all of them of the generation opposing continued U.S. involvement in Southeast Asia — had helped turn him around. It was because he listened to his kids that he was able to listen to the war's critics, and not just the Pentagon. While it won him admirers among the Harvard crowd — in much the same way his rejection of teacher loyalty oaths had two decades earlier — his position on Vietnam brought a very different reaction at home in North Cambridge. In a neighborhood where enlisting in the U.S. Marines or other armed forces was the patriotic alternative to going to college, Tip's position was a betrayal. There were those, even, who took it personally and despised him for it. With young townies dying each day in that far-off, unknown place on the other side of the world, he had broken faith with the faithful, even as he kept it with himself.

Though his opposition to the Vietnam War caused pain at home, the same moment was, in Washington, a juncture in Tip's career when the possibility of the Speakership first started to be tangible. There were several political incidents — you could even call them "accidents" — that contributed to this. The first occurred at the raucous, unforgettable Democratic National Convention of 1968. With antiwar demonstrators massed in the Chicago streets and turmoil in the convention hall itself, President Johnson, watching on television at his Texas ranch and getting angrier by the minute, managed to reach Chicago congressman and fellow Democrat Dan Rostenkowski by phone on the convention platform. With all the force of his considerable personality, not to mention his presidential authority, Johnson ordered him sternly to get things under control, pronto. "Take the gavel. Get some order in the hall," he demanded.

Rosty, as he was known, went to work. Grabbing the microphone from the convention chairman, House majority leader Carl Albert, he managed to restore order. Unfortunately for Rosty, the diminutive Albert never forgot what the burly Chicagoan had done to him. Especially once he got wind that Rostenkowski was dining out on the story of how he'd physically wrested control from him, making sure that anyone who'd somehow missed it knew of this affront to Carl Albert's dignity in full view of millions of people.

At this time, Representative Rostenkowski

had imagined himself the likely next Speaker, especially since he already held the elective post of chairman of the Democratic caucus. However, by having acted the bully at LBJ's bidding and then unwisely replaying his big moment for all it was worth, he was going to have to pay the price. Quite soon, he realized he'd gone as far as he was ever to get in the House leadership. When Albert himself became Speaker in 1971 and Louisiana's Hale Boggs took the post of majority leader, this left open the party's number-three leadership position of majority whip. Albert rejected Rostenkowski outright. To punish him further, and, obviously, to leave not the slightest doubt as to his vengeful purpose, he then recruited another congressman to run against Rosty for caucus chair, thus taking that job away from him as well.

At this point the choice of a new Democratic whip came down to a decision involving two men: O'Neill and Hugh Carey of New York. Unfortunately for Carey, a pair of fellow Irish-Americans from the New York delegation failed to support him as they might have been expected to. Putting down the future New York governor by labeling him too "high hat" and too "lace curtain," these two colleagues' blackballing

183

of Carey helped Carl Albert decide in favor of Tip O'Neill, awarding him the coveted position of majority whip in 1971.

Then, in the autumn of 1972, a tragic stroke of fate changed everything. A plane carrying Hale Boggs and three others was lost over Alaska, crashing in the wilderness, the bodies never recovered. With the help of Boggs's aide Gary Hymel and the endorsement of his presumed widow, Lindy, Tip O'Neill pulled ahead of the other candidates jockeying for the job to replace Boggs as majority leader. "You haven't got an enemy in the place," Florida congressman Sam Gibbons, the last to leave the field, told him.

Now, having paid his dues for two decades, Tip soon revealed he had little interest in laurel-resting. At this point, the only person standing between him and assumption of ultimate power in the Democratic caucus was Speaker Carl Albert. Within a year, O'Neill, the new majority leader, showed his nominal leader who was boss.

It's a fascinating side story that probably not many people ever paid any attention to. It had all begun when, in August 1973, Vice President Spiro Agnew found himself facing imminent indictment for extortion, tax fraud, and bribe-taking, among other counts, some of which had occurred back when he'd been a county executive and later the governor of Maryland. In an eleventh-hour gambit to try to save himself from the federal courts, he arrived at the Capitol with the intention of convincing the U.S. House of Representatives to assume jurisdiction, the same way they would for a president, hoping that he would avoid impeachment by the House and certainly removal from office by the Senate. Speaker Albert was ready to grant Agnew's request and even had begun to set the judicial process in motion when Tip O'Neill, his second in command in the House, refused outright to consider going along. Quickly, Tip managed to shut down Albert's efforts, thus killing Agnew's last hope to avoid prosecution in the criminal courts.

The majority leader would soon prove himself even tougher on Agnew's boss. Once the Watergate burglary scandal and the subsequent revelations about Richard Nixon's White House had spun out of control, Tip O'Neill became the chief engineer of the impeachment proceedings. Above the smoke of battle, Nixon himself would credit O'Neill as the man calling the shots that doomed his presidency.

On August 8, 1974, the night before Nixon's forced resignation, Tip's old friend

Jerry Ford — the Michigan congressman who'd been appointed vice president after Spiro Agnew had been forced to resign rather than serve a prison sentence — called him with critically important news: Nixon himself intended to resign the next day. At that moment he, Gerald Ford, would become the thirty-eighth president of the United States.

The two longtime pals chatted, seemingly hating to end the conversation and savoring the extraordinary moment between them. "Jerry, isn't this a wonderful country? Here we can talk like this and be friends, when eighteen months from now I'll be going around the country kicking your ass in." Once Ford granted a pardon to the impeached Nixon, Tip publicly denounced the decision, though, in private, he understood the judgment call and empathized with both men, each of whom he'd known for many years. "Although I thought the pardon was wrong, I didn't want to send Nixon to jail either." As he'd always said, he didn't like seeing a fellow pol "go to the can."

Two years later, O'Neill took his final step to the Speakership. Having exerted pressure on Albert to give up the office, he won the departing Speaker's go-ahead. With that in hand, he immediately began locking in his political base, asking friends, right to their faces, if they'd endorse him. Tom Foley, whom O'Neill would name majority whip, was in the Capitol room when O'Neill forged the phalanx of fifty or so members that would form his critical mass of support.

I was in the room when Tip conducted the grand inquisition. He had this staged. The fire was low and there was some kind of music in the background. He would say to whomever it was, 'I'm going to be a candidate for speaker. Do I have your support?' You had one millisecond to answer that question. I mean millisecond. There couldn't be any of 'Well, let me see . . .' You either had the loyalty as an orgasm of support or you didn't. The guy would say, 'Absolutely, Mr. Speaker.' The second test: 'I don't know who I'm going to have nominate me, probably Eddie Boland. But if I don't ask Eddie, can I ask you to nominate me?' 'Absolutely, I'm honored.' Tip was asking everybody whether they'd support him. He had about five standards. 'Can I count on your vote?' 'Can I count on you nominating me if Eddie Boland can't do it? I'm not asking yet. I just want to know if I can count on you to do it.' 'I want to have about fifty people supporting me for speaker. Can I count on you to sign on that line?' 'What about speeches? They have seconding speeches in the caucus for whoever's supporting whomever for the speakership. Can I count on you to be one of these?' 'Oh, absolutely!' And then out would come the hand, and the other guy had no choice but to take the hand and shake it. And Tip would say, 'Well, that's done,' or something like that. And over in the corner behind the speaker, somebody was taking notes back there.

He was carrying out the ritual of power he had been taught while still a senior at Boston College. He was doing what his father instructed him to do whenever seeking election. He was locking up his base. He was asking for his friends' votes, face-to-face. And now he had the winning cards right there in his hands.

The president and first lady back on the national stage.
The country never knew how close it came to losing its elected leader.
Seeing him now, healthy and on his feet, rallied America's spirit:
Ronald Reagan had once again given us a Hollywood ending.

CHAPTER NINE:
HERO

"The happy ending is our national belief."
— MARY MCCARTHY

The remarkable way Ronald Reagan responded to John Hinckley's attempt on his life just as his administration was getting under way marked a political turning point. Because of the courage and stoicism he demonstrated in the immediate aftermath — along with the wry quips he delivered so gamely in extremis — suddenly he was *more* than just a president. Now he appeared in the eyes of his fellow citizens as a full-blown hero.

It was an unprecedented situation. But with the savvy that characterized its operations, the Reagan White House had no trouble recognizing the opportunity handed them. It had taken a would-be assassin's bullet — an enormous price to pay, with the president's recovery less speedy than the public was led to believe — yet at this moment, owing to his grace, literally, under fire, their man was all but unassailable politically.

As a result, all obstacles to the agenda Reagan had been preparing to launch seemed puny, more like bad manners than Washington business as usual. His newly broad popularity appeared to guarantee Americans' ready willingness to accept his leadership as he steered the country in the direction he believed it must go. They were rooting for him as if he were an injured quarterback valiantly running for that touchdown: they felt he *deserved* the victory, and so were willing to hand it to him. For the opposing team, the Democrats — with Tip O'Neill their point man — it was nothing if not disheartening.

Up until this game-changing historic moment, my relations with the Speaker — for whom I'd now been working two months — had been tangential. Gary Hymel remained the out-front guy dealing with the press, Kirk O'Donnell led on political strategy and foreign policy, Ari Weiss on domestic policy and relations with the committee chairmen, and Leo Diehl was the ever-alert sentinel, managing the flow of corporate lobbyists and defense contractors always seeking the Speaker's ear.

My responsibility, a job special to that moment in history, was to check the morning papers for Reagan targets of opportunity. Zeroing in, I'd confect a quotable line or two. But being outside Tip's close circle meant I couldn't really barrel in to force my ideas on him. Rather, I needed at this stage always to be patient, strategizing my best shot at introducing a new thought — or attitude — into the Speaker's repertoire. As I gradually made my way into his political huddle, I sensed his growing alertness to my ideas, my gung-ho-ness, my eagerness to win. Like the kid who stands hopefully courtside as the bigger kids play basketball, I was running and catching the ball when it went out of bounds, earning my way into the game, waiting for someone to leave.

A week after the assassination attempt, O'Neill explained in his daily press briefing that the Democrats in Congress were writing a budget to help the "struggling class" of Americans, those men and women stuck in the middle who'd be hit hardest by the 16 percent inflation rate reported by the Labor Department. It was a phrase I'd developed back in my days working for Edmund Muskie on the Senate Budget Committee. The problem of the right public tone to take in the coming battle against the Republican onslaught was already an obvious, and awkward, issue for Tip.

"Well I expect that smiling radiance to be back at the White House for Easter," he told the assembled reporters the next day at his morning briefing. "He's a beautiful man, but I'm sorry he doesn't agree with my political philosophy." Knocking Reagan directly was understandably ill-advised; after all, the president had yet to be discharged from the hospital. Opting for a well-wishing approach befitting his status as Speaker, Tip was willing to add only the tiniest of digs — and a bland one at that. It made better sense to focus — for the moment, anyway — on the harm that was already being felt as a result of Reagan's cuts. For example, young people back in his district — so the Speaker recounted somberly — had made clear to him how fearful they were that cuts in the student loan program would kill their chances of staying in college.

The feelings Tip had for both the worried students and the recuperating Reagan were authentic, but, given his position, any concern for the president conflicted with his partisan role. He had a job to do, and despite what was happening now, he was well aware that a protracted fight lay ahead.

What's important to know about Tip O'Neill is that, after all his years serving there, he took a deep pride in being able to "read the House." The problem now was that its members were hardly exempt from the powerful emotional spell cast by Reagan's miraculous survival. For Tip's troops, just as it was for the rest of the country, it wasn't only President Reagan's survival but also the jaunty fortitude he'd exhibited. His spirit had moved an entire nation, the world, really. In an atmosphere of such widespread admiration for President Reagan, how could the House of Representatives *not* be representational? The chamber over which Tip held sway was, in every way, the "People's House," and recognizing exactly what was happening, he realized, sensing the mood around him, that there was nothing to be gained by trying to deny their sentiments.

Unfortunately, there were other instances where he was less well able to read a given situation. Since I worked *with* the O'Neill office, not truly *within* it, I didn't initially realize what was afoot when Kirk O'Donnell asked me to set up a weeklong schedule of media events for the Speaker just before Easter. I obliged — only to learn what was really going on when a savvy reporter decided to ask an uncomfortable question.

Wasn't it possible, the *Boston Globe*'s David Rogers challenged Kirk — with me in hearing range — that this carefully orchestrated effort to showcase Tip's on-the-job dedication was intended, in fact, to distract attention from the Speaker's upcoming two-week trip to Australia?

The lightbulb suddenly came on, and I realized, hearing Rogers, that what he was suggesting had been precisely the idea. I'd been made complicit in the business of spotlighting a heavy O'Neill presence in Washington, a pol's trick that would allow him then to skip town. He'd engaged in the preemptive attention-getting as a way of not having his absence loom large when he flew off around the world. With Reagan about to be released from the hospital and the first House vote on his economic program due in May, there was every reason to expect the Speaker to be working round the clock.

The plain fact was this: Tip had this trip planned for quite a while and was looking forward to getting a glimpse of life Down Under. No way would he forfeit a chance to visit the land of "The Wild Colonial Boy," where so many Irishmen had journeyed — freely or not — before. He prized these annual springtime junkets, taken each year by him and a close-knit group of congressional buddies, usually to a faraway, alluring destination. He, Dan Rostenkowski, and what amounted to a regular band of fifteen congressmen and their wives — including Republicans such as Pennsylvania's Joe McDade and Ohio's Ralph Regula — planned them to carefully but not overly feature the necessary obligations along the way. They'd meet with foreign leaders and pose for ceremonial pictures, leaving time for eighteen holes in the afternoon, and they certainly saw no harm in it.

Now, in early April 1981, they weren't about to give up the perk, especially with what looked like a long and difficult battle ahead once they were back home again.

Viewed against the old rules, O'Neill's steadfast fealty to his fellow junketeers made solid sense. Those annual trips overseas were, in a way, like camp, where you saw the same friends every year and anticipated the experience. You ate and played together, were often confined to the close quarters of an airplane cabin, and otherwise hung out morning, noon, and night. Such circumstances tightly bonded the travelers. The inevitable golf days and onboard poker games cemented the men's relationships, while the wives shopped, visited tourist attractions, and connected with each other in a way they couldn't back in their ordinary lives.

But, above all, what such trips — so often, and sometimes rightly, I admit, bashed in the press — can accomplish is the sort of outcome a journalist's investigative report is unable to measure or assess. They create the wide back channels and spaces where the necessary horse-trading can take place, both always useful in the complex game of politics. But, in the end, the greatest advantage of these excursions is that they offer to these travelers recognition of the shared humanity of a precarious career.

Appearance, though, is always what matters, especially when anyone's looking. Political junkets, even in the best of moments, carry with them an air of the illicit, of at least a minor crime being gotten away with; still, most take place and no one's the wiser. This time, too many people were watching, however, and Tip paid the price for being loyally — and stubbornly — unable to relinquish it.

"We were back in Washington working," dryly commented Billy Pitts, floor man for Republican leader Bob Michel, "and Tip was in Pago Pago." The public relations fallout was disastrous. A network news broadcast showed the plane carrying the traveling members of Congress on the tarmac at Hickam Air Force Base in Honolulu. What viewers saw on their TV screens was the aircraft just sitting there on the landing field, its passengers refusing to leave the plane, apparently too embarrassed. Alas for Tip and his companions, the Republicans could have confected no better portrait of the Congress, and its top leader, adhering to the old rules. It was as if the Democratic Speaker had reenacted the Republican ad showing him in the car that had run out of gas — only this time it was a government airplane.

Meanwhile, over at the White House, Reagan and his own men were moving steadily ahead with their planned onslaught on House members, regardless of where the Speaker was and what he was up to. Democratic congressman Tom Bevill from Alabama was in New Zealand with Tip when the call came from the White House, where the president was now back at work.

"This is President Reagan. What time is it, and where are you?"

"It's three o'clock in the morning and I'm in New Zealand," Bevill replied, still uncertain what it could be about.

"Have a good trip and when you get back to Washington, I want you to come in and see me. I want to sit and talk to you about the budget."

Reagan later told Ken Duberstein, one of his top congressional lobbyists, that when he learned it was 3 a.m. in New Zealand, he was tempted to announce, "This is Jimmy Carter," and hang up.

The next day, the president placed a second call, presumably at a more acceptable time of day, to the traveling House members. This time it was to O'Neill. "I'm having more luck with Demos. than Repubs.," Reagan jotted in his diary that night. "Asked Tip O'Neill if I could address a joint session next week. He agreed." He didn't bother noting he'd caught his rival far from the political playing field.

Democratic congressman Eugene Atkinson received his call from the president when he was on-air, doing a local Pennsylvania radio call-in show. It was the first time anyone in the country at large had heard the president's voice since the assassination attempt. Atkinson, who would switch parties and declare himself a Republican six months later, agreed on the spot to support the president on the coming vote.

But despite such a dogged methodology,

with its relentless tracking down of congressional votes in every state, Reagan's primary target of opportunity remained the South. If he could convince and count on those Democrats in Dixie who were willing to listen, he'd be assured of winning House passage of his overall spending and tax plan. When Tip returned from Australia and found himself facing the results of all those calls made from 1600 Pennsylvania Avenue across so many time zones, even to the South Pacific, he freely admitted the "tremendous impact" the president's intensive effort was having. In truth, he had no choice, since the clear evidence was all around him. Yet at that moment he was unwilling to take any blame for the situation, chalking up the surge instead to "the president's popularity."

The White House push for votes was being overseen by Baker and Reagan's full-time lobbyists Friedersdorf and Duberstein; already in high gear, they had a great deal to be pleased about. Now they and their fellow Republicans were about to be made even happier: Ronald Reagan, who'd been performing behind the scenes, was at last ready to step back in front of the audience eagerly awaiting him. The Speaker, in his daily meeting with reporters on April 28, the morning of Reagan's televised speech, saw clearly what his reemergence would mean — to him, Tip O'Neill, to the Democratic Party, to the system and its ideals that he so long had valued. Americans, he knew, would rally to the healed and shining hero, simply because in their adulation they couldn't understand what was coming and how it would affect them. The crowd, in short, would be responding to the highly satisfying sentiment of the moment, just as they did when singing the national anthem at a ballpark. How do you fight that?

That day Tip chose to offer, in his press briefing, simply a confirmation of the plain reality: "Because of the attempted assassination, the president has become a hero in the eyes of the public," he said bluntly. "Is that effective?" was the question he then asked, and answered himself: "I would have to presume it is. We can't argue with a man as popular as he is." He was facing the facts, at the same time as conscious of what was at stake as he'd ever been aware of anything in his life.

That same night, Ronald Reagan took his place at the podium before a joint session of Congress. The packed-to-the-rafters audience sitting there in high anticipation offered him an ovation as he walked in, even before he'd said a word. It soon swelled into a tumult he would later describe as "unbelievable." Only once it finally subsided did he begin to talk; his tone was humble, grateful, and affirmative. Speaking on behalf of himself and Nancy, he first told the crowd, "The warmth of your words, the expression of friendship and, yes, love, meant more to us than you can ever know. You have given us a memory that we'll treasure forever. And you've provided an answer to those few voices that were raised saying that what happened is evidence that ours is a sick society."

He went on to describe how Americans of all ages had sent letters expressing their good wishes and concern over his progress. One, from a small boy in New York, Peter Sweeney, had especially pleased him and he read it aloud. Wrote the worried second-grader, "I hope you get well quick or you might have to make a speech in your pajamas." Then, Reagan, ever the showman, paused before he finished with the child's charming postscript, an ideal punch line: "P.S. If you have to make a speech in your pajamas, I *warned* you."

As they watched, the White House operatives had every reason to be thrilled. Their man had come to Capitol Hill — where not everyone was a friend — and been interrupted *fourteen* times, three of which were standing ovations, by swelling waves of applause as he spoke. But of all those approving outbursts, it was the third standing ovation that most moved Ronald Reagan himself. It was at that moment that forty Democrats rose to join the Republicans in endorsing his call for an historic shift in U.S. fiscal policy.

"The old and comfortable way is to shave a little here and add a little there. Well, that's not acceptable anymore," Reagan declared. "I think this great and historic Congress *knows* that way is no longer acceptable." He'd been taking a direct shot at the Democratic opposition's attempt to propose an alternative to Reagan's program, one that asked for far more modest cuts in spending and taxes. Not only was he dismissive of it, but when that sizable clutch of approving Democrats got to their feet to applaud, he took it as their renegade seal of approval. "It took a lot of courage for them to do that," he wrote in his diary that night, "and it sent a shiver down my spine."

Tip O'Neill, his shock of bright white hair a beacon marking his presence on the podium behind the president, similarly registered what had just occurred. "Here's your forty votes," he whispered to Vice

President George H. W. Bush, seated beside him. He knew only too well those conservative Democrats sitting up there in "Redneck Row" — their chosen seats high in the back of the House chamber — and what they were up to. He recognized that voting with the administration and not with their own party was the only way many of them would stand a chance of reelection in 1982 in their basically conservative districts. (Among them were Democrats whose *aye*s were always in question, and now a few would even change them for good.) Yet there were no surprises: Tip had already identified them on the scoreboard he'd been keeping. "This is only the first skirmish in the war. The war is the election of 1982 and we will win the war," he was soon to declare, accepting the fact that the current battle was over. "You know a horse that runs fast doesn't always run long."

Publicly, however, O'Neill's response was gracious to the point of excess, as when he made his first comments to the press directly after the speech. "I was overjoyed to see the president looking so well," he said. "Like all Americans, I am deeply and humbly grateful that so many prayers have been answered." Calling Reagan "inspirational," he pronounced the speech he'd just heard "even poetic at points," saluting his performance as in every sense of the word presidential through his ordeal.

But he also showed his mettle. He presented a sizable list of factual errors that the address had contained. Yet, even so, he was careful not to blame Reagan himself for the mistakes, instead pointing the finger at White House staffers. "It is unfortunate in the extreme that some of those who provided statistical information for this data did President Reagan a grave disservice," he noted.

While the language he used was careful, it was obvious to those who knew him that his frustration came from the heart. Even if he'd been expecting the worst from the Reagan economic recovery program, that didn't make it any easier to witness so much that he'd cared deeply about and fought for so stoutly just tossed aside. More important, for Tip-watchers, the signs were there: he was becoming angry, even if he didn't himself yet fully realize it.

The next morning, weighing in once more, he was again first making sure to praise Caesar. "I have been saying all along that he is a great human being," the Speaker reminded the press corps, "but I don't think he appreciates what is in there. The vaccine program would be eliminated, colleges will close and a half million people will be denied the opportunity to go to school, many children won't receive hot lunches." And then he reiterated, "I don't think he realizes that those are the things in the package." It was a delicate balancing act — acknowledging Reagan's off-the-charts popularity, and at the same time spotlighting the extent of the potential, and terrible, damage he saw being planned in his name.

Then he managed to get off a nice shot: "All in all, I would like to remind you that Ronald Reagan was a Democrat himself not too long ago. I think he would have been at least as good last night reading our script rather than the Republican one."

The Republican effort to secure Democratic votes, as we've seen, was a marvel of efficiency and tireless effort. And, of course, their secret weapon was the president himself, his strength now recovered, and even more fired up than ever. Well accustomed to the discipline of many takes, stepping into his marks for each one, he played the role expected of him like the consummate professional he was. "We stroked and we stroked and we stroked and we stroked and we stroked and we traded," James Baker said, "and the president was very good at that, and willing to do it all day and all night." One of his gotten prey was that same Tom Bevill whom he'd reached on the phone in New Zealand. Outside the South, he was able to woo Jerry Patterson of California, Donald Albosta of Michigan, Andrew Jacobs of Indiana, Tony Hall of Ohio, and Gus Yatron of Pennsylvania.

Not surprisingly, there was a person standing firm who wasn't being won over, and that was Tip O'Neill. What conservative Democrats, as well as other wavering ones, regarded as tolerable cuts, the Speaker viewed as assaults on people desperately in need. Hedrick Smith, then chief Washington correspondent for the *New York Times,* recalls getting an urgent call from Godfrey Sperling of the *Christian Science Monitor.* At that time the weekly breakfasts Sperling hosted at the National Press Club, featuring prominent newsmakers, were a Washington institution and with Tip O'Neill as the upcoming guest, he wanted to be sure the influential Smith planned to come.

When the morning arrived, Tip didn't let his audience down. He arrived loaded for bear, defiant in his refusal to abandon — or see abandoned — the many critical programs he'd fought for. What most struck

Smith at the time — what he remembered best from that breakfast session — was Tip O'Neill's visibly simmering rage as he drew for his listeners a vivid picture of those programs and services scheduled to be closed down. With his decades of experience as a people's advocate, he could see that the citizens most harmed by the Reagan agenda would be those least able to protect themselves, and it was in order to be their protector that he, Tip O'Neill, had gone into politics in the first place.

Unlike Tip, Ronald Reagan had been propelled into the position he now occupied by a different set of concerns, and had entered the political arena through a route that little resembled the Speaker's. The president's son Ron — a perceptive observer of his dad — later would identify certain habits of mind that greatly frustrated Tip in his dealings with the elder Reagan at this time, as he repeatedly came up against them. Explained Ron Reagan: "Tenderhearted and sentimental in his personal dealings, he could nevertheless have difficulty extending his sympathies to abstract classes of people."

In Washington terms, in the late spring of 1981, this meant that whenever Tip would try to illustrate for the president the harmful effects of this or that imminent cut by citing an individual case — for example, a young woman forced to leave college because Social Security survivors' benefits had been eliminated — Reagan would quickly exhibit warm sympathy. What can we do to help this poor girl? Wanting to help out, he'd summon Ed Meese or another staffer to instruct them to go find the tuition money.

The problem, Tip saw — and found impossible, really, to understand — was that while Reagan could be made to take interest in, and even genuinely seem to care about a particular situation, he remained unmoved if the same hardship story was multiplied into a million similar ones. According to Ron Reagan, the impression left by this failure of his father — whether through inability or willed disregard — to make the leap from the micro to the macro came off as "an obliviousness that was, understandably, taken for callousness."

Which is exactly how Tip O'Neill took it. Increasing his sense of frustration was the fact that he and the Democrats could be seen moving inexorably toward a loss. "Am I getting commitments? The answer is no, to be truthful. Have I got disappointments? The answer is yes," he told reporters, speaking honestly. But when one asked if perhaps he'd turned into a metaphor for old-time, big-spending liberalism, he wrathfully put the questioner in his place: "The Speaker of the House is not a goddamned metaphor. God willing, I never shall be."

More and more, Reagan's own personal lobbying was continuing — and it continued to pay off. "More meetings with Cong. These Demos. are with us on the budget and it's interesting to hear some who've been here 10 years or more say it is their 1st time to ever be in the Oval Office. We really seem to be putting a coalition together."

The dilemma for Tip and the Democrats was immediate and ongoing. They were on a beach, an enormous tide was rushing toward them, and there was nowhere to look for safety. If they simply stood still, they'd be overwhelmed, and yet if they ran for it, they'd never attain the high ground again. "Support the president! That's the concern out there, and Congress can read that," he wearily told the press. "I've been in politics a long time, and I know when to fight and when not to fight."

Given the immense pressures of the situation, Tip began to find it hard to stay respectful. His every instinct now was to tweak Reagan, to try to find a way to land a punch. A week before the vote on the new White House–orchestrated budget he couldn't resist a cutting remark, one that came off, unfortunately, as all too predictable. Taking aim at Reagan's intellectual grasp of his own policies, he made a point of noting that the president had summoned Vice President Bush into a meeting with the congressional leadership to discuss the budget in order "to have someone explain it for him." The crack accomplished nothing, but it undoubtedly made Tip feel better. He knew he was losing and he didn't like it.

On the morning of the budget vote, O'Neill, seeing defeat ahead, took the only stand he reasonably could and still maintain his dignity. It was also the only way he could prepare to move ahead as he would need to. "When the results are over and the headlines are proclaimed, we will have written the record for the American people. . . . If Reagan is able to win tonight the monkey will be off the Democrats' back. The cuts . . . are the Reagan cuts."

On that day, May 7, the vote for the Reagan budget was 253 to 176. The president had won all 190 Republicans in the House plus 63 Democrats, a number far beyond those 40 southern conservatives who'd risen to their feet. Reagan was exuberant. "This was the big day . . . We never anticipated such a landslide. We felt we were going to win due to the conservative bloc of Demos but expected R. defectors so we might win by 1 or 2 votes. It's been a long time since Repubs. have had a victory like this."

For O'Neill the defeat was painful. And he took it personally now. "An old dog can learn new tricks if he wants to learn new tricks. This old dog wants to learn," he told members of the House, using a phrase I'd heard him say in the office. But his most forceful — and colorful — response came the next day, when, back at home and paying a visit to the *Boston Globe,* he found himself asked by one of the pressman, a North Cambridge fellow like himself, how things were going in Washington. His salty reply was perfect for the moment. "I'm getting the shit whaled out of me," he informed the man.

Otherwise, his public position and his fallback political strategy were one and the same for the time being. The idea was a simple one: don't blame him or his party once the going starts to get rough. "From now on, it's Reagan's budget. From now on, it's Reagan's unemployment rate. From now on, it's Reagan's inflation rate. You can't criticize the Democrats. It's Reagan's ball game."

Five days after its big victory, the Reagan team committed an unforced error, which had the effect of invigorating Tip. Richard Schweiker, the secretary of health and human services, released a proposal for radical cuts in early Social Security retirement benefits. For those who chose retirement at age sixty-two, instead of receiving 80 percent of the sum due them had they chosen to wait 'til age sixty-five, they would — if the Reagan administration had its way — now collect only 55 percent.

O'Neill's initial reaction was to follow the regular procedure for dealing with such a proposal, which meant allowing the House Ways and Means subcommittee to study it first. Then he thought again — and he got angry. Why roll over? What was being proposed was a travesty and he needed to speak out. Both his history and his conscience demanded it. "I'm not talking about politics," he told reporters. "I'm talking about decency. It is a rotten thing to do." The Democratic Party, he said, will "fight this thing every inch of the way." It was "nothing but a sneak attack on Social Security."

At this point, when I heard about the Reagan Social Security plan, I could think only of my own dad and so I did what I could to encourage the Speaker's anger. My sixty-one-year-old father, I knew, was planning on retiring early from his position as dean of the Philadelphia court reporters the following year. I knew he'd already announced his plans at work and would be unable to reverse them. I understood how vital their Social Security check would be to him and my mom, since they'd married young and worked hard raising five sons, sending them all to college. Inevitably there had been sacrifices all along the way, and they were looking forward now to taking it easier.

At this moment, I was behind the scenes in Tip's office, and, as I've said, not exactly working *for* him. But, because of my parents, I'm proud to take credit for the simple but heartfelt statement I wrote for the Speaker at the time.

"A lot of people approaching that age [sixty-two] have either already retired on pensions or have made irreversible plans to retire very soon. These people have been promised substantial Social Security benefits at age sixty-two. I consider it a breach of faith to renege on that promise. For the first time since 1935 people would suffer because they trusted in the Social Security system."

At the White House, Jim Baker suddenly

realized too late the horror of what was unfolding. "Whoever called Social Security *the third rail of American politics* got it exactly right," he said, as he made sure the administration extricated itself from the mess it had just landed in. It had never been so clear before this moment that a war was about to be waged, and words would be the ammunition.

On the same day, May 12, 1981, House Speaker Thomas P. O'Neill announced that Gary Hymel, who'd been his administrative assistant during his years as majority leader and now Speaker, was leaving. In the statement announcing his departure, Tip said it wouldn't "be easy to find someone to replace Gary . . . his shoes will be hard to fill."

I don't recall exactly the moment when I started to get my hopes up the Speaker would pick me for the job. But it was what I wanted.

Conservative vs. liberal.
The two men would argue philosophy even with no other audience than each other.

CHAPTER TEN:
FIGHTING SEASON

"Courage for some sudden act,
maybe in the heat of battle, we all
respect; but there is that still rarer
courage which can sustain repeated
disappointment, unexpected failure,
and shattering defeat."
— ANTHONY EDEN
ON WINSTON CHURCHILL

Once I'd begun working closely with Tip O'Neill, I found myself struck by the enduring commitment he felt. A complicated man, his political strength lay in the belief system he'd long adhered to, which was a simple one. In Tip's mind, government was there to make better lives for those governed. And the fact that he stuck to this conviction, willing to be on the "wrong" side when the country was tilting in the other direction, was, I believe, a particularly fine moment in American heroism. There is more than one sort of heroic behavior, and they don't all look the same.

In his daily life as a working politician who'd risen to a pinnacle of power, Tip O'Neill knew all the moves, could wheel and deal shrewdly, apply pressure as needed, put a word in the right ear. He understood most keenly the ways of those making the laws. In his world, seniority, procedure, and tradition were honored, while rewards and punishment needed to be fairly rendered. Always underpinning his visible actions was his less visible passion, making him a traditionalist ripe for leading a righteous rebellion.

The following *Time* magazine analysis gives a sense of the criticism that began to be leveled at O'Neill once he'd lost the budget battle. "At that moment, it was clear that the nation's most powerful Democrat had been badly, perhaps even fatally, wounded," Robert Ajemian wrote in mid-May. "It was obvious that he still had an emotional hold on the House. But the hold is loosening now, and it looks very much as if the job Tip O'Neill has worked a lifetime for is offering challenges he cannot meet."

Further adding to the unhappiness that *Time* piece created around the office was the feeling that Ajemian, a reporter considered a pal by Kirk O'Donnell, had betrayed a trust. Granting access is always risky — the power of the press ultimately belongs to he who holds the pen — and we all knew it, but that didn't make it any better. Or Tip any less angry. The truth is, he was already coping with enough.

An observer could see that the table had been turned. Suddenly Tip O'Neill, the veteran liberal, found himself in a position like that of Ronald Reagan back in the 1960s when his own party had little interest in hearing what he had to say. Through his early politician years, Ronald Reagan's name had been associated with his party's out-of-the-mainstream right, the hard-line admirers of Barry Goldwater — both conservative and libertarian — who marched to their own ideology.

During the Nixon years and after, out of step with Gerald Ford and other centrist Republicans, Reagan remained a Goldwaterite. Never taken quite seriously, he managed to find his national popularity only when conditions — the high inflation and interest rates of the late 1970s, the taking of the hostages in Tehran, the seeming weaknesses of Jimmy Carter — aligned the stars for him. Watching Tip in the late spring of 1981, he may even have been reminded of his own time in the wilderness. Ronald Reagan knew only too well what it felt like to be in ideological disrepute.

Fresh from his stunning victory in the Congress, Reagan was now about to look backward, though not to his days as a GOP outsider. Instead, he was headed to Notre Dame as president of the United States. He arrived on campus to deliver the class of 1981's commencement address as the Gipper, the embodiment of an ideal he'd portrayed on-screen in a role that had come to define him. It was life imitating art imitating life, and to make this even clearer, Pat O'Brien, Reagan's old pal and the top-billed star of *Knute Rockne — All American,* was also to get an honorary degree that day. And so a Hollywood reunion also took place in South Bend on that Indiana afternoon.

Fifteen thousand spectators had turned out, all aware of the historic nature of the event. Reagan was the fifth president to present a speech to Notre Dame graduates, yet the first who'd ever portrayed one of their own. "I've always suspected that there might have been many actors in Hollywood who could have played the part better," Reagan told his enthralled listeners, "but no one could have wanted to play it more than I did."

Recognizing not just Ronald Reagan's symbolic worth to Notre Dame, but also the value of that connection *to him,* the school now awarded the man standing there on the dais two distinct honorary memberships in its Monogram Club for athletic achievement: one for himself as president and another as a stand-in for the late George Gipp. Having once so movingly acted the part of Gipp, Reagan acknowledged that the nickname had been passed on to him. "Now, today I hear very often, 'Win one for the Gipper,' spoken in a humorous vein," he told the crowd. "Lately I've been hearing it by congressmen who are supportive of the programs that I've introduced." Then, after waiting for the laughter to die down, he got serious. "For too long government has been fixing things that aren't broken and inventing miracle cures for unknown diseases," he explained. It was his well-wrought theme, now perfected after decades of experience. "Indeed," he went on reassuringly, "a start has already been made. There's a task force under the leadership of the vice president — George Bush — that is to look at those regulations I've spoken of. They have already identified hundreds of them that can be wiped out with no harm to the quality of life. And the cancellation of just those regulations will leave billions and billions of dollars in the hands of the people for productive enterprise and research and development and the creation of jobs."

Back in Washington, Tip was gearing up to fight these very convictions. Though over the years he'd only infrequently, and with reluctance, agreed to appear on the networks' weekend interview programs, a new era now called for new tactics. As a guest on ABC's *Issues and Answers* on June 7, he denounced the Reagan tax cuts as a "windfall for the rich." Yet, with that, he was only warming up.

"I'm opposed to the Reagan tax bill," he further explained, ". . . because it's geared for the wealthy of the nation instead of being spread out among the working class of America and the poor people. The president truly in my opinion doesn't understand the working class of middle America, what it's all about, what they go through, because of the fact that he doesn't associate himself with those types of people. He has no concern, no regard, no care for the little man of America."

What Tip was doing, in fact, was proclaiming himself to America, stepping out of the background to declare who he was and why it mattered. He was careful to say he understood, of course, where President Reagan was coming from, and that he knew what made him tick, recognized his habits and his natural habitat. But, owing to "his lifestyle," Tip said, the president actually never met those people to whom he'd just been referring. "Consequently, he doesn't understand their problems. He's only been able to meet the wealthy. I think he'd do much better if he had brought in some people close to him who are from the working force of America, who have suffered along the line, not those who have made it along the line and forgotten from where they've come." Not that he was calling Ronald Reagan himself "callous" — he made that clear — but, he bluntly suggested, there must be "very, very selfish people *around* him."

Steven V. Roberts of the *New York Times* saw the Speaker's Sunday appearance as a political turnaround. "Mr. O'Neill, a hulking bear of a man with a large nose and a fondness for big cigars, does not fit the modern image of smooth-faced, blow-dried TV-age politician. Where he comes from, you win votes with handshakes, not makeup; by doing favors, not by being famous."

The *Times* reporter said it was significant to see O'Neill so aroused:

As a neighborhood politician who loves the intricacies of legislative maneuvering, the Massachusetts Democrat is not particularly comfortable with television. And as a 68-year-old grandfather who has spent most of his life in politics, he hates to give up weekends with his family to appear on television. . . .

But now Mr. O'Neill feels that the battle over the direction of the nation has been joined with President Reagan and his Republican troops, and the Democratic leader is under considerable pressure from younger colleagues to step out front and lead the counterattack.

Tip's shot at Reagan struck like flint on steel. All it needed was the right person to blow on the spark. At a White House press conference a few days later, ABC's chief White House correspondent, Sam Donaldson, fanned the flame. "Tip O'Neill says you don't understand about the working people!" he shouted just as Reagan was concluding a televised press conference. "That you have just a bunch of wealthy and selfish advisors!"

Returning to the microphone, Reagan took the bait. "Tip O'Neill has said that I don't know anything about the working-man," he began. His indignant tone was perfectly pitched. "I'm trying to find out about *his* boyhood," he went on, "because we didn't live on the wrong side of the railroad tracks, but we lived so close to them we could hear the whistle real loud."

It was a great line, but he wasn't finished — and he begged to differ. "And I know very much about the working group," Reagan asserted. "I grew up in poverty and got what education I got all by myself, and I think it is sheer demagoguery to pretend that this economic program . . . is not aimed at helping the great cross-section of people in this country that has been burdened for too long by big government and high taxes."

Sheer demagoguery. Intended as a mere rebuttal, Reagan had gone too far when he uttered those two words. Caught off guard by Sam Donaldson, he'd defended himself by attacking in return, and, in the process, badly misjudged the term he picked to denounce the Democrat's disagreement with his policies. To Tip, who'd been calling the truth exactly as he saw it, Reagan's phrase was nothing less than a shocking insult. The Speaker of the House stands second, after the vice president, in the line of presidential succession, and, to him, Reagan's slur was an attack not only on him,

Tip O'Neill, but on the historic dignity of the office he now held.

The news wires lit up with the story. At Washington's highest level, it looked like the gloves finally might be coming off! As the TV evening news programs prepared their stories, Reagan's target stood in his office, trying to make up his mind how to handle the situation. There were staffers who wanted him to allow the president's inflammatory comment to pass, while others were urging a swift, decisive counterpunch.

"Let it go, Tom." This was his longtime friend and senior aide Leo Diehl. He was of the old school, just like Tip, and believed politics belonged, for maximum effectiveness, in back rooms like this. There were a half dozen of us sitting in the antechamber to the Speaker's office where such sessions normally took place. He'd stopped there to get a sense of what his people thought he should do. It proved to be a heated moment. Leo, like Eleanor Kelley, Tip's executive secretary, was of the view that all TV camera crews must be stopped before they even get a toe inside, just the way you keep pesky door-to-door salesmen at bay.

As I watched, it was clear to me this man was no longer going to be comfortable in retreat — not now, not anymore. Ever since the election back in the fall, he'd been slowly having to accept the notion that, in Ronald Reagan's Washington, being Speaker of the House meant more than that basic job description up until now implied. Suddenly, here was a veteran politician who'd become, symbolically, the country's last standing Democrat. Expected to keep aloft the banner for his fellow liberals — who, to greater or lesser degrees, now cowered behind him — Tip O'Neill was in front of the curtain all by himself.

As the reality of all this — and the imperatives for change in the ways he'd always operated — started to sink in, it seemed to him both overwhelming and a galvanizing personal challenge. He'd had his political heroes, FDR the greatest of them, obviously, and channeling his indomitable spirit would be part of going forward. Yet Tip's own convictions and courage until this moment had, for the whole of his career, asked different things of him. Most crucially, he would now be faced with the seemingly impossible task of defending his party's principles on that national, televised stage where the highly telegenic Ronald Reagan had long been professionally at home. There were reasons why Tip's old pals and senior staffers worried about him and any intrusion by camera crews.

But, helping support Tip, not just sharpening his message but also getting him out front, even if it meant standing alone, was the reason I was in that room to begin with. So, sitting there on that historic afternoon, I expressed my opinion — perhaps a bit tremulously, I confess, but I knew what I believed — that retreat was not the answer. "You've got to fight this," I said, weighing in. My position was that we were already at war with the White House, and so the only question, really, was the right moment to abandon the political pacifism he'd been practicing, a stance arising both out of traditional courtesy to a newly inaugurated president and also in response to Reagan's nearly having lost his life to an assassin's bullet.

If Tip didn't punch back now, I felt, he'd be missing out not only on a necessary partisan shot, but on something much bigger — the chance to reshape himself as a leader willing and able to go head to head with his adversary. Were Reagan allowed to get away with accusing Tip of "demagoguery," it could stand for the foreseeable future as an accepted truth. Plus, it amounted to weakness to let the other guy have the last word, even if — *especially* if — he's the president.

For me it was the moment of truth. I said he had to fight, that anything else would signal Reagan's domination — and not just of the moment.

I wasn't the only one there in that meeting who hoped to see him offer a hard retort to Reagan, but I was the sole person who'd been hired to blow the bugle. I represented the opposite of business-as-usual, which is the direction he'd been slowly heading in and needed to now reverse.

"I'm going up to the gallery," Tip now said. At this, some of us looked at one another with deep awareness. He had decided to fight. First, he headed back to the door of his private bathroom. At six foot three and close to three hundred pounds, Tip's already imposing self was topped with a head of hair that remained defiantly thick for his age and always sent dandruff flaking onto his giant shoulders. When he emerged, I got a whiff of the richly old-fashioned scent I'd soon come to associate with his making himself camera-ready. Was it cologne? Or, possibly, hair spray? I wasn't sure and never asked. But it was included in his ritual and I respected it, knowing it was a part of his armor.

He then began the — extraordinary for him — ascent to the House's radio and television press gallery, well aware that all the correspondents, notified of his imminent arrival, had raced there ahead of him. As he took his position in front of the waiting cameras, Tip O'Neill looked straight into them and began speaking.

"I would never accuse a president, whoever he was, of being a demagogue," he said with dignity. "I have too much respect for the president, for the institution . . . and I assume in the future he would have the same respect for the Speakership."

He was responding to the assault that had so offended him in his own way — and I believe he did it perfectly, focusing neither on himself nor on his role as leader of the opposition, but rather on the significance of his constitutional post, as Speaker of the House. Reagan's accusation revealed, as Tip saw it, a basic ignorance of the civic protocol of his new home, an ignorance resulting in a regrettable show of political bad manners. Traditionally, presidents had understood and acknowledged the relationship that linked them, and respect for a Speaker was what was expected.

Tip had more on his mind at that moment than rebuking Reagan for his unseemly incivility. He wasn't forgetting what he was even angrier about, the elephant in the living room he couldn't ignore and that he'd come there to the press gallery to denounce — the White House economic program. It was clear to everyone who heard him that afternoon that the Speaker was really on the boil, and once he'd finished — his contempt informing every word — the question instantly asked was inevitable. "Well, I'd have to say the honeymoon is over," Tip informed the reporter who'd wanted to know.

Word of Tip's wrath quickly reached the Oval Office, where it definitely wasn't the message from the Hill its inhabitant was expecting to hear. Ronald Reagan preferred to avoid conflict whenever possible, and Tip's defiant planting of the banner spoiled the president's vision of their shared political landscape. Arising the next morning, he was eager to regain their previous footing. Reagan phoned the Speaker to apologize for the attack that had launched Tip on the warpath. Though he listened courteously, his adversary was uninterested in what he believed the president to be offering him, which was a truce.

"Old buddy," the Speaker replied, certain of his ground now, "that's politics. After six o'clock we can be friends; but before six, it's politics." It was Tip's town, and if he couldn't call every one of the shots, he was still his own man.

The day Tip went to the press gallery was when the lines got drawn. Nothing was the same afterward, not for Ronald Reagan, not for Tip O'Neill, not for the country, and not for me. The Speaker had stepped into his role as a late-twentieth-century media politician, accepting that it was both his duty and his fate. No matter what he'd thought of his abilities in the past, in the present he was happy with the decision to fight. So was I, of course; it's what I was there for. I now understood that he'd wanted Kirk and me to cheer him on, even as Leo and others worried about him urged caution.

Kirk O'Donnell, who'd quietly been supporting me all along in my quest to be named Gary Hymel's successor, now offered the latest update: "Your stock is sky-high!" he told me, pleased. We both recognized that Tip — who enjoyed the predictable routines and rituals of his life and whose own political instincts didn't urge an ongoing slugfest with an immensely popular president — had come around to our way of thinking. We all knew, too, that there were dissatisfied Democratic House members who felt the Speaker had been too obliging so far in his dealings with Reagan. A few had even been grumbling off the record to reporters, expressing their criticisms. Yes, even as each flinched clear of harm's way himself.

In retrospect, I think it's fair to say that the Republicans themselves actually set the stage for the rise of Tip O'Neill back in the fall when they'd run those ads with the look-alike actor. By casting him as the true face of the Democratic scourge they were running against, they'd put him in the spotlight and rendered him unable to hide. Once the GOP identified the idea of "Tip O'Neill" as a target, the real one's choices were clear: he could either be a sitting duck or else shoot back.

The next time Tip and Reagan publicly tussled, from their opposite corners of Washington, was two days later, June 18. The issue: who decides how taxpayer monies are spent. Since Reagan's budget framework had been overwhelmingly approved in the House of Representatives, he didn't see why those same politicians should decide how it was put in effect. As far as he could tell, the numbers were brazenly being manipulated so there'd be no real spending cuts. David Stockman, his White House budget director, disgustedly accused the House committee chairmen of playing games. The "Politburo of the Welfare State," he dubbed them, tarring them with a couple of brushes. Stockman would lampoon O'Neill as the "Hogarthian embodiment of the superstate he had labored for so long to maintain."

The president, out of patience with the tactics up on the Hill and wanting to put an end to it, now made a personal plea to Speaker O'Neill, requesting that all of the proposed Reagan cuts be considered in a single vote on the House floor. And if that weren't enough, Reagan made clear to Tip that he wanted the White House itself to craft this bill, deciding to the penny what programs should be cut and by how much. The answer he got in reply was short and to the point. "Did you ever hear of the separation of powers? The Congress of the United States will be responsible for spending," Tip parried. "You're not supposed to be writing legislation."

Then, when Tip characterized Reagan's proposed one-for-all bill as a power play, the president was ready. "I was a Democrat myself, longer than I've been a Republican, and the Democrats have been known to make a few power plays." That reference to his former party affiliation — and his later sincere congratulations on Tip and Millie's fortieth anniversary — signaled that he wasn't yet waging all-out war. The Speaker suddenly relented and agreed to take a look at what his Democratic House chairmen had been up to.

That night, in his diary Reagan offered a thoughtful take on the conversation that fully reveals his political street smarts.

Called Tip O'Neill — there is no question but that games are being played. The Dem. dominated Committees have put together their plans for implementing . . . [the Reagan budget]. Some did alright but a number of them claimed savings by putting in unrealistic figures they knew would not hold up. For example one of them called for eliminating 1/3 of the P.O.'s [post offices] in the U.S. Now they know we'd have to ask for replacement of those which means their claimed savings doesn't exist.

Tip was blustery on the phone & accused me of not understanding the const. — separation of powers etc. I was asking only that he allow an amendment to be presented on the floor for correc-

tion of the phony comm. recommendations. He wont allow that of course. He
is blocking our move to consolidate
categorical grants into Block grants.
Claims Cong. would be abdicating its
responsibility. In truth Wash. has no
business trying to dictate how States &
local govts. will operate these programs.
Tip is a solid New Dealer and still
believes in reducing the states to admin.
districts of the Fed. govt. He's trying to
gut our program because he believes in
big spending.

With the Reagan spending cuts set for a
vote in the House a week later, on June 25,
Tip persisted with his plan to have them
handled separately, standing against the
president's determined push for a single
yes-or-no. "Tip O'Neill is getting rough,"
Reagan wrote in his diary two nights before
the vote. "Saw him on T.V. telling the
United Steel workers U. I am going to
destroy the nation."

In the end, it didn't matter. Tip's dire
prophecies weren't enough to ward off a
crushing defeat. In an extraordinary step,
the House of Representatives voted to rebuff
the Speaker and permit an up-or-down vote
on the entire package of Reagan cuts. It was

an unheard-of act of rebellion, stripping the Speaker of the House of his historic power to decide what the House votes on. While the vote was close — just seven votes — it would demonstrate for all to see that Ronald Reagan was calling the shots, even under Tip O'Neill's own roof.

But Reagan's big victory wound up coming at a cost. With a strategy that insisted that his spending cuts all be included in a single bill, the White House encouraged a slapdash drafting process. Even in the final form in which it passed the House, the giant document continued to be an unedited catchall, one including such nongermane material as one Congressional Budget Office staffer's phone number. However, far worse a calamity was the inclusion in there of a measure eliminating the Social Security minimum benefit. It meant that three million seniors, many of them in their eighties, would be stripped of their $122 monthly benefits. This would cause panic among the Democrats — and also among many Republicans, who voted for the Reagan bill — once they'd realized what they'd done. They understood only too well what a weapon their opponents the following year, in the 1982 elections, could make of this blunder.

■ ■ ■ ■

On July 7, 1981, President Ronald Reagan made history by nominating Arizonan Sandra Day O'Connor, a moderate Republican Court of Appeals judge and the first woman ever to be tapped, to the Supreme Court. Speaker of the House Thomas P. O'Neill wholeheartedly approved, calling it "the best thing he'd done since he was inaugurated . . . the first time he's turned the clock ahead during his administration."

And then Tip turned around and made an appointment of his own.

The Speaker entrusted me with the job of helping him
take on Ronald Reagan. It was a thrilling challenge.

CHAPTER ELEVEN:
BATTLEFIELD PROMOTION

"I still believe that the mildest and
most obscure of Americans can be
rescued from oblivion by good luck,
sudden changes in fortune, sudden
encounters with heroes. I believe it
because I lived it."
— TED SORENSEN, *COUNSELOR*

I'd sensed it was coming. As I continued to
hear encouraging reports from Kirk O'Donnell, I also saw how each morning the
Speaker was regularly using the statements
I wrote to open his press conferences. And
that, of course, had been the idea from the
start. What caused the delay naming his new
administrative assistant was explained easily
enough in Tip terms and made sense to
anyone who knew him. As his son Christopher "Kip" O'Neill told me at the time, his
father had to have a person in that critical
job whom "he felt comfortable with." I'd

now met that test.

I'd been waiting nervously outside his office when Tip called me in. It was late in the afternoon and he'd asked me to come by. Naturally, I was on tenterhooks. "I want you to have Gary's press job," he announced almost the moment I sat down. "I like the way you carry yourself," he added warmly, by way of explanation. Even though I appreciated the compliment, I couldn't help but be disappointed. That's because what he just said had the same effect on me as back when I'd been offered the Capitol Police moonlighting job.

In this case, I immediately assumed he was slotting me into a second-rung position, one where I'd be reporting to Kirk. Then, after a pause, he went on: "It's a statutory position. It carries the rank and salary of administrative assistant." In fact, this was it! The big one!

As I got up to leave — feeling happy, fired up, and relieved all at the same time — I was already forgetting just about everything else my new boss had said, except that he'd promised we were "going to have fun." The fact that he said that made me feel great, and I believed him. As far as I was concerned, we were going to enjoy ourselves just the way David did when he took on Goliath. Helping load the slingshot was going to be my job!

Here's what ran in the *Washington Post*.

Tip Top Aide
By Cass Peterson, Washington, July 9, 1981
House Speaker Thomas P. (Tip) O'Neill, Jr. (D-Mass) has hired Christopher J. Matthews, a former Carter speechwriter and onetime aide to Senator Frank Moss (D-Utah), as his administrative assistant, replacing longtime aide Gary Hymel. Hymel was a key political aide as well as O'Neill press man, keeper of the gates, appointments secretary and King Solomon of space allocation.

Be careful what you wish for, they say. Well, I'd gotten what I'd wanted: all I had to do now was deliver.

From that afternoon on, I committed myself totally to the challenge I'd been recruited for. Standing at Tip O'Neill's side as he endeavored to level the Reagan White House's off-balance economic agenda was an honor, a responsibility, and a huge kick all at once. It was up to him not to let them get away with it — and each one of us on the Speaker's staff understood the necessity for this, as did an equally committed band of other House members.

Every morning when I pulled into my assigned parking spot by the East Front of the Capitol — where Jack Kennedy, among other presidents, had taken the presidential oath — and then sat down behind that big desk in the high-ceilinged room just across from the House chamber, it was a genuine high. At the same time, it was impossible not to remember my stint as a cop there in that building. Though it had been barely a decade earlier, it felt like a few lifetimes. Even fresher in my mind, though, were those two years I'd put in at the Old Executive Office Building, next door to the White House. It had been an incredible experience writing speeches for a president, and then spending those last days and nights heading to Election Day crisscrossing the country on the campaign trail.

That job, however, had come to an abrupt end on Inauguration Day, which meant I also had a personal issue with Reagan. Those of us on the Carter team had given the effort to defeat him everything we had — and then some — but we failed. Now it seemed as if I was being offered a second chance, and I intended to get it right this time around.

One thing for sure: I didn't want to miss out on anything that was happening, virtually minute to minute, in the Speaker's office. Being there, keeping watch over the action and helping Tip to respond quickly when the circumstances demanded, soon turned into an obsession, or maybe even an addiction — from morning to night, right through the weekend and back to Monday again.

The pattern was familiar. First, I'd been a junior legislative assistant in the morning, Capitol policeman in the afternoon. More recently I'd been an outsourced Speaker's advisor in the morning, a Democratic campaign operative in the afternoon. Now I was corner man for Tip O'Neill in the morning, and later in the day his roving envoy on the House floor.

Mornings were most important. From the minute I awoke until Tip's daily press conference at quarter to twelve, one thing and one thing only was on my mind: making sure that when the Speaker walked down the hall to begin taking questions he was perfectly prepared for whatever might be thrown at him. In politics, nothing good ever comes out of the unexpected. It helped that Tip started each day as a vacuum cleaner for information. "Whaddaya hear?"

was his invariable greeting to Kirk O'Donnell, Ari Weiss, and me as we sat there in his office.

"Anything special out there?" He continued probing, looking around at us expectantly. "Anything I ought to know?" We understood we needed to be sharpest when it came to this last query, that it required us being his eyes and ears. If any tidbit of information happened to be floating around Greater Washington, the existence of which might affect him and his stewardship of the House, he counted on one of us to make him aware of it. We knew we had to come through with no excuses and that he was expecting us to deliver the goods.

Not wanting to be caught off guard or unprepared in the day's press conference was one part of the equation, but the other was that Tip also never wished to be surprised in his role as *Speaker,* as the leader of the United States House of Representatives. Though he trusted us and others on his staff, it was the rest of the world — that is to say, his world, of Capitol Hill and its environs — that could and did harbor trouble. He relied on us to distill the essence of every Sunday's public affairs talk shows for him and to reduce the hot air spouted to the essential nitty-gritty he craved. Statements made on-air often required expert decoding — no pol ever went on *Meet the Press* or *Face the Nation* without packing an agenda — and those analyses we supplied as well. Then, too, if a Democratic colleague had been speaking against Tip or his leadership in the cloakroom, of course the Speaker had to know *that.* Somebody would always drop the dime, and thus one of us would hear through our networks who'd been dabbling in disloyalty or insurrection. Secrets were hard to keep even in so mammoth a building. "The walls have ears," the Speaker would remind us ominously.

Priding himself on his skills at reading the House, as I've said, he relied on us to help ensure his ability to do so. It was also imperative that each and every day he was on top of where all the legislative issues stood — which ones were headed to the floor, which were still in committee, which ones weren't going anywhere. "Where're we at on that, Ari?" he'd ask Weiss, who, though still in his twenties, appeared to have been born to this job. He was a prodigy who possessed the astounding gift, as I've said, of knowing the answer to any legislative question within minutes of arriving daily at his desk, right next to mine.

Basically, there was a division of labor, and here's how Tip described it in an interview with Hedrick Smith: "Ari Weiss was absolutely brilliant. Legislativewise, he was the fellow I followed. International and politics was Kirk O'Donnell. Local was Leo Diehl. The writer was Chris Matthews. I had four extremely able and talented people."

Before long we'd arrive at the question of what that day's targeted statement — focusing on a topic of current interest — was to be. These "scripted" comments were always the centerpiece of his press briefing. I'd have suggestions ready to present, as to where we might go and what I thought would work, and then I'd pitch them to him. His reactions, when he approved, would vary from a sober approval to an appreciative chuckle. It was easy to know when he liked an idea. However, if he didn't go along or wanted tweaks, he made it clear. "That's not me!" he'd exclaim. Or else he'd instruct, "Drop that last line." His was a self-protective, or maybe I should say self-defining, editing process: he knew who he was and he was simply sharing that knowledge.

Once the brainstorming session was over, anyone watching would have seen me race down the corridor to my desk next to the Speaker's ceremonial office. Once there, I'd knock out the daily statement we'd decided on as if a stopwatch were ticking off the seconds. What a kick it was to each day prove myself fast enough to knock out the Speaker's statement so that it would be sitting there, neatly ready for him to pick up and read to open his meeting with the press.

Once the Speaker had gone in at noon to "open the House," the afternoons were mine to wander the floor. Such access to "the floor" of the House of Representatives was a grand perk, and before long I was familiar with its landmarks and its people.

Just off the back row was a door leading to the Democratic cloakroom. There are four cloakrooms in the Capitol — one for each party off both the House and Senate chambers. Legendary multi-purpose rooms, they're where the serving pols go to snack, answer phone calls, or relax. In a corner was a fellow named Raymond, selling boiled hot dogs, tuna sandwiches, chips, soda, and coffee, allowing members to dash in and grab a bite. In those days before cell phones, "Chez Raymond," as we liked to call it in a mock French accent, stood off from the double row of old-fashioned telephone booths that were another of the room's classic features.

Entering from the House floor, the first person you encountered was the "Master of Phones." The presider in the cloakroom, his job was facilitating communications between the leadership and the rank and file. It's always his business to know as much as anyone ever could, especially with regard to what time the House was going to adjourn each week. He also somehow managed to keep track of the departure schedules for those Democratic members who left town on the weekends to head home to their families and districts. The Master of Phones looked out for them, ensuring they'd make whatever train or plane they were expecting to catch.

Also there in the cloakroom were a few tables and a cluster of worn-in leather chairs, a pair of overstuffed couches, and a television. In the old days, some of the senior members would settle in comfortably to enjoy the classic black-and-white movies that came on at 4 p.m., eventually falling asleep for all to see. For his part, Tip O'Neill liked to claim one of those trusty armchairs and, cigar in hand, wait for members to come up and tell him what was on their minds. By making sure to stay tuned in like this, he was better able to "read" the House. The Speaker loved being there and available to listen.

I was fascinated by the floor and its human geography, and soon familiarized myself with the different members, where they sat and with whom — and what these choices meant. It was easy to spot the cliques. Up in the back and hugging the center aisle, and therefore closest to the Republicans, was "Redneck Row." That was home to the southern Democrats, the members who were the Speaker's biggest worry; they were the conservatives who were now voting heavily for the Reagan program. Tip understood what their reasons were — backing of stronger defense and opposition to "big government" — but he was playing a waiting game, hoping they'd see the light and come home to the Democrats, to him.

Down on the far left side of the chamber, looking toward the Speaker's chair, was the "Pennsylvania Corner." Party stalwarts one and all, the guys sitting there represented the blue-collar citizens of Pittsburgh, Johnstown, Scranton, Wilkes-Barre, and the machine Democrats from Philadelphia. Their leader was Jack Murtha, a combat veteran from Vietnam who'd run a car wash before getting elected. Jack was a pal of the Speaker's and soon turned into my great booster, the friend most openly appreciative of all my contributions to Tip's public standing and approval ratings. He was strong on defense, and his vote could always be counted on when there were military issues at hand. Jack was also well versed enough when it came to House rules to know when and how to slip a congressional pay raise through, despite the watchful eyes of a fellow Pennsylvanian, Bob Walker, a Republican from Lancaster. Murtha's skill in this regard would have made him an extremely popular guy even had he not been one already.

Still, it wasn't so easy to identify the loyalties of every Democrat by his location on the floor. While the conservative southern members were easy to peg, there was another faction in the caucus who were harder to locate and label. These "Watergate babies" — so called because they'd been elected in 1974 and 1976, following the Nixon White House scandals — often came from politically moderate suburbia, taking seats held previously by Republicans. They'd won as a result of deep-seated voter reaction to crimes uncovered in Washington — abuses of power reaching all the way to the top and shocking the country. These members tended to be much more independent than the Democrats from big-city party organizations; they were also more reform-minded. Arriving on Capitol Hill from all over America and aggressively wielding new brooms, they were intent on limiting the clout claimed by senior House members while simultaneously strengthening their own.

The Speaker held a mixed view of these Young Turks. While recognizing the excellence of their educational backgrounds, their overall sophistication, and the undeniable commitment they brought to the job, he was less able to accept how so many strangers had appeared suddenly on the landscape and secured congressional seats for themselves. Their arrival on the scene, as he saw it, showed no understanding of or respect for the old ways. What Tip and his cohorts had done was "rise through the chairs," progressing from seats in the state legislatures to seats in the U.S. House, in a time-honored fashion. The post-Watergate representatives were making a point of doing it differently.

"The interesting factor was that people were elected to Congress who under normal circumstances never would have been elected," he said. Because of this, Tip believed, the new members were able to have a sense of independence from traditional Democratic Party allegiances. Their justifications for this, he saw, were several. "They didn't help me," the new legislators would say — "they" being the Democratic establishment. Or: "They didn't finance my campaign." Or else: "They didn't help me along the line." Finally, you'd hear this one: "I won *despite* the Democratic Party."

One group of younger members was actually bipartisan. This was the "Gym Caucus." Late in the afternoon, they'd arrive on the floor, their hair wet from playing basketball over in the Rayburn House Office Building subbasement. There, behind unmarked steel doors, was where you'd find the House gym. Claiming medical necessity for the fierce contests they waged on the court, the Gym Caucus liked to refer to their pickup games as "heart attack prevention." Since it first opened in 1965, the facility has always been restricted to House members, and this exclusivity has only added to its mystique. Former members have lifetime privileges, with the sole nonmembers permitted to use it being the House officers — doorkeeper, clerk, sergeant-at-arms — who were nominated by the Democratic leadership and elected finally to their positions by the members.

The Speaker, certainly no jock at his age, had his own habits when it came to gym-going. Whenever I'd hear him say to his secretary, Eleanor Kelley, "I'm going over for a rub, Ella-nah," I knew he'd be clutching a handful of cigars he planned to share on arrival. The steam room camaraderie provided him with yet another opportunity to keep his ears to the ground, yet another way to read the House.

The annual Gym Dinner is one of Congress's great rituals. I was eligible to attend, and despite the unexciting setting — the staff cafeteria in the Longworth House Office Building — and the basic American comfort food — New York steaks, baked potatoes, corn on the cob, apple pie á la mode — knew it to be a coveted ticket. Turning down events and sending regrets are regular features of Washington life, especially for a busy legislator, but the Gym Dinner is an occasion none of them ever wants to miss.

There was no program, no entertainment, no toasts or speeches, nothing except the meal, which was served buffet-style, with members — past and present, from both parties — joining each other at long tables. Each guest waited in line, helped himself to his meal and a bottle of beer, and then surveyed the room to grab whatever seat was open. No one stayed long, only hung around for just enough time to feel joined to a greater whole, this venerable political body that had seen so much history and yet would always be the sum of its diverse parts.

My own first Gym Dinner took place a mere two weeks after I'd been named administrative assistant to the Speaker. It turned out I wasn't the only newcomer that evening: Ronald Reagan was another. Vice President George Bush, a Texas congressman in the late 1960s — back when the Rayburn Office Building was just completed and the gym newly open — had brought along the president for what seemed to me a very clear reason, the indisputable potential for goodwill. As I saw the lines of Democratic members, as well as Republicans, patiently waiting their chance to pose for a picture with Reagan, affable as always and sporty in his glen plaid suit, it didn't surprise me. Anyone who's ever spent more than a couple of hours on Capitol Hill knows only too well that the working politician loves photos of himself with the powerful. Not only are these mementoes the standard decoration of every office but they also serve as highly effective eye-catchers in constituent newsletters. Seeing the Democrats' eagerness, still, was sobering, simply because at the same time it was business-as-usual, it was also a perfect symbol of the party's current dilemma.

The Gym Dinner, purely an insider evening, is off-limits to the media. At that particular one the other attendees were, in fact, flattered that the president would take the time to join them on their own turf. It presented no photo ops beneficial to him — except, as I said before, in the individual goodwill sense. If it had been George Bush's idea to bring Reagan, it was a shrewd one, and Reagan knew it. His diary entry that night read: "Six-thirty a drop by at the annual 'Gym Dinner' of the House — Carter never went." A week later the House was to vote on the third section of the White House program — the 25 percent cut in the federal income tax.

When it came time for this third jousting match over the Reagan economic program, the Democrats were a bit more prepared. This time, not just Tip O'Neill but Ways and Means chairman Dan Rostenkowski went on national television to respond to Reagan's latest prime-time appeal.

In a maneuver to hold the middle class, the Speaker declared the vote on the Reagan tax bill a question of whom you support. If you're looking out for the better-off, you vote for the Reagan program; if not, you vote the Democratic tax cut proposal. Our analysts isolated the pivot point at $50,000. If you made more, you benefited from the Reagan plan; if less, you'd be wise to vote the Democratic option. We christened it "the $50,000 Question" after the TV quiz show of the 1950s. The flaw in our case — I was the one who concocted it — should have been obvious. Congressman Tom Downey of Long Island voiced the belief that many voters making less than that figure could well imagine themselves rising past it. Our attempt at ripsnorting populism wasn't going to be much use.

In the end, the result was 238–195 for the historic Reagan tax cuts. Forty-eight Democrats sided with him on the key vote; nearly a hundred joined the Republicans on the bill's final passage. Jotting these numbers into his diary, Reagan added: "This on top of the budget victory is the greatest pol. win in half a century. Tip O'Neill & his leadership called me and with complete graciousness congratulated us on our win. Now we must make it work — and we will."

But what Tip recalled saying to him in that congratulatory phone conversation, and what Reagan could have therefore neglected to record, was, "These are just the innings. The ball game will be up in 1982." Was this merely bravado or something more? For the Speaker could well see worse trouble ahead when the next freshman class — many of them bound to sail in as supporters of a popular president's mandate for change — arrived on the House floor. The current coalition of Republicans and southern Democrats, as long as every one of them was on board, already was sufficient to crack the magic number — 218 votes — that made for the majority in the House necessary to pass a bill.

Over the past six months, Tip had had to face not just Ronald Reagan's enormous crowd appeal — which translated as widespread public support — but also the admiration and well-wishing the president had gained after the assassination attempt. Therefore, the Speaker had proceeded carefully. He'd trusted his natural tendencies to caution. Moreover, Reagan had had the Speaker's goodwill; they'd connected in genuine, if not deep, ways. Still, in Washington terms, that counted.

Owing to these factors, Tip had held back, wanting to fight but not wanting to obstruct. He'd intended that the Democrats should present smart and convincing alternatives to Reagan's program yet, at the same time, no roadblocks, which he felt could easily backfire. It was Kirk O'Donnell who'd offered the basics of this summertime strategy. "The key was, don't get caught being a defender of the status quo. Don't get caught obstructing the political process. Give Reagan his chance." It was more important for Tip to save his troops than to logjam Reagan — meaning that if the Speaker had delayed the earliest budget votes well into the summer, preventing the tax cut from being passed in early August as scheduled, he and the Democrats could find themselves blamed for any negative consequences.

The only problem was, in following this scenario, Tip O'Neill looked like a leader spinning his wheels or even in retreat. It certainly gave the crepehangers their opening, and so a *New York Times Magazine* cover story in August portrayed the Speaker as on his last legs. "Is Tip O'Neill ready to join his old cronies in retirement?" the piece asked with cruel frankness. "The Speaker is a proud man who will not easily be driven from office. But he knows that he is considered a burden by many Democrats, too large a target in the legislative battles and on Election Day."

Just as I came into my new position, it seemed that Tip remained stuck in a public relations black hole. He'd been judged by popular opinion and found wanting. "What I had to get used to in 1981," he'd later describe it, "was being criticized not only by the press but by the man on the street — or, to be more precise, the man in the airport. . . . Some of them shouted insults like 'Leave the president alone, you fat bastard!' Now and then one would be supportive, but friendly voices were all too few."

Throughout this difficult and discouraging period, what kept Tip O'Neill strong was, as I've said, his unswerving commitment to the role of government as a force for good in its citizens' lives. It was his firm conviction that he was *acting* on his beliefs — just as Ronald Reagan was. He felt that the Reagan program would ultimately fail. He believed the economy would worsen and that the victor of 1981 would end up punished by the voter in 1982.

I could only respect my new boss for his toughness in sticking it out. Every day he arose to face the abuse he knew would be hurled at him. He was a politician out of step with the times and he was willing to live with that fact. Yet he also held this unexpected natural advantage. What I came early to realize was that this big, overweight guy with his shock of white hair had the goods in a way we just hadn't been seeing. The truth was, many people *liked* his looks. What was the Speaker of the House *supposed* to look like, anyway? Yes, he was an editorial cartoonist's delight — and never more so than in those tough summer months of 1981 — but what was written on his face, his character, was unmistakably genuine.

Tip himself would frequently worry about his appearance, and just as frequently say so. But, as the weeks passed, what I began to see was how great he looked, how special, how unlike any other person. He was Tip O'Neill, and he looked exactly like who he was. As Republican Bob Dornan of California once said, if Martians came into the House chamber they'd know instantly who the leader was. David Rogers, an astute Tip-watcher on the *Boston Globe,* had this to say about the veteran politician from North Cambridge: "Whatever carping comes with any defeat, the political facts are that no Democrat today commands more affection in the House than O'Neill or is in any position to challenge him as Speaker."

The problem was the timing, which seemed to be running against him. As the summer of 1981 drew to an end, the national verdict was decisive. Reagan had rolled up the score, victorious on the three big votes — the budget, the spending cuts, the tax cut — and O'Neill had won none. Columnist George F. Will, falling back on what was fast becoming a cliché, dismissed Tip as "a cartoonist's caricature of urban liberalism on its last legs." He predicted O'Neill was in his last term as Speaker.

Congressman Charlie Wilson was, as usual, more colorful. A Democrat from southeastern Texas, he was known for the zest with which he approached both whiskey and women. Considering Reagan's successes in enacting his programs and his own fellow Democrats' seeming inability to stand in his way, Charlie succinctly summed up the political situation's potential for serious disaster as he saw it: "I sure as hell hope that sonofabitch doesn't come out against *fucking.*"

The Speaker and Norm.
Tip O'Neill's appearance on *Cheers* was as natural as the foam on a Sam Adams.

CHAPTER TWELVE:
TURNING

"It's the long road that has no turning."
— IRISH PROVERB

By August 1981, Ronald Reagan had proven his legislative might. Victorious in every test of strength so far, he was about to bring to bear the full force of his presidential punch. "Learned the Air Controllers will probably strike Mon. morning," he noted in his diary over the weekend of July 31. "That's against the law. I'm going to announce that those who strike have lost their jobs & will not be re-hired."

The Professional Air Traffic Controllers Organization, known as PATCO, had a history of calling job actions — a slowdown in 1968, a mass "sick-out" in 1970 — in order to force the government to the bargaining table. Since air traffic controllers served in the Federal Aviation Administration, such tactics were the PATCO leadership's way to evade the law banning strikes by government employees. In 1980, the union had become more aggressive, protesting its differences with President Jimmy Carter by refusing to endorse him for reelection, instead giving its eleventh-hour backing to a Republican, Ronald Reagan. Now they were going further, violating not just their contract but federal law.

On August 3, 1981, PATCO's members made good on their threat and walked off the job. Their demands involved workplace rules, pay scales, and a shortening of their high-pressure workweek to thirty-two hours. A further requirement on the table called for excluding PATCO from the rules governing the rest of the civil service. What justified this audacity was the union leaders' calculation of their bargaining position. They timed the strike to coincide with a peak airline traffic period. Would any president dare to incur the anger of travelers who'd booked their flights and would now be forced to forgo not just planned departures, but in many cases, their family vacations as well?

Sitting in the Oval Office, President Reagan was ready, unwavering in his intention to stand firm. For the past three decades he'd had a decidedly low tolerance for what he saw as union arrogance and troublemaking. Having prepared a plan of action, he now carried it out with ruthless confidence. "The strike was called for 7 A.M. I called the press corps together in the Rose Garden & read a statement I'd written yesterday. I included in it a paragraph from the written oath each employee signs — 'that he or she will not strike against the U.S. govt. or any of its agencies.' I then announced they would have 48 hrs. in which to return & if they don't they are separated from the service."

Two days later, with the PATCO membership refusing to return, Reagan fired the 11,345 controllers who were disregarding his back-to-work order. Much worse, he went on to ban them for life from federal service in *any* capacity. That, however, was not the end of the punishment. In a final blow, the administration acted to decertify PATCO. Once the recognized union of the air traffic controllers, it now did not exist.

Reagan's swift action and near-dictatorial command of the moment sent out shock waves, and not just through organized labor. Seven thousand commercial flights had to be canceled the first day. But by breaking PATCO, he showed in a single executive judgment call how different he was from his recent predecessors. This first-year president's take-no-prisoners stance also carried a clear message that was missed by no one on either side of the ideological fence. Future Federal Reserve chairman Alan Greenspan, a supporter, applauded Reagan's toughness, pointing out that the precedent Reagan was setting would empower corporate employers around the country facing contentious labor disputes to act similarly.

On Capitol Hill, Tip O'Neill's reaction was layered. Publicly, he showed sympathy for the strikers, reminding listeners that Reagan's "two-fisted" leadership style also was the mark of a man unwilling to compromise. The Speaker called the mass firings yet another "result" of the new economic order now being advanced in the country. He threw out a sarcastic jab as well, reminding labor leaders inclined to wonder that PATCO had chosen the wrong party to do business with. "That's what happens to a union that supported the president of the United States. That is what is going on. The same thing is happening to the people out there who supported the president. They are *really* getting it." If you'd thought voting against Jimmy Carter and for Ronald Reagan was in your own best interest, Tip was saying, it was time to think again.

When he was commenting more privately, around the office to staffers, Tip was forced to acknowledge the political muscle Reagan was displaying — and not just domestically. A massive contributor to both parties, Dwayne Andreas, the CEO of Illinois-based Archer Daniels Midland, was an influential international agribusiness figure to whom every senior politician paid attention. With multimillion-dollar deals that took him frequently to Moscow, he enjoyed regular contact with highly placed officials there. That summer, returning from the Soviet Union, he reported to Tip that the Soviet top brass had shared with him their healthy respect for the new president. The Russians, he said, credited Reagan, in contrast to his predecessors, with the strength of will to qualify him as a true leader.

As invincible as Reagan seemed that August, there were also trouble signs, certainly the kind a seasoned political watcher might have spotted. David Stockman, his budget director, had informed him he needed perhaps a half trillion dollars in *additional* spending cuts over the next years if he didn't want to see the federal deficit balloon further. "If these numbers were out," Reagan retorted, "Tip O'Neill would be wearing a halo." By the time he got to his diary to record his thoughts, though, the president sounded more upbeat. "We have our work cut out for us. Our goal of balancing the budget by '84 is doubtful. I'm still optimistic that we do it."

Whatever the numbers seemed to call for, there was one program Reagan no longer had any intention of messing with: Social Security. The White House remembered the politically scarring push to cut early retirement benefits back in May. The House of Representatives had just voted overwhelmingly to restore the minimum $122 payment, another Social Security issue that had shown itself to be potential political poison. At the same time, the Speaker continued to bear down on Democratic colleagues who'd shown any inclination to pose further threats to America's millions of beneficiaries.

This included those who, with the best of intentions, foresaw future problems with the system if it wasn't fixed. When Texan Jake Pickle, the Democratic chair of the Social Security subcommittee, began work on a reform measure, Tip simply moved to stop him in his tracks. To accomplish this maneuver, he called on Missouri Democrat Dick Bolling, a loyalist and chairman of the Rules Committee, which controlled when and how legislation got to the House floor. "Jake, we are all proud of your work," Bolling told Pickle, "but I want to say one thing. As long as I am chairman of the Rules Committee there won't be any Social Security legislation in this Congress." The decree had come directly from Tip O'Neill himself.

Reagan, never a slow learner, was now prepared to keep his hands, too, off the country's most cherished program. "I'm withdrawing Soc. Security from consideration & challenging Tip & the Dems.," Reagan wrote in his diary on September 23, "to join in a bipartisan effort to solve the fiscal dilemma of S.S. without all the politics they've been playing." With the 1982 midterm election season soon kicking into gear, Reagan, intending to neutralize the issue, announced the creation of a Social Security commission the purpose of which would be to address the system's financial health. There would be fifteen members: five chosen by the president, five by the Speaker, and five by the Senate majority leader, Howard Baker. It seemed the very essence of a Washington solution, this burying of an issue in another layer of bureaucracy, even if a bipartisan one at that.

But the truth for Reagan in this case was that he'd pretty much handed the issue over to the opposition. He could see no way to reclaim it to his advantage. If the failed May proposal to penalize early retirees and the June vote to eliminate the minimum Social Security benefit weren't enough, Reagan's own history of pushing to make the system "voluntary" in the 1960s had left a trail of cookie crumbs for the hungry Democrats, who'd have no trouble following it all the way to the Oval Office.

Suddenly came a tragedy — and all such horrific events arrive with no warning — that shocked the country: the assassination of Egyptian president Anwar Sadat. Two days after the PATCO strike was called, President Reagan had welcomed the Egyptian leader to the White House for what he saw as highly successful meetings. "I'm encouraged that between us maybe we can do something about peace in the middle east," Reagan jotted down the night before Sadat's departure.

The deadly attack took place as Sadat was reviewing a Cairo military parade that annually celebrated the Egyptian army's crossing of the Suez Canal during the 1973 Israeli war. The assassin was an Islamic extremist serving in the Egyptian military. "It's hard to describe the shock & sorrow . . . ," Reagan wrote in his diary that night.

"Even though their visit was short we discovered we had a deep feeling of friendship for them. Maybe it has to do with a state visit. You start out with knowledge of each other & immediately get into the problems you mutually want to solve."

The afternoon the world learned of the assassination, I went with the Speaker to the National Cathedral. There we honored, in a hastily scheduled prayer service, the Egyptian leader who'd made peace with Israel, now slain on account of that extraordinary act. I remember well the Call to Prayer echoing through the Gothic nave of the mighty sanctuary. In the aftermath of Sadat's death at the hands of a fundamentalist fanatic, to be sitting there amid the Christian prayers gave me a great deal to think about.

For four years, I'd served Jimmy Carter, the man who in 1978 at Camp David had brokered the historic deal between Sadat and Menachem Begin, Israel's hard-nosed prime minister. Now I was working for Tip O'Neill, an Irish-American Catholic, mourning a Muslim who'd made the ultimate sacrifice as a result of what he'd dared to do. The mood in the cathedral seemed to me to embody a commitment to interreligious affection I could not have previously imagined. It was a moment when I have to say I experienced a feeling of being with my new boss in just the right place.

In the fall of 1981, after a spring and summer in which Republicans had dominated Washington with their promise of blue skies, the country's barometer dropped. The political weather was about to change. The Democrats hadn't lost just the presidency but also, effectively, control of Congress, and the ripple effect of that was making itself felt. Pounded by high interest rates, the tight-money economy began to slip downward. Whatever it was the Democrats were doing — shaking themselves off after a bad season of defeat and beginning to worry about the next year's election — they weren't quite prepared to see Tip O'Neill as their savior.

But anyone paying attention knew of the Speaker's conviction that there'd have to come a reckoning, sooner or later. Given the swift passage of Reagan's custom-built economic program on Capitol Hill, the president would have to shoulder a portion of blame for its alarming aftermath. "We haven't obstructed," Tip explained. "I think we fought a good fight as far as the Reagan people are concerned. We stuck to our timetable. We passed the largest tax bill and budget bill in history. It's the president's now. The ball is in his court — the deficits, the interest rates and unemployment." He didn't need to say any more; he'd made his point.

As the days passed and the warmth of the Republicans' triumphant summer continued to fade in the chillier fall political climate, there continued to be no good news regarding the economy. Watching closely and feeling a certain satisfaction even as he lamented the increasingly difficult reality for his fellow citizens, the Speaker simply kept pressing his case. For example, the rising jobless rate: it certainly, he pointed out, could be laid at the administration's door. "They got their cuts and said that America would be happy and go forward with a strong economy. It looks like a house of cards. . . . We understand that one million more people have been laid off. The pie-in-the-sky projections seem to be tumbling."

With the president's economic plan fixed in his sights, O'Neill zeroed in even more closely on a crucial notion: accountability. If Ronald Reagan had convinced the electorate that his fiscal agenda would be to their benefit, then it was the president's duty to stand up and defend its effect when it wasn't. "As an American, I hope it works," Tip told the press. "After all, it is his baby now. . . . He would like to say it was left over for him, but the American people truly believe we have given him what he wants."

Look what they get for it, he kept insisting. Take a family making $20,000 a year and due a weekly tax cut amounting to the princely sum of $2.34. In return, he said, they could easily find that their kids' student loans had been cut, or maybe now they'd be billed more for school lunches, while, by necessity, state and local governments would be making up the difference for a wide variety of services by raising these already strapped families' property taxes.

As mid-October arrived, Reagan made news by admitting publicly that the country could be considered in a "slight recession." Days later, he was back in the headlines with a different, equally embarrassing confession: the balanced budget he'd promised to have in place by 1984 wasn't going to happen. "Not probable" was how Treasury Secretary Donald Regan chose to describe the chances of achieving it, but the word choice fooled no one. The man who'd been swept into the White House a year earlier by a landslide majority was paying the price of his rousing legislative success.

The veteran critic of government decision-making was now obliged to be its defender.

Timing is everything, as Tip liked to say. As the economy began its autumn slide, the public needed to assign blame. Had the Democrats spent the summer months pushing back on the Reagan agenda, they'd be taking the heat for the current bad news. Kirk O'Donnell, who'd been the one pushing the Speaker to keep the trains moving during the spring and summer, now felt confirmed in the strategy he'd counseled.

With the turnabout occurring, the Speaker seemed suddenly to have more spring to his step. In politics there's a large divide between losing and being defeated, and now, it seemed to me, Tip was living the difference. Once it began to appear that President Reagan was wrong, it stood to reason that the man who'd been his chief critic, and mocked for it, would look right to have opposed him.

In November, Tip gave a speech to the alumni of the Fordham University Graduate School of Business, during which he shared one of his favorite stories:

Jakie Bloom was a good man, a poor but generous shopkeeper who allowed all his customers to buy on credit during the

Depression. But now Jakie's in his seventies, and he's despondent because his dear wife has passed away. His friends take up a collection to help him out, and Jakie Bloom is gradually able to put his life back together. Over the next few months he becomes a new man. First he gets a hair transplant. Then he loses some weight and buys some fancy clothes.

Next, Jakie grows a beard, starts working out every day, and moves down to Miami. Soon he takes up with a beautiful lady half his age.

They walk along the beach, he with his new look and she in her red bikini. Suddenly there's a tremendous storm, and Jakie is struck by lightning. A moment later he finds himself in heaven, where he demands to speak to the Boss.

"This isn't fair," he cries. "All I ever did was good, and now, in the twilight of my life, I'm finally having a little fun. How could you do this to me?"

"Jakie!" says the Lord. "I didn't recognize you."

Tip told that story for a reason. Its purpose was to spotlight the dangers of changing who you are. By late autumn of 1981, with a string of difficult, discouraging months behind him, he believed he'd weathered the worst. Most important, he'd managed it by sticking to the set of beliefs he'd held his entire political career. The self-description that he was a "big-spending liberal" satisfied him. Government, he had no doubt, *should* be there offering a hand whenever needed. Inseparable from this basic idea of such federal responsibilities was his conviction that they were best paid for by levying taxes on those who could well afford them.

With Tip O'Neill, there was no such thing as lip service, and he resisted any hollow rhetoric. He knew who he was and what he believed, and he had no need to fake it, ever. Crowd-pleasing for its own sake wasn't a practice he had any use for, a stance rare for such an old-school pol. Once I drafted a statement for his daily press conference that took a hit at Reagan for increasing the deficit. "That's not me," Tip said, rejecting it. An admitted "big spender" for good causes like health and education, he refused to strike a pose with his grip tight on the federal purse strings.

In November, with the whole world watching, Ronald Reagan took a pie in the face at embarrassingly close range, thrown from inside his administration. The latest issue of the *Atlantic* brought an interview with his budget director titled "The Education of David Stockman." In it the thirty-five-year-old former Michigan congressman revealed to writer William Greider what he described as the two deep secrets of Reagan economic policy. First, he explained, the current spending and tax policies didn't — and couldn't — add up to balanced budgets. The only way the deficit was ever going to be eliminated under Reagan, according to Stockman, would owe more to what one skeptical senator dubbed a "magic asterisk" than any honest math. The asterisk was Stockman's audacious bookkeeping notation indicating deficits to be shrunk by spending cuts *not yet identified.*

The budget director's other headline-making disclosure was virtually a gift, wrapped and ribboned, for Tip O'Neill. Over the past months, Reagan had said his tax cuts were intended to benefit Mr. and Mrs. Hardworking American, denying every inch of the way that they'd been designed to help the rich. Yet, according to his budget director, the actual goal of the Reagan plan was to cut the 70 percent bracket, the one at the top. The middle-income tax cuts were — in the words of David Stockman, there in black-and-white in the *Atlantic* — window dressing, included in the president's program only "in order to make this palatable as a political matter." The whole exercise, Stockman revealed, was a "Trojan horse" to bring down the top rate. He even unmasked Reagan's "supply side" economics as the same old "trickle down" policy favored by Republicans, just with a new name.

Reagan's shock at such disloyalty comprised a mix of disbelief, confusion, and anger. "If true," he wrote in his diary, "Dave is a turn coat — but in reality he was victimized by what he'd always thought was a good friend." So, what did the president mean by that? He seemed to be proposing that Stockman had shared his personal take on the Reagan cuts, and the economic agenda to which they belonged, with his journalist pal Greider, not realizing they'd be printed. Yet the revelations Stockman made and the misgivings he'd expressed obviously had their basis in his budget director's very real concerns. Didn't it bother Ronald Reagan that his top fiscal architect was worried that the structure he'd overseen seemed wobbly? Whether it did or not, though, wasn't what mattered at this all-hell-breaking-loose moment: inside the White House the decision made by the president's counselors was not to panic but to spin.

Up until now the story had been one of revelation. Thanks to Stockman's whistle-blowing, Americans suddenly had a chance to peer at the inner workings of the Reagan economic operation. What they saw was a jerry-rigged mechanism built on principles of economic elitism and powered by manipulative bookkeeping. Troubling as this was, fixing it, or even promising to do so, wasn't in the White House script. Instead, Jim Baker and his colleagues now quickly prepared a scenario intended to shift the media's attention by offering what they tried to package as an even more devastating angle — betrayal from within. The Reagan team was pinning their hopes on being able to change the story from the bombshell Stockman had dropped to the spectacle of a treacherous young budget director who'd self-servingly put himself above the president. They were behaving like the Great Wizard of Oz when he attempted to again hide his gears and levers.

But the damage had been done.

As an exercise in spin, what now took place followed what I've discovered is the basic two-step familiar to any veteran news watcher. First, you admit you have a problem. Next, taking advantage of those precious moments when you've won the public's trust by coming clean, you then go all out with your preferred notion of what precisely the problem is. In this case, the White House team decided to make use of an old-fashioned but still familiar metaphor. After all, David Stockman wasn't very old given the critical job he held, and given the fact that he'd grown up on a farm, the White House now scheduled him to be "taken to the woodshed." In other words, he was expected to present himself at an officially arranged sit-down with the president of the United States, where he'd be dealt with severely and the appropriate punishment would be administered.

"You're going to have lunch with the president," Jim Baker told him. "The menu is humble pie. You're going to eat every last motherfucking spoonful of it. You're going to be the most contrite sonofabitch this world has ever seen. When you go through that Oval Office door, I want to see that sorry ass of yours dragging on the carpet." Stockman was now not just a turncoat but a scapegoat, with little choice regarding the new role he'd been assigned.

Tip O'Neill naturally saw right through the White House ploy. The issue for him wasn't that Stockman had talked out of school to a journalist but whether he'd believed what he'd told him. And if he didn't, then what had been the point of the whole exercise? Since the Reagan economic program had seemed dubious to Tip from the beginning, he was perfectly able to accept what he'd read in the *Atlantic* as the plain truth straight from the horse's mouth. Besides which, having known Stockman as a colleague during the two terms he'd served in the House before joining the Reagan administration, the Speaker thought of him not just as hardworking but also as straight-shooting.

"Dave, in his heart and mind, advocated exactly what the Democrats have been saying all along," he said. "He was carrying the ball for [the White House] and I think is probably the only knowledgeable person in their organization who knows the budget system. He knows it inside and out." Meaning, if anyone had a right to sound off about it, Stockman did — and trying to distract Tip and the rest of the country by making the budget director out to be a very naughty boy simply wasn't going to work. "George Bush called it 'voodoo economics' and they made him vice president. Dave is saying the same thing, and I don't know where he is going to go," the Speaker commented wryly.

Even in the wake of the Stockman incident, Tip still found himself admiring his opponent. It was always complicated, watching the man he called "one hell of a pol" to reporters and deploring at the same time everything he stood for. "I think he's going to remain popular, to be perfectly truthful with you," the Speaker told the *Washington Post*. "People like him as an individual, and he handles the media better than anybody since Franklin Roosevelt, even including Jack Kennedy. There's just something about the guy that people like. They want him to be a success. . . . He's cutting the heart out of the American dream to own a home and have a good job . . . and still he's popular."

"You know, I said to him one day that ninety-seven percent of the economists that I talk to think your program's not going to work. And he laughs and says, 'Well I guess it's the three percent that I talk to that have been right all along.' How can you dislike a guy like that?"

As Tip's administrative assistant, I, too, felt the unsettling effect of Reagan's dual nature, the way his charm and affability seemed separate somehow from his unswerving ideology, even as those qualities remained in service of it. And I was very aware of the dilemma it caused for the Speaker, a man who'd been drawn his entire life, ever since those Barry's Corner days with the other boys in North Cambridge, to the warmth of camaraderie. When Reagan would say to him, "Look, Tip, I'm resetting my watch, it's six o'clock," he was intuiting a truth about his rival and cannily plugging into it.

On December 9, Tip's sixty-ninth birthday, President Reagan hosted a party at the White House for him. Beginning over lunch, the mutually enjoyable bipartisan celebration continued well into the afternoon. At one point, the president, by habit never much of a drinker, rang for one of the White House attendants to bring up a bottle of champagne. The tribute he then offered was as over-the-top as it was unforgettable. "Tip, if I had a ticket to heaven and you didn't have one too, I would give mine away and go to hell with you."

Mike Deaver would recall the moment: "It was an old Irish toast he had heard somewhere. Well, Tip's eyes were all filled up, you know, it was just incredible. And they left the dining room with their arms around each other's waist and Reagan took him down to the elevator and Tip went out on the South Lawn and beat the shit out of

Reagan with the press." I've got to hand it to Mike. His overall sizing up of the relationship between his boss and mine strikes me as pretty close to the truth. "Reagan," Deaver said, "thought Tip was absolutely wrong and pigheaded. And Tip thought Reagan didn't understand anything about this country except the rich. But there was a lot of respect that both of them had for each other."

Even when the Speaker went on the attack, the president, hearing Tip rail against him, simply brushed it off. He'd tell staffers not to get upset. He seemed to see Tip clearly and accept what he saw. "Tip was an old-fashioned pol," Reagan wrote. "He could be sincere and friendly when he wanted to be, but when it came to the things he believed in, he could turn off his charm and friendship like a light switch and become as bloodthirsty as a piranha."

His son Ron believed the regard in which Reagan always seemed to hold the Speaker was real. "He was fond of him," he told me. "He'd say so around the house." Just as I know Tip took his feelings — positive and negative — about his opponent home to Millie and his kids, the president did not leave Tip at the office.

■ ■ ■ ■

Now the two were headed for their second round. A year that had been shattered by an assassin's bullets had given the new American president his greatest policy triumphs. The coming twelve months would test his wisdom on where and how to defend them.

Shape of the Table.
When President Reagan came to Capitol Hill to negotiate
a budget deal in April 1982, Speaker O'Neill suspected a setup.
Here he sits uneasily at Reagan's side, but only for the picture-taking.
Later, he would take the seat across from Reagan.
Others at the table are Senate Majority Leader Howard Baker,
House Majority Leader Jim Wright, and White House aide Ed Meese.

CHAPTER THIRTEEN:
SUMMIT

"Always be able to talk."
— KIRK O'DONNELL

The Reagan winning streak had made it a tough year for the Speaker. As the Democrats departed the White House at the start of '81, the Republicans' media consultants were still wringing mileage from their caricature of the portly, white-haired, old-school pol left high and dry by the roadside. Imagewise, Tip O'Neill was the exact opposite of the new GOP president, who was handsome, athletic, and always ready with a grin and a quip.

Given his blunt manner, frequent cigar, and seemingly out-of-date convictions, the man from North Cambridge, Massachusetts, seemed the perfect embodiment of his own party's current unseductiveness. Yet wounded as he was by the continual conflicts of the first Reagan year, with one difficult month following another, Tip had hung in there and survived. Most vitally, he'd made a name for himself — out there in the world beyond Capitol Hill and the commonwealth of Massachusetts — not just in spite of the distinctively unfashionable persona he presented but, perhaps, *because* of it.

To those paying attention to the struggle in Washington, Tip O'Neill had been out front, taking on Reagan when others of his party and philosophy looked to be heading for the tall grass. His goal was to make Reagan pay for each victory with a heavier burden of responsibility. He wanted the American people to demand every inch of what the new president had promised.

A pragmatic politician above all, Tip was rising above the daily frustrations in order to play the longer game. You had to believe, and he did. Few in the Speaker's own camp specifically blamed him for losing the legislative fights over spending and taxes — battles that, more than likely, no one on their side could have won.

The good news was that Tip had started to make headway connecting the man in the White House to charges that stuck, among them Reagan's on-the-record — and never believably enough repudiated — opposition to Social Security, as well as his preference for relaxing among wealthy friends mostly at home in Bel Air or Palm Springs. A man can be judged by the company he keeps, and the idea was to paint a portrait of a president not just out of touch with mainstream Americans but blithely so.

Nonetheless, a campaign of strategic retreat — which is what, essentially, Tip O'Neill had been waging — only succeeds up to a point. As Winston Churchill warned after Dunkirk, "Wars are not won by evacuations." While, in 1981, losing those House votes had been bearable, failing to win legislative seats in the critical election year of 1982 would not be. According to standard political wisdom, the opposition party is *expected* to pick up congressional seats in the midterm contests. A failure to do this would be humiliating and shocking.

For Tip O'Neill, what now lay ahead would be a war of aggression, and the strategy was a simple one: stand, fight, and conquer. But more than this, the opposition troops he led needed the symbolic boost a strong victory that November would provide. In the sports lingo he well understood, Tip was going to have to beat the spread.

For Ronald Reagan, the arrival of 1982 brought different challenges and also an emerging peril: the U.S. economy was sinking into deep recession and the jobless rate edging toward double digits. As this all-important index rose, so, naturally, would the country's impatience with the administration's direction and the possibility of dangerous shortfalls. The Gipper — his speeches rich with sincerity — had promised to cut taxes, boost defense spending, and banish the deficit all at the same time. Those doubting whether he could actually manage such an astounding feat now saw their skepticism proved correct.

The balance of power was starting to tilt, in ways affecting both parties. To maintain an appearance of confidence in his program, President Reagan needed the backing of that same congressional coalition that had supported him before. But with the economic figures plunging around them, even the GOP legislators, now most concerned with holding on to their seats, were showing less enthusiasm. On the other side of the aisle, the rebel Democrats looked as if they might be coming home. It would take Reagan's most persuasive efforts, plus a display of White House muscle, to keep those restless recruits content with what they'd previously bought into.

■ ■ ■ ■

When it came to Tip O'Neill, I could see the shift in the political winds had breathed new life into him. No longer the beleaguered warrior I'd encountered when I first signed on the year before, he now seemed ready to defend mightily all that he cared about, and to do it with gusto. Along with his increasing zest for combat came a change in my role.

When first we'd met, I'd been the media-savvy young guy fueled by partisan belligerence and brimming over with attention-getting ideas, most of which Tip had regarded warily. It was as if I'd arrived from Mars to tell him what life was like out there, only in this case the alien environment was requiring you to be camera-ready at all times and the only language you had to speak was sound bites.

Over the months of our working together, Tip and I had learned much about each other's strengths and weaknesses. The respect I had for him from the start now was mirrored in the growing acceptance he began to offer me. Ronald Reagan had been dubbed the "Great Communicator," but my colleagues and I knew two could play at that game and even on the same turf: television. My particular job was to stand behind Tip every step of the way, making sure he had the right weapons, as he advanced onto this new battleground.

There were others cheering on this effort, and though I've mentioned the two most important allies I had before, still I want here to make a large nod to both again. Kirk O'Donnell had been with the Speaker since 1978. Those four years had left him confident enough to call him "Tip" while in the room with him and tough enough to act on such presumption. Kirk believed that the moment to fight had arrived, and, having helped put me beside Tip to begin with, he now backed my operation all the way. Tony Coelho, the chairman of the Democratic Congressional Campaign Committee, an early booster, too, remained staunch. Chosen by his fellow Democrats to reverse the party's fortunes, Tony never lost sight of his assigned mission. He played a critical early role in urging the Speaker to step out from the procedural shadows — the behind-the-scenes world where he was most at home — and become the fighting firebrand their fellow House Democrats cried out for.

When it came to the part that television, by necessity, now was going to play in Tip's life, it was necessary to acknowledge a pair of his deep-seated certainties. One, the Speaker was convinced his looks worked against him; on this, he was virtually unshakable. Plenty of handsomer guys were out there on the floor among his troops — ask him, and he'd name them with no trouble — but not only that, he also recognized how many Democratic legislators were far more articulate than he. In the same way that Richard Nixon had been only too conscious of John F. Kennedy's personal glamour, Tip O'Neill knew, when he looked in the mirror, that he didn't see Ronald Reagan's face staring back at him. But while Nixon's opponent had been simply a dashing and privileged rich man, Tip's had once been an actual movie star.

Yet, since Tip wanted nothing more than to continue as Speaker, a job he'd fought for and treasured, he couldn't argue with the task assigned him. Men of his generation understood the life predicament of having no choice; what was dished out, you took, and then you gave your utmost. Yet even with the fate of the party he loved resting in his hands, a Tip O'Neill wouldn't turn on a dime. While he accepted the necessity of TV cameras, he did it in his own way. Though still banning them at his daily press conferences, he instead took part in what became a popular daily ritual.

Arriving for work at the Capitol early each morning, he'd find network cameramen waiting for him. As he'd get out of his car on the East Front Plaza, the eager television crews stood watch. Accompanied by their field producers, the congressional correspondents then would vie to get his comments on breaking stories. For both sides, it was a fruitful solution. By the time he arrived in the office — to meet with Kirk, Ari, and me in preparation for the morning briefing — he'd not just run a small gamut of TV cameras and lived to tell the tale, but satisfied the networks, which now had fresh tape of House Speaker Tip O'Neill to broadcast on the evening news. It wasn't the most polished of settings, but it got him in the daily story and got him there early.

This simple compromise that Tip accepted — showing himself to the press, however briefly — turned out to have a significant effect beyond its immediate message-delivering benefit. Because of this greater regular visibility, the Speakership, as embodied by Tip O'Neill, became institutionalized as a position of authority that involved *speaking out* at a national level and not just a parochial one within the Congress. Suddenly "Speaker of the House" meant more than the title of a figure belonging to the back corridors of Capitol Hill who symbolized legislative deals the general public couldn't really follow and so yawned over. In this way, as he took on the freshly defined role shaping itself around him, Tip's job allowed for a counter-pulpit to the bully pulpit of the presidency. It was an idea new to the Washington stage. It delighted me that I was able to pitch the man I worked for as the natural, inevitable anti-Reagan.

Here's a quick example: If the wire reporters covering him failed to run any important point the Speaker had made at his daily press briefing, I didn't gnash my teeth. I'd merely wait a half hour, then pick up the phone to put in calls to selected White House reporters. "Did you hear what the Speaker said about Reagan today?" I'd ask. Invariably, whoever was listening would say, "Wait a minute . . . ," and then I'd hear them roll a sheet of paper into their typewriter or flip open a notebook.

That's how it was in those days, when the news cycle was more leisurely — before the incessant real-time jamboree of cable — *Hardball* included — Limbaugh, and social media. During this crucial period in 1982, the absolute top goal for those of us committed to pushing back the Republican gains — both legislatively and electorally — was to keep the heat on in any way we could, with Tip leading the charge. Yet it was easy to see that the Speaker from Massachusetts was, at that political moment, too liberal for the country at large, and so our goal was to turn this fact from a negative into a rousing advantage. The key was his continuing to focus on specific issues like Social Security, where the American public — above all the Reagan Democrats who'd switched teams to follow the Gipper — had no quarrels with Tip's longtime, fiercely held views. They meshed perfectly with the familiar truth that, in an economic downturn, the middle tends to identify with those worse off than they, fearing their own turn might come next. (In good times, the middle identifies with those better off, in hopes of joining them.)

Such was the look of the battlefield as the opposing forces examined and solidified their positions in 1982's early months. Ronald Reagan needed to ensure the country remained patient, thus allowing his program its chance to stimulate economic recovery. Tip O'Neill had the task of roundly bringing home the other side of the argument, which equally meant the argument over *him.* Lampooned in 1980, derided in 1981, he could now be seen as rightfully openhanded when it came to those in need. Here was no lobbyists' fat cat but rather an experienced paternal figure long committed to a regular flow of monthly Social Security checks into America's mailboxes, and also to keeping them hefty enough to pay for inflation. Listening to the advice of veteran pollsters like Pat Caddell and Peter Hart, O'Neill learned to adjust his political grip. The sharpest shot he now took at Reagan had no trouble hitting the bull's-eye: not that Reagan was tough on the poor, but that his real constituents were the rich.

It was the night of Ronald Reagan's first State of the Union address and he'd come to the Capitol early. For reasons of security he needed to be in place even before the Secret Service walked their bomb-sniffing dogs through the House chamber, and so while he waited, he needed to be held in a suitable room in the building. The one selected was the Speaker's ceremonial office, right next to mine. It was where the Speaker's daily press conferences took place, the ones currently showcasing his regular criticisms of the president and his policies. After a bit of hesitation, I walked through the door and introduced myself. He was standing in the middle of the room surrounded by a few staffers I didn't recognize. "Welcome, Mr. President, to the room where we plot against you." Technically, we hatched our plans in the Speaker's back office, but it was as good an icebreaker as I could manage.

In any case, Reagan was having none of it. "But it's after six! The Speaker says in Washington that's when we put politics aside." It was the first I'd heard of it, but, of course, I didn't argue. He then promptly disarmed me by speaking as confidentially as if he'd always known me. "Like opening night," he said, admitting his jitters. On a nearby table I noticed a cup of tea with a slice of lemon that he'd undoubtedly requested. Later that evening, when he got back to the White House, he wrote in his diary: "I wonder if I'll ever get used to addressing the joint sessions of Cong.?" The boy from Illinois had been a bona fide movie star and then governor of our nation's most populous state, and still he felt the weight of history. "I've made a mil. speeches in every kind of place to every kind of audience. Somehow there's a thing about entering that chamber — goose bumps & a quiver."

The speech he delivered swerved away

from his ongoing war with Congress over spending and taxes. It was no time to hold up a scorecard on his economic program, which would end up doubling the national debt in his presidency. Instead, he offered an off-the-topic case for returning more than forty federal programs to the control of the country's state and local governments. The "new federalism," he called it. The Democrats, however, weren't buying either the topic or its fancy moniker. Here's how the Speaker responded at his daily press conference.

Question: There has been some talk that the "new federalism" proposal is simply a diversionary tactic, to avoid discussing the economy. Do you think it is?
Speaker: Did I think it was? Yes. He avoided the No. 1 issue at the present time, which is unemployment.

It was Reagan's proposed deficit, as evidenced in the budget he presented to the House in February for the upcoming year, that started the new round of fighting. "Met with bi-partisan leadership on budget then with Repubs. alone," he recorded. "Then signed the bud. & sent it to the hill. Tip O'Neill still thinks I'm depriving the needy.

Told the press I associate with the country club crowd. He plays more golf & I don't."

The president, as Tip already knew, loved having a repertoire of horror stories of Democratic regulations and spending habits that he could pull out for every occasion. The trouble was his habit of casually blurring the edges between useful anecdote and established fact, a habit popular on the partisan luncheon circuit. These Reagan assertions — always vaguely plausible and always at the expense of liberal programs — drove Tip crazy: What about the Medicaid rule that hospitalized a young girl for a decade — at huge cost to the government — when her treatment could have been administered just as well at home? What about the rich kids in upscale suburbs receiving free school lunches? What about the well-off college students getting food stamps? There was simply no stopping him; the president was incorrigible when it came to his relish of such tales. For him they vividly, and believably, portrayed a world where Big Government and Bleeding Heart types were allowed to hold sway.

Irritated anew by Reagan's hard-line conservatism, Tip decided he'd had enough and felt justified in letting loose publicly. Accusing Reagan of turning his back on his origins, he claimed the president had "forgotten his roots." Though he cultivated an average-guy image whenever he could, the Democrat argued, he spent too much time "associated with that country-club style of people." The gloves were off at this — and Reagan took the opportunity for a hard jab in reply. "I've only played golf once since I've been president, and he's an inveterate golfer, and I'm sure he *must* have to go to a country club to play golf."

The Speaker got off a well-placed punch of his own, accusing the White House of trying to sell the country a "Beverly Hills Budget." It stuck. The phrase nailed Reagan squarely as a Southern California *swell* who preferred spending his evenings and weekends with multimillionaires. It was meant to sting and did. Meanwhile, the Reagan budget, with its proposed $90 billion–plus deficit, hit Reagan's Republican allies with what amounted to sticker shock. "There is unrest among the troops over the budget problem," he noted unhappily in his journal.

Early in 1982, I started to keep my own record of my experiences in the trenches of Washington warfare. "Tomorrow we begin the long-run fight for the year." I realized how decisive the year would be, with so much riding on it in the years to come. If

Tip lost this election, there'd be no coming back.

Then, two days later I noted: "President hit hard at press conference. Press treatment is cold; the President's attempt to charm his way through rough moments ran very thin today. The best he could say about economic outlook was that there would be a return to normalcy sometime this year. We need to build argument that Reagan program is responsible for economic problems facing the country. I notice a growing consensus that the Democrats should pick up seats in the House this Fall."

What I'd seen was that the polls were starting to show a hard swing away from the Republicans and toward the Democrats as the "party of prosperity."

Not long after, on a snowy afternoon in March, I got a personal sense of why Tip O'Neill enjoyed such genuine loyalty in the House. We were sitting, the Speaker and I, in one of those Learjets used by corporate executives. As we took off, I couldn't stop thinking that just weeks before, an Air Florida jetliner, departing this same airport and with too much ice on its wings, had plunged into the Potomac River.

With this recent tragedy on my mind,

thinking of my wife, pregnant with our first child, and watching the wintry sky outside the window, I caught the eye of the giant man sitting in the plane's backmost seat. I wondered what perversity of chance-taking led him to take the seat farthest to the rear, making it all the harder for that little aircraft to strain through the snow that had surrounded its wheels and still kept coming down hard. "What are you worrying about?" asked the face beneath the Irish tweed hat. Well, for one thing, I thought, the prospect of slipping through the ice of Lake Erie, never to be seen again. I mumbled something about "the weather" and began shunning eye contact in order to better attend full-time to the white-knuckled hell of that frost-covered porthole.

Why, you must ask, as I certainly did that March afternoon, was he taking this trip on such a day? The answer is that he'd made a promise and was keeping it. Dennis Hertel, a young congressman from the Detroit suburbs, wanted the Speaker of the House on hand to bolster his credibility at a couple of fund-raisers. In the coming months I would often remember the trip on that Learjet in such terrible weather and see it as a metaphor for Tip's fateful decision to face off with Reagan. It was as if up there in the media skies he'd been doing battle with the gale-force reality of early 1980s Reaganism. I'm not saying Tip O'Neill didn't worry. I'm saying he didn't let people *see* him worry even when everything he stood for was being jostled and thrown into the wind, even when his long, hard-fought-for career was at stake.

"I was the lone voice out there crying — you might say whimpering — last year," Tip admitted as the winds began to shift in his direction and he watched congressional allies who'd virtually abandoned him now come drifting back. "But I won't be alone this year." The reversal of fortune he was experiencing wasn't a matter of poll numbers alone. It was also evidenced by the fact that, over in the White House, President Reagan was showing signs of badly needing his support.

Only with the Speaker's backing could the president secure the votes in the House he needed, the ones required for the difficult steps to cut the massive government deficit. Yet even as he was aware of his importance to the man in the White House, Tip wasn't hopeful about a deal. Reagan, he said, had seen too many John Wayne movies and equated compromise with retreat. Tip's own hard-line position was simple: there would be no reductions whatsoever in Social Security, and unless Ronald Reagan himself proposed it, no discussion, either. This dynamic laid the groundwork for one of the biggest battles between Tip and the Gipper. As stubborn as he was, Reagan was also in a corner. Not even the Great Communicator would find it easy to sell the public a budget with so large a deficit. He and his fellow Republicans had campaigned successfully on the argument that high deficits cause inflation and high interest rates. To stanch the red ink, he needed a deal. The problem was that the conservative Democrats who'd helped form the previous year's coalition in the House and handed him his historic budget victories needed to rethink their defection. How could they stick with all this White House–endorsed red ink now that they were facing reelection?

This was where the situation stood late in March just as cherry blossom season began. If Ronald Reagan were to get out of the crisis with some measure of his presidential dignity intact, the Democrats would have to come on board and help rescue him from the mast he was clinging to. That went double for any messing with Social Security.

Despite Tip's over-my-dead-body stance,

the White House ambition was to draw the Speaker into a deal that would make him a partner in any slashes, including the egregious ones. When it fell to Chief of Staff Jim Baker to make the initial approach, he set off for what he intended as a highly discreet meeting with Tip at the Speaker's suburban Maryland residence. That it happened on Tip's actual home turf, with the proud Baker traveling out to the Speaker's modest condo, was a sign of the administration's rising panic.

Tip, who had no reason to keep the rendezvous secret, afterward let reporters in on just what had happened. Baker had come to him, he said, asking permission to meet with two key Democratic committee chairmen: Oklahoma's Jim Jones of Budget and Illinois's Dan Rostenkowski of Ways and Means. But he wasn't telling the press everything; he knew what was actually afoot beyond the good manners. Baker's appearance in his living room, and the elaborate courtesy that it spoke, was a message in itself. By carefully seeking Tip's approval to schedule those meetings with his congressional colleagues, the White House was implying the Speaker's imprimatur could be attached to the results.

With such a scenario now being plotted

around him, Tip was faced with a dilemma that lacked a simple solution. He knew if he refused such an extremely correct offer to allow those Democratic members even to discuss the red-ink problem, he would undoubtedly be made the villain of the piece. Therefore, he'd have to agree. At the same time, there was a giant hazard ahead that he couldn't ignore.

O'Neill saw the cunning that caught him in the Hobson's choice. "He thought that Baker was the toughest political opponent he ever came across," his daughter Rosemary recalled. The political reality guiding the Reagan forces was their need to rope in the Democrats. As Tip understood, the only safe route for the Republicans at this point, burdened as they were by the looming specter of monster fiscal humiliation, was to win political cover from his side. This meant securing his out-in-the-open partnership. Participating, however, would mean he'd have to personally agree to painful economies, most likely ones including cuts to Social Security.

The White House request to meet with Jones and Rostenkowski, two Democratic colleagues more accommodating than he, demanded an equally shrewd response. O'Neill decided to agree to the proposed meetings with one caveat. The White House could have all the get-togethers they wanted with the moderate Jones and the deal-loving Rosty. However, as far as the Speaker was concerned, just one person would be representing him in budget talks. That was his ever-loyal chairman of the Rules Committee, Missouri's Richard Bolling. And the White House had to accept it. Tip wanted a stand-in he trusted in any such dealings.

Throughout these curtain-raising preliminaries to what, a few days later, would wind up as a ballyhooed face-to-face between Tip and Reagan, I never knew how far he was willing to go. Would he actually have agreed to cut Social Security benefits if the offer had struck him as fair? In Tip's vocabulary, that would have been a bargain that, at minimum, raised taxes on the wealthy to match any cut in the social safety net. In the meantime, Bolling's task, as Tip's surrogate in the meetings Baker wanted, was to listen, discuss, probe for a deal, and, above all, protect the Speaker.

My own attitude was to fight. "I think we should not compromise," I wrote in my journal. "We should push the President hard and get what we can. Why should we give in on anything if Reagan doesn't want to give in on Kemp-Roth?" This shorthand referred to Reagan's signature 1981 tax cuts bill that had been jointly sponsored by New York congressman Jack Kemp and Delaware senator William Roth. That victory had defined the country's direction, as dictated by Reagan's agenda since the summer before, and its reality constituted the Democrats' defeated position now.

To push for even a partial repeal was asking Reagan to repudiate Reaganism. I could never see it happening. Quite frankly, I wasn't even rooting for such a deal. My view was that, if Reagan, against all odds, could have been talked into concessions on the timing of his tax cuts, the Democrats would still be wrong to accept it. It was an unequal trade. Reagan would only be adjusting details of his tax cuts by a year or so. The Democrats would be betraying their fifty-year commitment to Social Security. For me, any Democratic deal that compromised that bond would never be as good as no deal at all.

The Speaker realized it wasn't that simple. There were moderate Democrats, he knew, ready to agree to an arrangement with the White House. They were letting it be known they were open to accepting a swipe at the Social Security cost-of-living adjustment in return for a partial delay in Reagan's proposed three-stage cut in income taxes. I compared them, if somewhat indiscreetly, to the British prisoners of war in *The Bridge on the River Kwai*. Meaning, those guys were getting so involved in the intricacies of deal-making with the enemy that they forgot they were doing it primarily to save Reagan's skin. After all, it was *his* administration, and *he* was the one faced with a greatly flawed budget he'd shoved into being and now needed badly to fix.

One political case for buckling to the Republicans on the budget was that it would change the subject. The pollsters working for our side had issued a warning to the effect that whenever "the budget" became the headline in partisan debate, it benefited the Republicans. What the opposition party needed to focus on was "the economy." Budget, as a concept, played up the Democrats' reputation as big spenders. To speak of the economy, on the other hand, put the accent on the rising jobless rate. This argued for giving up legislatively on the *budget,* while keeping up the media drumbeat on what Reagan had done to the *economy.*

When it came to how the public was viewing the protracted efforts over the budget, Reagan knew what we knew. As an actor he'd naturally never liked bad reviews, and as president he must have hated them all the more. Fed up with media talk about the worsening recession — "Is it news that some fellow out in South Succotash someplace has just been laid off, that he should be interviewed nationwide?" he asked sarcastically after watching a Bill Moyers documentary on its impact around the country. He badly wanted the national conversation off the "economy" and back to the "budget" fight. "I called Tip O'Neill," he jotted in his diary. "I'm not sure he's ready to give. Tip is truly a New Deal liberal. He honestly believes that we're promoting welfare for the rich."

In early April, a day after the shock of lousy poll numbers — "I'm slipping badly," he wrote in his journal — Reagan began making weekly Saturday radio addresses. These five-minute live broadcasts were designed to be a media magnet for the weekend. The Sunday newspapers habitually provide end-of-the-week analysis of the political scene. Reagan's carefully scripted commentary often trumped the op-ed pages with the public. It was a masterful use of traditional media by an old pro. Radio was where Ronald Reagan had started, after all.

It became my task — one I shared with my Senate counterpart; we alternated weeks

— to enlist House members to sit in front of a radio mic and present the formal Democratic response to air after the president's Saturday talk. I would discover to my dismay how many Democrats didn't want to go head to head with Reagan, how only a few would agree to respond to him in real time. Overwhelmingly, those who stepped forward wanted to have their five-minute "responses" an hour after Reagan's address written and ready the day before. Here's a note in my journal for Saturday, April 17, 1982. It concerned the congressman Toby Moffett, who was willing to take the plunge despite extraordinary family circumstances. "Toby Moffett, his wife in labor from 8 AM this morning, is about to respond to Reagan's radio address." Looking back, I give the Moffetts — both of them — credit. Even under normal family circumstances, heading into a studio to talk back to a president with the whole country listening had to be stressful.

As those spring days passed, the White House set up a situation that amounted to an ambush waiting for Tip to walk into it. If he didn't participate directly in a budget deal that briskly trimmed Social Security payments, he'd be tagged an "obstructionist," the very label he'd sacrificed so much to dodge the previous year. To heighten the melodrama quotient, President Reagan would now motorcade to the Capitol, symbolizing the heroic "extra mile" he was willing to go in order to strike a compromise with the Democratic Speaker. After this bit of political theater, and depending on how Tip responded, the president would either applaud him for at last agreeing that Social Security needed cutting, or else lay into Tip if the Speaker held firm.

So the two of them were about to go head-to-head, purportedly on Tip's home turf. It would be a battle of wits, deciding who would come out the grand compromiser, who the roadblock. It would play to Reagan's strengths as a showman but also to the Speaker's proven ability once the pair of them were in the room together.

O'Neill was a master of the backroom negotiation. He worked them all the same way. Each time there was a dispute within the caucus to be settled, he would summon all parties to his working office. There he would sit behind his giant desk, the one used by President Grover Cleveland, light up his cigar, and hear the arguments.

He would never move from behind that desk while the arguments rose and fell. He was the judge, after all, and never in a rush to offer his verdict. My guess is that he liked it when the room grew hotter, stickier, closer. It wore down the contestants for his judgment, made them hunger for the fresh cold air of the Capitol they knew awaited them just outside those doors.

He had this other technique, which is so absurd as to not be believed: He would bellow loudest at the congressman he had decided well beforehand to support. This way, the loser would leave his office feeling that the Speaker saw his argument even if he did not end up siding with it. His prestige was that great, his cunning that sharp. After all, he *knew* these guys.

The Reagan people also liked to leave nothing to chance. Always a smooth operation that preferred no surprises, in this case they were careful to preemptively spin for the media the "real story" of the meeting about to take place. Reagan's spokesman, Larry Speakes, authoritatively put out the word that ongoing negotiations between the two sides — the White House congressional liaison team and the House Democrats — had progressed to the point where it was now all over except for the cherry on top. Meaning, the presence of the two top guys, Reagan and O'Neill, was being required merely to sign off on the final deal. The "chief stumbling point," Speakes explained, remained taxes, nothing else. His clear implication: whatever you may have believed up until now, Tip O'Neill is ready to swallow a cut in Social Security.

David Broder, the much-respected *Washington Post* columnist, saw the Reagan-O'Neill encounter that April as an historic matchup of men with differing philosophies but equal conviction.

After 45 years in public office, O'Neill is easily caricatured as a bumbling relic of the political past, a ward heeler who threatens harm to the Queen's English every time he puts down his cigar and opens his mouth. Reagan, the movie actor and television host who took up a second career in politics as he was approaching retirement age, is just as easily caricatured as a lightweight charmer with a gift of gab but no talent for sustained leadership.

Each man has come to know the other's caricature is a lie. O'Neill learned last year that Reagan is as tough as he is charming; and Reagan is learning this year that O'Neill can be as stubborn about his convictions as the president is himself. . . . But Reagan and O'Neill are not just stubborn Irishmen; they have convictions, and those convictions were forged a long time ago. Reagan is certain he did not become President of the United States in order to raise taxes. And O'Neill is equally convinced he did not become Speaker of the House in order to reduce anyone's Social Security. . . .

For O'Neill, a rollback in promised Social Security payments is the first retreat from the promise of decent, dignified retirement that the sainted FDR made the cornerstone of the New Deal. . . . For Reagan, an increase in the tax rate contradicts the first principle of the philosophy he has preached since he left the Democratic fold, the belief that the only way to curb big government is to slow the torrent of taxes on which it feeds.

Despite what amounted to a journalistic benediction from Broder, the "Budget Summit" clearly seemed a setup. For one thing, the Speaker's office was presented with the White House's rules for the engagement, which, most significant, dictated that only *principals* were to attend the Capitol meeting, meaning *no staff.* Such an attempt at control made an absurdity of what was scheduled to happen, since staff experts, laden with their facts and figures, are standard operating procedure during such sessions when legislation is being finalized. In short, the Reagan people were practically telegraphing the fact that this face-to-face would have a great deal in common with David Stockman's "woodshed."

When I called Jim Baker to say that the Speaker wanted to bring Ari Weiss with him, he stood firm. "No staff," he reiterated. At this point, I pointed out the obvious. "You're staff!" It was a point Baker, with his mandarin sensibility, seemingly hadn't taken in. He then attempted simply to brush aside the Speaker's reasonable request while proposing we "be gentlemen about this." In any case, when I told the Speaker of the rebuff, he was unimpressed. "I'm bringing Ari."

President Reagan, one could deduce already, certainly wouldn't be coming alone. When he arrived in the Capitol at the agreed-upon day and time, so did a full White House entourage. You'd think he was traveling to China. It was definitely *not* to be a quiet, out-of-the-way meeting to reconcile a budgetary stalemate. As I turned the corner to the Senate lobby that afternoon — the meeting was to be held in the President's Room, just outside the Senate chamber itself — I saw a mass of reporters, held back by the stanchions. It was clear the White House media-meisters had something big in mind. To be fair, Reagan, too, had suspicions about what *he* might be walking into. "The D's are playing games," he'd written in his diary two days earlier. "They want me to rescind the 3rd yr. of the tax cut — Not in a million years!"

As I would learn later, the meeting began with Tip demanding a change in the seating arrangements. The place cards had him next to President Reagan, an unusual placement for two men about to begin tough bargaining. O'Neill's first order of business was to take a chair directly across from the president.

Reagan tried breaking the ice with an Irish story:

Mary, suffering from morning sickness, is asked by a doctor for a "specimen." Not knowing what he means, she goes to ask her neighbor Deirdre. When she gets back to the house, she's got a black eye and bloody face. Her husband Michael wants to know what happened. "I stopped to ask Deirdre what a specimen was," she replies. "So she told me to piss in a bottle. I told her to shit in a hat, and the fight was on."

Tip was not to be charmed. "Mr. President, the nation is in a fiscal mess," he began sternly. "Last year you were going to win on everything you put up. Now the economy is going bad. If we don't have agreement there will be massive deficits. I know you people don't like to hear it, but you're just advocating trickle-down economics. Your program has failed, and you should take the lead in admitting it."

"I've read that crap about my program," Reagan shot back. Reaching into his cinematic memory, he tossed out a scene that seemed to fit. "We haven't thrown anybody out in the snow to die. . . . It has not failed at all. It hasn't even started yet."

Meanwhile, out in the corridor, where I was positioned, I saw Lesley Stahl of CBS, whom I knew from my Carter days. She pulled me aside to say that the White House staff was putting out the word that the Democrats were the ones proposing to cut Social Security benefits. I went ballistic, furious that anyone would buy such a fiction and only too aware of its potential for real damage. When I delivered this news to the Speaker during a break in the "summit," it confirmed his worst suspicions. What the White House foot soldiers were peddling in the hallway, I learned from him, was exactly what Reagan's lieutenants were conniving to accomplish inside.

When he and the other Democratic leaders had walked into the room they'd found on the table a working paper, placed by the White House. It was labeled the "Bolling Proposal." It was only then, when the Speaker and I compared notes, that we realized what the game was.

Also, who was winning. Dick Bolling, with Tip backing him, had apparently come around to giving Reagan's people what they'd been looking for from the start. For his own reasons, Tip had allowed Bolling to counter the Republicans' aggressive move on Social Security benefits with a smaller one, a slight (1 percent) cut in that year's adjustment for inflation. The problem was, the Speaker had strayed perilously close to the abyss. By taking this step he'd left himself exposed to the charge that he, Tip O'Neill, was the one initiating it.

It was the White House overreach that saved him. The instant I told him what story they were pushing outside the meeting — that he, not Reagan, wanted to cut Social Security — his limited interest in cutting a deal was gone.

Their gambit had failed. They had attempted to mouse-trap too large a mouse.

When he reentered the room, O'Neill confronted Reagan with what I'd just passed on to him. Point-blank, he asked the president to state clearly whether he was the author of this move on Social Security or not. The moment of truth had arrived.

"Now, *wait* a minute," came his reply. "This is the proposal that came from the *Congress.* It's on the table because *you people* put it on the table!" Burned before, Reagan was adamant. The only cut in Social Security he'd accept was one that came out of a compromise between the two parties on Capitol Hill.

That was Reagan's answer. Tip was ready with his own: "We didn't specify this cut in Social Security."

The Bolling Proposal represented Tip's good-faith effort to help Reagan reduce the federal deficit. He'd been willing to accept a minor delay in Social Security's cost-of-living adjustments. What he would not cooperate in was being played for a fool. Thus he walked away from what they were trying to do, and, by doing so, protected not just Social Security but himself.

The meeting ended with an odd episode.

Out of nowhere, Tip's lieutenant, Congressman Jim Wright of Texas, offered a trade. He asked Reagan to slash the final installment of his tax cut in half, from 10 to 5 percent, in exchange for a grab bag of spending cuts. Reagan's response was not fit for a family newspaper. "You can get me to crap a pineapple," he said, "but you can't get me to crap a cactus."

Once the meeting was adjourned and the White House press corps safely back home in the West Wing, Reagan's aides went back to spouting their company line — it had been the Democrats themselves who'd proposed cutting Social Security. But no one was really buying it. The nation's revered retirement program would remain for the Republicans a hovering albatross.

Still, the face-to-face hadn't been a total failure. The two partisan leaders would always have fundamental differences, but the meeting's impresario, Jim Baker, was surprisingly happy with their "chemistry." The Speaker agreed. "I wasn't any more of a stubborn Irishman than he was." Asked whether he thought the White House had been setting him up, O'Neill refused to blame Reagan. "I would have to honestly say, in my opinion, that the president of the U.S. wasn't any part of it, but I think there are wily minds around him, and that's what *they* had in mind from the start."

There were moments when, for all the public wrangling, the backdoor cooperation could still surprise me. A very human example involved Mitch Snyder, well known in Washington, D.C., at the time as a militant, highly creative advocate for the homeless. Inspired by the radical priests Philip and Daniel Berrigan, whom he'd met in federal prison ten years earlier, Snyder had become a committed activist for the poor.

In the early months of 1982, Snyder embarked on a hunger strike that went on for sixty-three days, over two months during which he took nothing but water and lost fifty-seven pounds. Mitch was a grandstander, to be sure, but at the same time deadly serious. What he was starving himself in protest over was the recent naming of a nuclear attack submarine the *Corpus Christi,* Latin for "Body of Christ." For a man now dedicated to pacifism, whose heroes were priests and who himself passionately lived the communitarian teachings of Jesus, it was an affront he couldn't overlook, despite the fact that the U.S. Navy customarily named certain classes of vessel after American cities, in this case a well-known port town in

329

South Texas. To Snyder, the choice of name was a blasphemy committed by the federal government and condoned by officialdom.

I was alerted to what was happening by a friend, the satiric journalist Nicholas von Hoffman. He urged me to get Tip O'Neill to intercede so that "this guy can go out and get a cheeseburger." I had a thought, which began with the fact that the Speaker recently had spent the evening at the apartment of syndicated columnist Mary McGrory, who frequently threw informal dinners and liked to have a lively mix of guests. The party, I knew, had concluded with Tip, among others, standing around Mike Deaver, one of Reagan's triumvirate of top advisors, as he played the piano. It occurred to me, remembering that, that Tip might be willing to call on Deaver to try to keep Mitch Snyder alive. When I explained the problem, Tip said okay, to go ahead and get the guy on the phone.

Deaver wasn't in his office but returned my call later. When I explained about Snyder's hunger strike and its motivation, he seemed irritated. Not only because I'd contacted him for such an odd-seeming reason — right when we were already embroiled in a lively partisan standoff — but because he seemed to have little patience for would-be martyrs like Snyder. "It doesn't seem like a very good reason to kill yourself," he commented dryly.

Thinking Deaver uninterested, unimpressed, and thus unwilling to help, I was, it turned out, wrong. Though Deaver had given me little reason to expect he'd take the matter right to the top, in fact, that's exactly what he did. Within days after our conversation, it was announced that the latest nuclear sub in the U.S. Navy would now bear the name USS *City of Corpus Christi,* with Mitch Snyder accepting the deal.

Those of us who took part in this unusual rescue mission felt a reassuring glimpse of humanity as we regarded our opponents; they'd listened and made a difference. It happens that the day Mitch Snyder's hunger strike was brought to an end was the very one on which President Ronald Reagan rode in that motorcade up to the Capitol to meet, summit-style, with House Speaker Tip O'Neill.

For Mike Deaver, his stint as Mitch Snyder's savior would be a precursor of a late-in-life vocation. Soon after leaving the White House he'd come afoul of the law that governed lobbying. His required community service was to work with homeless people in the same building near the U.S. Capitol that housed Mitch's shelter. This introduced Mike to a world he'd never known before. The man who once advised Ronald Reagan on image-building became a much-beloved counselor to the down-and-out. Through love and attention, he convinced dozens of homeless men to give up alcohol and better their lives. At his funeral, held in the National Cathedral, the great Johnny Mathis, whom he had also helped, sang "Amazing Grace." But it was the quiet personal testimony of the men he had saved that made the most eloquent music.

As the Speaker once said to me, "You never know what's in another man's heart."

When Reagan faced big deficit trouble in the summer of 1982,
Tip O'Neill made the decision to back him up.
The Tax Equity and Fiscal Responsibility Act (TEFRA) was,
for both men, a match of good government and good politics.

CHAPTER FOURTEEN: PARTNERS

"The future of this economy is now in the hands of Tip O'Neill."
— SENATOR BOB DOLE

While they'd disagreed in their "summit" meeting, in the aftermath Tip continued to reserve final judgment on the president. Still reluctant to blame him for the harm resulting from his administration's policies, Tip expressed it this way: "I don't think he believes his program is hurting anyone because he doesn't know it. He doesn't realize the severity of his cuts. *If he knew, they wouldn't go that far.*" As for Reagan, he had his own sense of his opponent, and it was one tempered with affection. According to Max Friedersdorf, "We would go in and want the president to fire back at him, say something nasty about Tip, and he would just laugh and say, 'That's just Tip being Tip. That's just Tip.' "

In the early summer of 1982, nothing had changed, at least not with regard to these two American leaders and their disagreements over federal spending. Farther away, in the disputed Falkland Islands, the Argentine forces had just surrendered to the British. Iraq and Iran were still locked in a nasty war, and at the beginning of June, Israel invaded Lebanon. Inside the Capital Beltway, the battles involved only the weapons of political persuasion.

In fact, a writer for United Press International took the Falklands as a point of comparison: "It may be easier for the United Kingdom and Argentina to settle their dispute than for President Reagan and Speaker Tip O'Neill to come together on a spending and taxing plan for the United States that satisfies both. It also is likely that if Reagan and O'Neill do find the basis for an agreement, there will be plenty of howling about it — including charges of betrayal — in Washington and elsewhere."

However, there was a difference that needed to be acknowledged. Unlike the year before, the two sides had arrived at a rough political balance. The rise in unemployment — the April 1982 jobless rate was the highest since before World War II — and the spiking federal deficit had pushed Reagan into the sort of tough corner unimaginable just months before. Those who had so celebrated his rise to power were suddenly looking at him with the sort of suspicion bestowed on every president when the economic numbers begin to go against him. Worse still, he was finding himself pummeled by his allies on the right, as not being sufficiently hard-nosed.

The fact was, neither the Republicans nor the Democrats were in full command of the circumstances as the slide in public confidence continued. Recognizing, finally, that there was no chance whatsoever to pass his still hoped-for progressive budget, the Speaker gave halfhearted backing to a centrist fiscal plan devised by party moderates. Yet, even that option was brought down in a chaotic night on the House floor. Myself, I will never forget the sight of California's archliberal Phil Burton, who clearly had been drinking heavily, going from member to member threatening him if he didn't vote "Nay" on the Democrats' budget.

"You can forget that fuckin' judgeship," he barked at a fellow Californian about to retire. Not everyone buckled, of course. With the face of a besotted Burton looming over him — imagine Harpo Marx in hell!

— Henry Waxman stood his ground and voted with the party. "He's trying to bring down the budget!" I appealed to the Speaker, who was circulating among the members. "What can I do?" he answered. "He's *drunk!*"

Yet the loss on the budget vote had its silver lining. Now, as Tip had warned all along, the rising deficits were Reagan's burden to carry, his red ink in the ledger. O'Neill's Democrats, moreover, were showing new strength. While they didn't pass their preferred budget, they cast 202 votes against a successful Republican budget, which finally prevailed, a considerable gain compared to the previous year's 176.

As the best showing against Reaganomics since its champion had taken office, the latest vote appeared to signal a political uptick. But just as we were about to enjoy that possibility, a discouraging *Wall Street Journal* piece appeared. Worse for me, it was I who agreed to the Speaker's being interviewed by one of the *Journal*'s Washington bureau reporters. "Like an aging prizefighter, he has been battered in the early rounds by President Reagan. So he is looking to the final bell — Election Day, November 2 — to redeem his reputation."

The Speaker, quite reasonably, wasn't

happy with this portrait of himself as a guy on his way out. Nor was he happy with me. In fact, he was irked enough that, later the same week when I happened to mention the name of a respected CBS correspondent, his displeasure came through loud, clear, and recriminatory: "Is he another one of your asshole media friends?" ("Asshole has become one of TPO's big words lately," I duly noted in my journal.)

I wanted to tell him that I'd let that reporter — and others — in because my job was to help him become what he could become, and the only way to do that was to be publicized. And the only way to do that was to let people write about you. And the only way to let them write about you was to let them take shots at you. This is the only way to become a figure in American politics. You can't customize it. You cannot come in and tailor it. All you can do is go in, allow reporters to see who you are, and let them make their own judgments about you. It's a distillation, not an accumulation. You can have twenty brickbats thrown at you, and what matters is what comes through. And what would come across, eventually, was *who he was:* a big guy with a good heart and a lot of guts.

Fortunately, Kirk O'Donnell appreciated

my situation and, as a veteran observer of Tip's moods and idiosyncrasies, was able to offer a bracing consolation. "Around him, you're expected to bat a thousand!" One of the downsides of having the Speaker think I was a media "expert" meant that if anything went wrong, I must have done it on purpose. Take my word for it: Tip's team in those tense, high-stakes days was a place neither for the amateur nor the sensitive soul.

At the same time I was learning — and learning to accept — three of my boss's discernible aspects. One of them was Santa Claus: you had a problem, he'd do anything for you. The second was Black Irish. Skeptical of motive, this Tip was always ready to suspect the worst. Third was politician. Fortunately for the planet — and me — the first and third of these comprised the working Tip O'Neill coalition. All he wanted was to do good, to win, and, despite all his denials, be *liked*.

It was at this time that Tip made a rare appearance on *Face the Nation*. Joan Barone, then the weekly program's producer, begged me to get him to agree to come on. In favor of it, but knowing Tip's reluctance to do the Sunday rounds, I suggested she ask her father, Walter Shorenstein, to make the request for her instead. Knowing how fond the Speaker was of her dad, a deep-pocketed, generous Democratic fund-raiser from San Francisco, I thought the ploy would work, and it did. As I'd guessed, Tip couldn't say no to his old pal and, when the time came, he made a special point of prepping seriously for his appearance. It happened to be the weekend of the Democrats' big midterm convention in Philadelphia, which, obviously, was Joan's reason for wanting him that Sunday.

As he always did, Tip brought Ari Weiss, his indispensable aide, along to brief him on legislative issues. However, Ari, observant in his Judaism, was unable to travel on the Sabbath and come to Tip's hotel. The briefing, as a result, was held where he was staying, with Tip traveling to him. It was an incident I considered characteristic of my boss, and one of the things I liked best about him. Here he was, displaying his respect for a young staffer's religion, at the same time showing the humility of his need for that young man's counsel. Then he went on television and knocked Reagan's block off. "When I see him he says, 'My program is working, I'm not hurting people.' Well, it's not and he is."

The starting day for Reagan's second-stage 10 percent tax cut was the first of July.

To mark the occasion, the Senate Republican Conference got wildly creative and ordered a seventeen-foot "World's Record Apple Pie" to display on the grounds of the Washington Monument. "It's time for the doubters to eat humble pie," declared Senator Roth of Delaware, opening the ceremonies on the historic National Mall. Before him stood several hundred people waiting patiently to get their metaphoric slice of America's new economic bounty.

Unfortunately, the festival of Republican success did not proceed as its organizers had anticipated. The day before, I'd phoned Mitch Snyder, the local homeless advocate who'd staged the dramatic hunger strike over the naming of the *Corpus Christi*. When I told him what the Republicans were planning, he seemed interested in attending.

Here's how the *New York Times* covered the event so optimistically scheduled as a GOP celebration:

As the Senator spoke, four men dressed in pillow-stuffed coats and wearing signs identifying themselves as "Reagan's Millionaire Friends" pushed their way through the crowd of several hundred people. Before anyone could stop them, they leaped into the pie, stomping and squishing the apples and shouting, "It's all mine, It's all mine."

Momentarily stunned, staff members of the Senate Republican Conference who had worked hard to arrange the event, sprang to the defense of their pie, leaping into the apples and attempting to drag out the offenders. By the time the Park Police showed up, almost everyone involved was covered with goo.

"All the local news shows played it big," I wrote gleefully in my journal that night. "The Committee for Creative Non-Violence vs. the Republican Senate Conference, TWA, Holiday Inn, Pepsi Cola, the Heritage Foundation. On some of the TV news programs it came off as if the demonstration was the *purpose* of today's event. It was not clear at all that the pie was to celebrate a tax cut."

Now came more street theater. Just two weeks after the pie-soaked melee, President Reagan himself showed up on the Mall. It was a sweltering Washington Monday and he was there to cheerlead at a rally staged by his canny White House showmen. In yet another attempt to turn the nation's attention from his proposing the largest federal deficit to date, the pastry metaphor had been abandoned in favor of what the president termed a "people's crusade." Standing in front of a crowd of roughly five thousand tourists and government workers — not to mention a goodly contingent of Republican National Committee staffers — he was loudly demanding that lawmakers approve an amendment to the Constitution *requiring* the federal budget be balanced, penny by penny. Commented House majority leader Jim Wright, "It's like the saloon keeper demanding that everyone take a vow of total abstinence."

I managed to pull together a modest-sized protest on the other side of the Capitol to coincide with the Reagan-led spectacle. It featured Democratic stalwart Claude Pepper, the eighty-one-year-old congressman from Miami who was the country's best-recognized advocate for seniors. The old New Dealer called the proposed constitutional amendment a "sneak attack on Social Security." That night on the evening news, the Pepper-led rally of a hundred or so people nearly won the attention of the significantly larger gathering on the other side of the Capitol. In my journal I noted happily how the coverage we got must have galled "the White House people who did so much to put the day together and had so much to work with."

Not completely satisfied with that success, I had the idea to plan a Democratic rally on August 4, the one-year anniversary of Congress giving its final approval of the Reagan economic program. My notion was to stage an event focusing solely on the jobs issue — the July unemployment rate had hit 9.8 percent — and away from the budget one. To ensure the most attention, I decided to hold it at 1600 Pennsylvania Avenue at the highly unusual hour of 4 a.m. The battle cry would be "Wake up, Mr. President!" This way we'd be playing not just to the mounting jobless number but also to the White House occupant's reputation for keeping gentleman's hours when it came to his workday.

The Associated Press reported on the 200 members of the steel and autoworker unions who picketed the White House:

Marching on the sidewalk under light provided by television news crews and White House floodlights, the demonstrators chanted slogans that called for more jobs and reversals in administration economic policies.

"I don't think we expect the President of

the United States to come out to the fence and say good morning, but what we're trying to say is that both the president and country ought to wake up to what's going on," said Kenny Kovack, a steel lobbyist and organizer of the noisy but orderly demonstration. . . .

Betty Robinson, another union lobbyist who helped organize the demonstration, said the idea for the 4 a.m. rally came from the office of House Speaker Thomas P. O'Neill, Jr.

My lone concern in planning the event was that the tired, angry workers might speak badly of both political parties. To keep things warm toward our side, I'd asked several Democratic members of Congress from Pennsylvania and Maryland to greet the protesters at 5:30 a.m. with coffee and donuts. Among them was the Speaker's close pal Jack Murtha, already then a multi-termer from southwestern Pennsylvania, who seemed to relish the odd occasion.

The "Wake Up, Mr. President" demonstration was also covered on the morning news shows on NBC, CBS, CNN, and on radio throughout the morning. It would also make the evening news that night. Steve Delaney, reporting on *Today,* commented,

"It's hard to come up with a new idea, but the Steelworkers and the UAW did it."

"Ten-strike!" yelled Congressman Murtha to Tip as the Speaker arrived in the office at his normal hour. "Is this one of yours?" my boss then asked, turning to me. I would take that question over any other form of praise — and the truth was, it carried with it an emotion he rarely expressed: wonder.

Despite this success, the fun and games were nearing their end. It was time for action, not theater. Democrats now held the high ground on the "economy" for the basic reason that the country was continuing its downward economic spiral. What both sides agreed on was the need to shrink the towering deficit being forecast for 1983. Moreover, steps needed to be taken to convince the money markets that the U.S. government was on the job, willing to take those corrective measures now so critical not only to the country's fiscal health but to its international financial standing.

Stung to find himself in such a dire predicament, Ronald Reagan was desperate for a rescuer to appear. That knight in shining armor turned out to be Bob Dole, chairman of the Senate Finance Committee. Dole, an old-time fiscal conservative, crafted a bill made up of loophole-closers, tax hikes on cigarettes, telephone bills, medical expenses, travel, investment income, as well as well-hidden business taxes. Reagan's insistence on referring to this piece of legislation as a tax "reform" bill was entirely disingenuous. Purely and simply, the Tax Equity and Fiscal Responsibility Act of 1982 (TEFRA) as devised by Dole and his committee — with the help of Jim Baker and David Stockman — was intended to raise $99 billion in additional federal revenue over the next three years.

Ronald Reagan now saw this tax increase — marked, for public relations value, daintily just below $100 billion — as the sole option for quieting the fears of the public. So did Tip O'Neill and for a similar reason: for the good of the country. Both saw the sacrifices. For Reagan, it meant joining with Democrats to raise taxes; for O'Neill it meant rescuing a Republican administration in an election year.

Tip and Reagan each now faced intraparty challenges. On the Democratic side and disagreeing with the Speaker, there were numerous lawmakers who saw no reason to join forces to help prevent Reagan from heading over the abyss. As far as they were concerned, the deficit problem he faced was entirely of his own making. He'd *wanted* the big tax cuts . . . and got credit for them from the public. He'd *wanted* the big defense buildup . . . and got credit for that, too. Now, ran the Democratic thinking, since he'd wanted them so badly, why shouldn't he also get the credit for the fiscal dilemma brought on by his policies, including the fast-rising unemployment numbers?

Tip well understood their concerns but saw matters differently. For one thing, he already had heard whispers of a Republican campaign theme that, during the run-up to Election Day, would anoint him again as the obstructionists' poster boy. Steve Roberts of the *Times,* in fact, had recently mentioned to me that he'd learned in his reporting of a GOP TV campaign already in the works. The Speaker also lived with the inescapable fact that Reagan's personal popularity was hardly tarnished despite the presence of his fingerprints clearly spread across the administration's achievements to date. "Every time I ask someone, 'Do you like the president?' they say, 'Yes.' "

As the House vote on the fate of TEFRA drew close, my own thinking, sitting there in the Speaker's office, centered on what positioning most benefited the Democrats. "If it fails," I wrote in my journal, "the focus shifts to the fiscal crisis in Washington. As long as the focus remains on the economy, the Democrats *have* the economy." Keeping that in mind, our only choice was to push as hard and as skillfully as we could to make the tax increase a bipartisan effort.

For his part, Reagan backed TEFRA by managing to convince himself, as I said, that it was a "reform" bill, not a tax hike. Even his diary notes refer to the measure as a "tax bill," never a tax increase. Call it cognitive dissonance. But with government deficits heading through the roof, he, Ronald Reagan, being the government's chief executive, had to get TEFRA passed in the House and knew it.

For Tip O'Neill, this was a crucial moment. In raw political terms, it was time for the kill. He could let Reagan sink in his own soup. He could not lift a finger to help him pass this tax "reform" bill. He could let the deficits just grow and grow with nothing done to stop them, all the time the public and the markets watching. But he chose not to.

Instead, he jumped into the void and went to work helping Reagan out of the very tight spot he'd gotten himself into. Tip, too, was for TEFRA — for the pragmatic reason that the deficit *needed* to be cut. But the Speaker was experienced enough in the ways of

Washington, however, to be able to spot the downside of doing the right thing.

So Tip also set conditions. Number one, Reagan himself needed to be out there pitching the tax bill. The brainchild of Bob Dole and clutched at by the president, it should be up to the fellow for whom it did the most to take to the hustings and try to sell it. It was primarily the Republicans, Tip and the Gipper both knew, who would prove the hardest to sell.

"I want him to use that smiling countenance and sweet-talking voice of his and be hard-knuckled with his Republicans along the line just as he did last year," Tip asserted. Everyone in Washington knew how Ronald Reagan now seized Dole's offered lifeline, even if he wanted to call it something it wasn't. Certainly, Tip did. "Senator Dole has shown the wisdom to produce a tax bill that will at least begin to correct the excesses of the 1981 tax bill. It is time for the president himself to show the same courage and the same wisdom. It is time for the president himself to face economic reality. It is time for the president himself to fight for the tax bill."

The Speaker's second condition was this: he wanted a majority of House Republicans voting for the bill. He was willing to send out his posse to help the economy — and Ronald Reagan — but they weren't going to be the lone riders. "The Republicans are not for any tax bill, so there is a problem. Some of my people are asking why they should vote for a tax bill when it is a Republican recession. If his own party doesn't want to vote for it, why should we? But we have to help bring deficits down."

A week before the vote, Reagan found himself getting it from both sides. One particularly unwelcome critic was the Buffalo congressman (and former Bills quarterback) Jack Kemp. This was the very man who'd done much to popularize "supply side" economics in the late 1970s. He championed the belief that Republicans should make lower marginal tax rates, not deficit reduction, their primary goal. But now Kemp was calling the most famous convert to "supply side" onto the carpet. "Met with Jack Kemp (alone) & then in leadership meeting. He is adamant that we are wrong on the tax increase. He is in fact unreasonable. The tax increase is the price we have to pay to get the budget cuts." If only to himself, the president is finally admitting that he, Ronald Reagan, is backing an increase in taxes.

Nothing is simple in such tricky situations.

As the right was laying into their hero Ronald Reagan for what they see as turncoat behavior, Tip O'Neill was starting to get impatient with the man he thinks he had a deal with, who's not living up to his end of the bargain. "There is a rumor," the Speaker teased the press, "that the White House people don't want him to go on TV. But, if he doesn't, he will have problems." In other words, if he can't go out there and *be* Ronald Reagan, what's the point?

When it was announced that the president asked for a prime-time slot to explain to the nation his support for the bill, I suggested to the Speaker that he name Tom Foley, No. 3 in the Democractic leadership and a respected intellectual from Spokane, Washington, to give the response.

Tom had long been a friend to me, one who always backed what I was doing, and when he got the word, he asked me to write what he would say. Unfortunately, as soon as he had my draft in his hands, his verdict was that it was too tough. I'd let my enthusiasm get the better of my judgment, Foley persuaded me. I'd taken too partisan a tone for the occasion. The beginning I'd come up with knocked pretty much every aspect of Reagan's presidency to date, and only after that did I get into the business of pushing for the new tax bill. The speech had been a lot of fun to concoct, I have to admit, as I imagined it being heard by millions of fellow Americans. Tom's advice was to skip the nasty preamble and keep it simple. *The president says we need this tax bill and the president is right.*

Foley was right, too. He delivered his preferred version well and was a big success. The Speaker was especially pleased. Ever the "reader" of his colleagues, Tip was alert to the effect Foley had had. "Some of the people in our party who were more reluctant last week are more willing to listen today," he noted, gratified.

The two speeches — Reagan's and Foley's — were broadcast on a Monday night. On Tuesday, the New York Stock Exchange had a near-record day of trading, with the Dow showing its biggest jump in history. Apparently, we were watching good politics validated by Wall Street.

The TEFRA vote was set for Thursday. On the day before, O'Neill put the vote in political perspective, *his* perspective. "The tax bill will not repeal Reaganomics," he said in a morning statement. "Congress cannot with one vote correct the excesses and inequities of two years. But it is at least a step in the right direction. It is a step away from 'trickle-down' economics and a step toward common sense. I urge my fellow Democrats to support the bill because it is the only opportunity Congress has this year to restore sanity and fairness to national economic policy."

That same Wednesday, Tip appeared at the White House in a show of unity. Reagan recorded the occasion with his usual descriptive brevity: "Interesting photo opportunity in Rose Garden with Tip O'Neill, Bolling & our leaders as a bipartisan group *for* the tax bill. Tonight a dinner in the W.H. for a group of undecideds."

I awoke the morning of the vote with my own doubts. "Tax vote comes today. Watching television and reading the press I get different impression than from the floor. Members are voting for this bill. I mean by that the average members who vote on the basis of national politics. I just don't see support for this beyond the good-thinking group of 50–70 and the leadership. I heard yesterday that the Democratic Conservative Forum was going to vote against the bill. Now the polls show [the] people against it. Need to make clear: that this is vote necessitated by the failure and excesses of Reaganomics."

As they usually were, the big vote was

scheduled for a Thursday night. I'd come to love such occasions, despite the grievous losses of the previous year. With the House chamber filled, the Republican leader, Bob Michel, the Democratic leader, Jim Wright, and finally, the Speaker, would "close debate." It was like the summations in a courtroom drama, the moment when those in attendance sit quietly, offering their respectful attention.

This occasion was different. After two years of battling the president, Tip O'Neill was joining Reagan in the fight. Both were battling from the center outward. Reagan needed to shrink the deficit; Tip needed to move the country's attention off Washington and back to pocketbook issues back at home.

It had been a stressful day for the president. That morning, his father-in-law, Dr. Loyal Davis, a pioneering neurosurgeon, had died in Arizona, where he was living in retirement. Here's Reagan on how the day had gone: "Nancy wasn't alone — thank Heaven Ron & Doria were there. But it seemed awful to be here & not be with her. All day I sat at my desk phoning Congressmen on the tax bill and tonite it passed with 103 Repub. votes & more than half the Dems. 226 to 207. Tip O'Neill made a speech to Repubs. telling them why they should support me. *It seemed strange — both of us on the same side.* The Sen. took it up tonite and it won 53 to 47. Again some of our ultra pure conservatives deserted. Now I'm packing to leave for Phoenix & my Sweetheart."

The vote on TEFRA, while little noticed in history, was a true profile in courage by the House majority. There was really nothing in the bill to benefit either Republican or Democrat — not really. How could you go home and brag you'd just raised taxes? That said, something *had* to give. With the country still punished by high interest rates, a spike in federal deficits could have killed the hoped-for recovery.

I remember standing near a Democratic member from upstate New York, Henry Nowak, as he cast his "Aye" vote. "My opponent doesn't have an issue," he said, if only to himself. Then, pushing his member's card into the voting slot, he said: "Now he does."

After the vote, the president called Tip to thank him for his support. In return, the Speaker offered a treasured story. "Did you hear that the Irish gave the bagpipe to the Scots and they took it seriously?" Yes, it was a gift, what they'd done, but one of unclear political value.

My own diary — "Friday — August 20. Leave for vacation today — (with a new baby!) New Jersey tonight, NY Sat. Mass. Sunday. Tip did solid job on floor yesterday. He [is] quoted throughout paper today saying that young Republicans should vote for Reagan because 30 of them came to the House on his coattails. Peter Hart [the pollster], Kirk tells me, will be happy at fact that Tip is not acting partisan but being cooperative in his opposition."

Mary McGrory appreciated the irony of the occasion. A liberal true believer in Jack Kennedy and Gene McCarthy both, she had a good deal in common with Tip O'Neill, whom she much admired, being an Irish-American from Massachusetts just as he was. However, Mary had beat him to Washington, having come to live and work there in 1947, six years before he arrived as a young first-term representative. From their different vantage points, they were both old-guard Democrats now and seasoned watchers of the partisan wars.

In her *Washington Post* column of August 24, she wrote shrewdly of the startling history that had just been made, coming to the conclusion that "bipartisanship can be fun."

It happened last Thursday when House Speaker Thomas P. (Tip) O'Neill Jr. (D-Mass.) lumbered to the well and had the incomparable experience of lecturing the opposition on the subject of loyalty to Ronald Reagan.

Seldom does statesmanship come in the form of sweet revenge. In the dead still of the chamber, O'Neill instructed the younger House Republicans on their debt and duty to their leader.

What the Speaker had told the potential Republican bolters was this: "You are here because of Reagan. You are here because he was elected president of the United States. He brought you to the Congress of the United States, and now we are on the eve of an election and he is asking for a change of policy. Are you going to follow the leader that brought you here, or are you going to run? I ask you just to think of that."

McGrory applauded his statesmanship. "If he could put aside his differences with the president ("We seldom agree," O'Neill said), they could, he told them. One hundred and three Republicans gritted their teeth, and voted for the bill Ronald Reagan had to swallow so hard to accept."

It had "seemed strange," wrote Ronald

Reagan, this joining together with Tip. But it would prove good politics — for both of them.

Winning twenty-six seats in the U.S. House of Representatives more than doubled the postwar average for the opposition party in a first presidential midterm election. It was a big victory for Tip O'Neill.

CHAPTER FIFTEEN:
TIP AT THE TOP

"Who is the happy Warrior?
Who is he That every man in arms
should wish to be?"
— WILLIAM WORDSWORTH

Time zips by on Capitol Hill. When I worked there, I found myself often reminded of those old reel-to-reel tape recorders. You know the *flip-flip-flip* at the end of a tape when it runs out? During this period of my life, each year passed so quickly I never realized the tapes were running out. Looking back, I think it must be because I never escaped from the intensity of what I was engaged in for long enough to actually feel the passage of time.

In late August 1982, King Sobhuza II of Swaziland died. The world's longest-serving monarch, he was known worldwide for his many wives and hundreds of grandchildren. Since my time and work in his country

363

meant a lot to me, I realized I'd like very much to attend his funeral with the American delegation. It turned out not to be that hard to arrange. My hunch — that the Reagan administration's list of officials wanting a quick out-and-back to this little-known southern African destination would leave room for at least one more — was correct. And off I went. My companion on the journey was the great jazz star Lionel Hampton, for decades an ardent Republican. Somehow, he'd gotten the idea that my stint teaching modern business practices to shopkeepers in isolated Swazi villages entitled him to introduce me as the young fellow responsible for the country's economic development. I couldn't manage to convince him otherwise, so finally gave up trying.

The funeral was a spectacle, though in no way resembling what I'd expected. In my imagination, there'd be a traditional Swazi ceremony with plenty of dancing, excitement, and wild emotions. What we actually witnessed from the American delegation's seats in the country's enormous soccer stadium was a Christian service traditional enough that it might have been taking place anywhere. The only real hint telling me I wasn't in Kansas was the unforgettable sight of the late Sobhuza himself dressed in full military regalia visible in an upright coffin that featured a full-length window.

Once the ceremony that had brought me there was over, I headed out to the distant town I'd lived in. Temporarily putting Capitol Hill out of my mind, I rediscovered the sensations of rural Africa. Yet here I was, thousands of miles away, and, suddenly, startled to be reminded of my current life back home. It happened when an old acquaintance, Mr. Mbabama, the provincial health officer back in my day, expressed to me his curiosity about how it happened I'd been "sent over by the Republicans."

And speaking of Republicans, this was an occasion when at least one got playful — at my expense. Ken Duberstein, the White House aide who had okayed my request to join the delegation, now sent word — as the trip was ending and I was headed back — that, in fact, I'd been issued only a "one-way" ticket. Keeping me in Africa, I understood, getting the joke, was a surefire way to keep me from making more trouble for the administration!

When I returned home, the Speaker was already hard at work on the campaign trail, out stumping for his troops in their districts. One trip took him, with me along, to Connecticut. When we got there, the congressman was waiting, prepared to share a photo op at a popular local tavern. It was an idea that didn't sit well with Tip. "I hate campaigning in barrooms," he growled quietly. I understood he was too familiar with far too many stories of men who'd wasted away their lives in such places, along with their struggling families' money. He knew the tragedy behind the cozy image of the corner saloon.

As we headed back to D.C., flying south over the bright lights of the New York megalopolis, both of us suddenly found ourselves focusing on the fact there was just a single lonely pilot up in the cockpit. The folks paying for the plane — the local congressional campaign committee — had obviously watched their budget when it came to Tip's transportation costs. "If anything happens to that pilot," the Speaker told me, not at all kidding, "I want *you* up there."

November 2 — Election Day 1982 — was two months away. Ever since World War II, partisan scorecards show an elected president's party will lose an average of twelve seats in the first midterm after he's taken office. That figure had turned into the benchmark for each party, one surging forward, the other falling back. To be counted the winner in 1982, we figured, given the recession, the Dems needed to pick up seats well beyond that dozen.

Both sides had hardworking pollsters whose business it was to pinpoint their winning issues and nail what topics to avoid. At this moment, the country's 9.8 percent (and rising) jobless rate — which could be blamed on Republican policies — was a big plus for the Democrats. Conventional wisdom had long maintained that if voters felt worse trouble lay ahead, they'd go to the polls to back a change of direction. In this election, that meant voting Democratic.

President Reagan, meanwhile, was energetically working an old angle, trying ploys that would help position him as the outsider in Washington, not the guy in charge but the one *taking on* "the Government." To launch this charade, in late August he resolutely vetoed a large appropriations bill, making him the tightfisted keeper of the purse, despite the fact that its total cost fell within the Republican-endorsed budget lines. It was a fight he'd been spoiling for, giving him an opportunity to take on the capital's powers that be.

The Speaker recognized what the White House was up to and labeled the veto a "political tactic" intended to draw attention away from the failure of the administration's economic program. "The president would rather have people talking about his fight with the Congress than his losing battle with unemployment." A letter signed by the Democratic leadership — this included the Speaker, Majority Leader Jim Wright, and Majority Whip Tom Foley of Washington State — made the same point. "The politics of the veto are all too obvious: it distracts attention from Reaganomics." It was the now familiar contest: the Republicans wanted the headlines on "the budget," the Democrats on "the economy."

Watching all this, I didn't like the way Reagan, with his grandstanding veto, was drawing attention to the appropriations fight. It made it appear that we on the opposing side were doing exactly what the public feared Democrats invariably do — that is, spend any money they can get their hands on.

It turned out I was wrong, at least tactically. Yes, a "spending bill" was the wrong place for Democrats to pick a pre-election fight. But it's not such a bad idea, at any time, to be seen *fighting,* especially when you might just win.

Jim Wright, for one, welcomed the conflict.

He had no problem calling himself a tax-and-spend Democrat. With the veto override vote just minutes away, the Speaker asked Ari Weiss and me if we thought he should go on the floor to speak. We were both for it. This was turning into a big Democratic moment and he belonged squarely out front. I left the room to find out if the Speaker had been accorded his usual privilege to close debate on a major issue. He had. When I gave him the word, he decided to take the opportunity.

Wright, speaking first, performed brilliantly. The veteran congressman from Fort Worth said that Reagan was pulling the Republican members around with a ring in their noses like a "prize bull." His fellow Democrats in the chamber loved it. When it came his turn, the Speaker took the high road. He'd only been accorded three minutes.

What *made* his performance was the way he handled an interruption, an unusual occurrence when he had the floor. Millicent Fenwick, the old-money, rather crusty, pipe-smoking Republican from New Jersey, took her place at the GOP microphone, declaring more than once her wish for the Speaker to "yield." After putting her off until he finished his remarks, O'Neill finally gave way to the older, distinguished woman. "I would be glad to yield to the young lady," which won huge laughter and applause.

He closed by urging Republican members to "do a good deed" and vote to honor the integrity of the Congress's budget. Tip O'Neill's decision to get out in front of the appropriations vote, affirming his leadership, had been the correct one. Upsetting predictions, the House voted to override Reagan's veto. The lopsided tally was 301 to 117. Eighty-one Republicans joined the Democrats across the aisles in giving the president his first licking since coming to office.

Here's what my journal entry says: "Monday — September 13. The vote on the supplemental appropriations override was Thursday. I was upset over the past 2 weeks, that we were making such a big deal over this. We were allowing Reagan to simply draw our fire and make 'spending' the issue rather than let people's attention revert to their home and pocketbook issues." Once again, I was trying to steer the national debate away from a Washington budget fight to the national unemployment rate.

I was desperate for a way to shift attention to one simple, smart question. "Why have we got the highest jobless rate in 40 years?"

I asked rhetorically in my journal. "Need a major event/instrument to focus attention on unemployment and Democratic Party's commitment to creating new jobs."

A few days later, the Democrats, with Tip spearheading the endeavor, introduced a "jobs" bill. However, it was no surprise when the Republicans bashed this legislation as a "billion-dollar ballot box bailout bill." The implication was that the government would fund only phony, "make-work" jobs. Republican House leader Bob Michel was out on the House floor trashing the Democratic proposal with this very argument.

Rather than let him get away with it, I decided to do a bit of digging. I recalled research I'd done a decade earlier for Senator Moss, during which I'd spent days pulling together a list of public works projects in Utah, ones approved but not funded. Operating on a hunch now, I called the chief engineer of Peoria, the heart of Bob Michel's congressional district, and asked how many bridges were below safety code. The man on the phone came up with a list, complete with names and addresses where necessary repairs in the structures had been identified but not funded. I gave what he'd sent me, along with the jobless number for

Peoria, to the Speaker.

I never realized how tough the Speaker would get with his old pal Bob Michel. Tip tore into him on the floor, listing with unusual specificity the precise location of each dangerous Peoria bridge, throwing in for good measure the charge that the Republican leader should have been on the ball and used his clout with the U.S. Department of Transportation and other agencies to get those bridges fixed. In short, he was calling him out for failing to serve the constituents who voted for him and trustingly depended upon him to serve their interests. Obviously upset at Tip's invasion of his back-home politics, Bob Michel headed to the back of the chamber. His press secretary, Mike Johnson, was waiting there for him, but there was little consolation he could offer. "In Peoria, Reaganomics is going to play a lot better than Tiponomics," the red-faced Republican leader shot back before heading to the back of the chamber. I just have to add here, looking back, what wonderful people Bob Michel and Mike Johnson were and are.

As September gave way to October, the election grew more intense. Time works that way, no matter what party you belong to.

Even though he'd come aboard for the bipartisan tax-raising bill just weeks before, Reagan still was bent on portraying himself as a man apart, as a citizen-politician at the gates of Washington.

Remember that big July rally on the West Front of the Capitol? Well, Ronald Reagan had gotten such a kick out of it he now was coming back for an encore. Unfortunately for him, his previous crowd-pleasing act — his call for a balanced-budget amendment to the Constitution — was beginning to wear thin. What he hoped to do was trap Democratic members of Congress who could be accused of being against a balanced budget. The problem was, even true believers were now more driven by the country's real economic predicament than the ideological appeal of constitutional change.

To his chagrin, the president saw the balanced-budget amendment now fail to win the two-thirds vote needed before it could be submitted to the fifty states for ratification. Twenty independent-minded Republicans had joined the Democrats to kill its chances.

As anticipated, Reagan tried turning the legislative lemon he'd just been handed into lemonade — what else could he do? He played the aggrieved crusader. "Voters across America should count heads and take names. In November we must elect Representatives who will support the amendment when we propose it again in the spring. Today I share the deep burning anger, I think, of millions of Americans." He attacked what he called the "stonewalling" by O'Neill and other Democrats who'd kept the House from having scheduled the vote earlier.

Since the *Washington Post* pronounced that the vote denying Reagan the balanced-budget amendment "boosted the stock" of O'Neill, I was happy with the result. Yet at the same time, I remained uncertain how this upset actually was going to play in the coming election. Here's how I framed it in my journal: "The problem is that the Democrats never really made a public case against the constitutional amendment. We needed some hook, some easily understood and accepted reason why the amendment was not the answer. I don't think there *is* one." In the voters' minds, why shouldn't there be a mechanism forcing politicians to do what they themselves have to do at home, balance the checkbook?

I further worried that Reagan could make the election about the refusal of the Congress — "Washington!" — to let him make the big changes he'd called for. Again, it was about not being the roadblock to voter intentions. Basically, I was fretting that the vote on November 2 wouldn't hinge on the worsening economy — the jobless rate was now above 10 percent — but on Reagan's righteous presidential anger at an unbending Congress.

But if morale was any guidepost, matters were suddenly looking up for the Democrats. Here's the Speaker describing how he saw his success story in fighting Reagan: "I was the only voice that was really criticizing them. I kept hammering away and hammering away and hammering away. A lot of my people were running away, frightened of 'em, scared stiff of 'em."

But for Reagan's speechwriters, the Speaker still remained a target. Here's the president at a campaign rally in Irving, Texas, unkindly equating Tip O'Neill with Pac-Man: "Somebody told me it was a round thing that gobbled up money. I thought that was Tip O'Neill."

During his swing through the Southwest, a script had called for Reagan to be much rougher. A copy of a speech released earlier to the press had him saying, "In Washington, the nine heavenly bodies are Mercury, Venus, Earth, Mars, Jupiter, Saturn, Pluto, Neptune and Tip O'Neill." Reagan was either too nice or too prudish to imply that his sometime buddy — after 6 p.m. — was known as "Uranus." He'd not been willing to go *that* far.

Tip, too, preferred to tease rather than insult. During a White House briefing on foreign policy, for example, Reagan had to excuse himself. He told the Speaker and the other congressional leaders present that he was going to get his picture taken with a group of handicapped children. "Your heart would die for them," he said as he left the room. O'Neill saw his opening. "Mr. President, don't forget to tell them that Tip O'Neill is fighting for their budgets!" he called after the departing Reagan.

In mid-October, during his regular Saturday radio address, Reagan spoke of his early presidential hero, Franklin Roosevelt. He explained that "fear" was now again the country's real problem, just as it had been in the 1930s. However, he wanted to be sure his listeners knew that, this time around, the Democrats weren't the solution but rather the problem itself.

But the president wasn't to go unchallenged. Until this moment Tip had delegated other House Democrats to broadcast the official opposition reply. Now, finally, he was going to do it himself. It was a great moment for us corner men. I planned to have the Speaker tape his five-minute address on Friday in Boston, then send the transcript to the wires and major newspapers that afternoon with an embargo. That meant they couldn't publish or broadcast the Speaker's remarks until the next morning.

From my journal: "By letting the wires go with the story at 9 AM — and also letting the radio stations begin running it then, we created a story that TPO was on offense and Reagan on defense. I called Peter Milius, an editor at the *Washington Post,* on Saturday and asked if they could put TPO in the lead and Reagan in the jump. He said, 'You can kiss my ass.' "

But he was just kidding. In the end, the strategy worked and we got the story we wanted: Tip and the Gipper fighting on even terms.

Here's how it played in the *Post:*

Democrats took the offensive yesterday for the first time in their weekly radio battle with President Reagan, bringing in House Speaker Thomas P. (Tip) O'Neill Jr. (D-Mass.) to elevate and sharpen the dispute

377

over who should be blamed for the condition of the economy.

In a taped message released three hours before the president's live broadcast, O'Neill charged that the administration's program "is not working because the program is not fair — and just as important, because the people themselves know it is not fair."

It was the first time a Democrat of O'Neill's stature had taken part in the Saturday broadcasts and the first time the party launched a political assault rather than responding to Reagan's remarks.

Steven Weisman's coverage for the *Times,* topping the front page, was even better in setting up the match.

Reagan and O'Neill Exchange Charges Over the Economy

President Reagan and the Speaker of the House, Thomas P. O'Neill Jr., exchanged accusations on the economy today as the off-year election campaign went into its final 10 days.

Sounding their principal themes in a campaign that is viewed by both sides as a referendum on the Reagan Administration's economic policies, Mr. Reagan charged the Democrats with proffering "fairy tales" and Mr. O'Neill said the Administration had deliberately thrown people out of work. . . .

Just as Mr. Reagan appealed for patience, Mr. O'Neill sounded the principal theme of the Democrats this fall: that the Administration's policies were unfair.

The Speaker's rare appearance on the airwaves did what we'd hoped: put him out in front where, suddenly, he sounded as impressive as I was convinced he deserved to be.

An election eve account by the Associated Press's Tom Raum recognized both the strategy and its effectiveness:

Not long ago, some members of his own party dismissed O'Neill as ineffective and politically over the hill, as he lost one budget battle after another to Reagan. Today, the speaker seems to have reclaimed his status as the Democratic Party's chief spokesman.

He is making more radio and television appearances, and his enlarged press staff is cranking out almost daily O'Neill attacks on Reaganomics. One was a poster that carried this message: "Voodoo Economics: Stay the Curse."

Kirk O'Donnell had a favorite political maxim, which I've quoted before — *you make your breaks.* We would prove that rule in the final days of the 1982 midterm campaign. With the entire House of Representatives, and a third of the U.S. Senate, up for reelection, we now did what was absolutely mandatory if we were going to prevail. We came up with a way to put the red-hot Social Security issue front and center, where it couldn't be missed.

As I said, it was a break we'd made in the final week before America went to the polls. I'd been working to make good use of what appeared a highly exploitable leak from the White House. Word was that the Reagan people might use the congressional "lame duck" session following the election to attempt once again to downgrade the role of Social Security as it was known and loved. This was obviously worth every second I could put into following up the truth of it, and I was highly motivated, wanting to be careful to pitch it to the right person for a thoroughgoing follow-up.

I decided on the *Post*'s Spencer Rich, who often wrote about government agencies. As

I tried to convince him to run with the story, I wound up listening as he asked me to help find a mass letter sent out by the National Republican Congressional Committee, one that discussed Social Security. I steered him to Eric Berkman, a House Democratic staffer who I knew could get ahold of anything, and who had contacts even in the White House.

On the Wednesday before the election, Spencer called and said he'd received the Republican mailing from Eric and was intending to go with the story for Thursday. Incredibly, that GOP fund-raising letter he now had his hands on included a questionnaire that suggested ways Congress might reform Social Security. It invited contributors to vote on several options for fixing Social Security. It promised the votes would "let the [bipartisan] Commission know . . . how you want Social Security reformed before they finalize their report." Ballot choice No. 1 was to make the system "voluntary."

Eureka.

Could Reagan still claim he'd since changed his mind, that he no longer held such a position? Not anymore. Here was a promotional mailing from his very own party that starkly implied otherwise. It was the Thursday morning before the election. I called Kirk, who said we should instantly get out a statement from Tip demanding that the president "repudiate" the mailer. I reached the Speaker up in Cambridge. When he phoned back from his first stop that morning, I gave him the news. "We got a break on Social Security," I reported happily.

The Speaker's stern rebuke to the president, calling for him to disassociate himself from the GOP mailing, made the UPI wire immediately, which in turn triggered the TV networks. The key was, here was Tip pinning the campaign committee's goof on Reagan himself, making it hard to blame anyone else. That afternoon, as Air Force One arrived in Casper, Wyoming, the press jumped Reagan, demanding he answer the Speaker. The story led the networks' news programs that night as the top item. From that moment on, our job was to keep Social Security alive and burning as the central, overriding issue through Election Day.

Now there was no more prelude. Our mighty efforts were either going to be rewarded . . . or not. Walking to the Speaker's office the day before the election, I'd suddenly recalled how, back in 1980, CBS had led its election eve news broadcast by focusing not on the tough battle coming to a close but on the fact that it was the first anniversary of the Iranian hostage crisis. I remembered how it had hurt.

Two years later, on another election eve, my mood was different. This time around, Tip O'Neill's assault on Ronald Reagan and his party's problem with Social Security was the lead story on the *CBS Evening News*. The tables had been turned.

Tip O'Neill enjoyed a plate of beef stew as the returns began coming in, receiving the election results in his back office. I watched him savor each incoming phone call bringing good news: the young House members he'd been worried about had come through safely and were reporting in.

There'd also been scores to be settled that got taken care of. During the campaign, an arrogant young Republican congressman from Long Island had attacked the Speaker as "big, fat and out of control, just like the federal government." At one point, he'd gone so far as to pin a REPEAL O'NEILL campaign button right on President Reagan's lapel.

"I wouldn't know him from a cord of wood," the Speaker insisted, pretending to be unbothered. The House, after all, was a very big place, and this guy wasn't one of his own. But the devoted Leo Diehl felt otherwise. He'd been with Tip through every election since 1936 and had no intention of permitting the offender to go unpunished. The next thing the Democratic hopeful in that district, Bob Mrazek — who hadn't stood much of a chance before — knew was that large contributions were flowing into his campaign treasury from unexpected sources. Diehl had quietly alerted the Speaker's friends that a certain disrespectful Republican needed to be taught a lesson.

"For a while there, I had no idea where we would get the money we needed to run a decent campaign," Mrazek would recall. "Then, out of nowhere, three weeks before election day, the money started pouring in, from Chicago, from *everywhere.*" The icing on the cake of election night, 1982, was Mrazek's win. Leo was triumphant. "I think the 'Repeal O'Neill' kid got repealed."

Albert Hunt, then of the *Wall Street Journal,* would write: "The one clear winner election night was Thomas P. O'Neill. He had suffered more than any other political leader in the past two years. But his strategy . . . paid off on election night."

As the election results rolled in, Tip

couldn't help declaring, "It's a great night for the Irish." He'd fought the election on three issues: the recession, Social Security, and "fairness." His tactics had paid off. After two years of intense frustration and unwilling accommodations, he'd retaken effective control of his beloved House, picking up twenty-six seats. "We don't want anyone to eat crow," he declared once it was all over. "The country is in too tough shape for anything of that nature." Instead, the Speaker called for "bending" on the part of both Democrats and Republicans. "And so we will extend to him the hand of cooperation to see, whether in the best interest of America, we can turn this unemployment around," he said.

The evidence of what took place the next morning appears, unadorned, in my journal: "November 3 — We won!"

Later that month, the *New York Times* columnist James Reston wrote this about Tip and the Gipper. It would prove an excellent testament of the new political order that emerged from the 1982 election. Reston, a world-renowned journalist, had just turned seventy-three.

They are an odd couple, but they have

some things in common. Both know they don't have the votes in the new Congress to put over the programs they prefer. Both are coming to the end of a long political journey. The Speaker will be 70 on Dec. 9, and the President will be 72 next Feb. 6.

What they also have in common is an important chance to do something together in these next two years for the defense of the nation at home and abroad. The Speaker wants to leave behind a Social Security system that will endure, even if he has to amend its benefits, and the President probably wants to depart in peace and get control of both the economy and the nuclear arms race.

Together, they might even do it, and being Irish, they might even try.

Fixing Social Security for the long term in the winter of 1983 was the great bipartisan achievement of the Reagan presidency. It required an elegant choreography that had both the president and Speaker agreeing to the deal in tandem. Here the two celebrate St. Patrick's Day with Republican leader and Tip pal Bob Michel.

CHAPTER SIXTEEN: DEAL

"Americans are conservative. What they want to conserve is the New Deal."
— GEORGE F. WILL

It was Kirk O'Donnell, the Speaker's counsel, who gave me a way to see how to operate effectively in the political arena. Over the years, the rules of action I first heard from him have evolved and grown into my own everyday primer. From the start I grasped their simple, practical wisdom. They deserved to be at the core of any working pol's personal handbook — that is, if he knows what's doing.

It was Kirk who had the smarts to dub Social Security the "third rail" of American politics. He was certainly right, of course — and this brilliant image had a very specific meaning for him. As a kid growing up in Boston, Kirk had been taken from an early age on the old MTA, only to be haunted by those scary signs that warned, NO TRESPASS-ING. DANGER THIRD RAIL. The prospect of the horrific fate he might suffer should he fall onto the tracks gave him nightmares he never forgot.

During the 1982 election, Kirk's imagined nightmare had become the Republicans' own. The Democrats had made sure of it. But another of Kirk's great expressions — which is the key to understanding what next happens — is one I've already mentioned (when it equally applied). "Always be able to talk," he liked to say. And that's what the two parties started, slowly, to do.

Following the midterm elections, and the gratifying Democratic triumph, I began to sense a positive shift in our dealings with the Republicans on Social Security. "If we are truly to avoid a disaster," the Speaker had said even before the election, "both sides have to give a little." November behind him, the calendar now pointed to mid-1983, when the Social Security fund faced its due date. "The old-age trust fund is already operating at a deficit," the *Washington Post* had reported the previous month, "and will be able to get through to next July only by borrowing from Medicare."

Reagan, viewing the same deadline, saw a deal with the Democratic Speaker as a way to silence "Social Security" as the Democratic battle cry in 1984. For this, he was ready to pay a price. Just as he'd been willing to accept a tax increase in 1982, he was now prepared to allow another breach in his no-tax firewall. To stanch the bleeding in the Social Security system, he would make a second compromise: if a hike in the payroll tax that every worker contributes to the retirement fund was essential to a deal, he was ready to do it.

On January 3, the *Washington Post* reported the following: "Administration sources have suggested that Reagan is signaling his willingness to consider tax increases as part of a bailout, while O'Neill apparently has sanctioned a compromise proposal that postpones benefit increases for three months." The rough basis for a deal was now on the table: Democrats would get an increase in the payroll tax, while Republicans would get their downward modification of benefits.

Around this time, I shared my optimism with Ken Duberstein, one of the top Reagan lobbyists. Later I worried I'd been so candid. The fact is, I *was* optimistic about what direction we were headed in — after the strong Democratic showing at the polls — and I was in no mood to keep it secret.

It was easy to see that in the coming round both sides had strong reasons to be open to deal-making.

Reagan's people, especially Jim Baker, were eager to have Social Security be a non-issue as the 1984 campaign started to get under way. Once again, an election had produced two kinds of verdicts, depending on which side was receiving it. The most recent contest for voter loyalties had told the Republicans they needed to call it quits when it came to targeting Social Security as a way to reduce the federal deficit. For Tip O'Neill and the Democrats, the message was, "Never be blamed for hurting the system." Both parties needed to keep Social Security sound. That meant making adjustments in the present to assure its solvency for future generations.

Back in September 1981, President Reagan had created the bipartisan, fifteen-member National Commission on Social Security Reform. It was chaired by Alan Greenspan, known, at that time, for having been the Ford administration's head of the Council of Economic Advisers. The group was preparing a report expected to be ready at the very end of 1982, but, as January 1 approached, the struggling commission asked for and received an extension, which made it now due on January 15. That fell amid Congress's annual two-week break between swearing-in day and the onset of legislative business. It was the period when the Speaker and his pal Dan Rostenkowski enjoyed splitting their time between Palm Beach and Palm Springs, giving paid lectures to corporate retreats and playing golf.

Because it was during the break, it was a date that would find me out of the country, for I'd been fortunate enough to be offered another opportunity to visit Swaziland, this time with Kathleen and our six-month-old, Michael.

The United States Information Agency ran a regular lecture series, which sent "American Participants," people from various backgrounds, to meet with their counterparts in other countries. They asked whether I'd like to do a quick trip to Swaziland, Zaire, and Nigeria during the two-week hiatus. Once I'd been given the word I could bring Kathleen, then a reporter for ABC's Washington affiliate, I jumped at the chance.

The three of us flew off right after the swearing-in of new legislators, at a moment when the Social Security negotiations remained on course. Or so I believed. However, when I dig back through the history of those critical days in early 1983, I see it was more touch-and-go than I realized.

The Greenspan Commission, it turned out, was at odds over the right mix of greater payroll taxes paid by workers into the system and lower benefits. The Democrats on it had been pushing for more revenues in the system, while their Republican fellows were insisting on lower payments to retirees. The result, as the deadline neared, remained a stalemate — an echo of the ongoing historic standoff between the parties — with the Democrats hoping to make the system of greater value to those who need it most and the Republicans looking for ways to reduce the burden on those paying in.

Back in December, Tip had said publicly he might be willing to support a tax on the Social Security benefits for those making more than $25,000 a year. The Speaker believed such a progressive tax solution would be a fair part of the deal.

But a very large question remained: who would be the first to show their cards?

Two senior U.S. senators, Bob Dole of Kansas and Daniel Patrick Moynihan of New York, now stepped in to play key roles in the drama. On the first morning of the new Congress, January 3, 1983, the *New*

York Times op-ed page featured a piece by Dole headlined "Reagan's Faithful Allies," which brought an unexpected result. "Through a combination of relatively modest steps," the Republican wrote, "the system can be saved." Having just read Dole's article on the Senate floor, Moynihan walked over and tapped his colleague on the shoulder. "Are we going to let this commission die without giving it one more try?" the Democrat asked.

As the commission attempted both to solve its complex assignment and also to work through its partisan differences, Greenspan, as chairman, proved nimble. Throughout 1982, as they studied and debated, he made a point of keeping both the president and the Speaker aware of the deliberations. At each step of the way, he'd check in with Jim Baker, who'd assure him Reagan was on board. To make sure every provision was okay with the Speaker, he'd rely on word from Robert Ball, Tip's key man on the commission.

Ball had been administrator of the Social Security system under Kennedy, Johnson, and Nixon, and was strongly committed to its robust preservation. Ball's liaison inside the Speaker's office was a young staffer named Jack Lew. "He didn't make a move

that we weren't aware of," Lew later would
tell me. "He'd leave the meeting and call
me, or if I needed to, I'd call the Speaker.
And it was all very safe — in the sense that
we were never negotiating anything directly."

The unspoken but paramount truth here
was that both Reagan and O'Neill were
conviction politicians. Each man embodied
the philosophy of his party. If Reagan
pronounced a deal okay, the Republicans
would be ready to accept it. The same held
for the Speaker and the Democrats. Between
them, they carried an overriding political
authority. Once they came together, the
perilous situation could be resolved.

With the January 15 deadline looming,
Reagan worried aloud. Now he was the
wary one when it came to touching benefits
in any way. If he did, he said, "the same old
political football would be seen going up in
the air like a punt on third down." Even up
until the day before the commission's report
was due, he refused to budge. "I'm not going to make choices on this until I see what
the entire thing is they're going to recom-
mend," he declared. Here's the *New York
Times* report: "Mr. Reagan's wariness of
Social Security was evident Friday when he
refused to endorse the statement of his chief

of staff, James A. Baker 3d, that he might accept a combination of payroll tax increases and restraints on the growth of Social Security benefits."

Duberstein described the political minuet this way: "We weren't going to put our head back in that noose, and the Speaker wasn't going to come forward unless the president came forward, and so we just danced around and danced around."

The fifteenth of January fell on a Saturday. Not until that night was a way found to make the deal without fear. It was like the exchange of a hostage for ransom in a life-or-death kidnapping. For six hours during the late afternoon and early evening, the deal was held up because the two sides could not agree on the wording of the agreement. Each also had to feel confident it would not be left holding the bag. The kidnapping parallel is apt: the hostage and the money needed to be delivered at the same precise moment.

In the end, two separate statements were issued, and in the interests of simultaneity, the president announced both his own agreement to the deal and also the Speaker's.

Here, first, is the White House's own careful wording of the outcome:

It is my understanding that the Speaker and the majority leader [Howard Baker] find this bipartisan solution acceptable.

Each of us recognizes that this is a compromise solution. As such, it includes elements which each of us could not support if they were not part of a bipartisan compromise. However, in the interest of solving the Social Security problem promptly, equitably, and on a bipartisan basis, we have agreed to support and work for this bipartisan solution.

I believe the American people will welcome this demonstration of bipartisan cooperation in offering a solution that can keep a fundamental trust, while solving a fundamental national problem.

The Democrats' statement was every bit as meticulously phrased. Reagan had made sure Tip O'Neill was fully implicated, and the Speaker did likewise. He called the plan "acceptable to the president and to me, one which I can support and which I will work for."

The agreement consisted of an increase in the payroll tax, a delay in cost-of-living increases, and a requirement that federal employees enroll in Social Security. It would also subject retirees making $20,000 or more of other income to pay federal income tax on half their Social Security benefits.

That night, Reagan recorded the historic moment in his diary: "S.S. team came by early evening. I okayed a proposal. Within the hour they phoned — we have a deal supported by Tip et al. Vote on commission was 12 to 3 — the 3 hold outs were Dem. Waggoner & 2 R's. Armstrong & Bill Archer."

The fact that the three holdouts were on the right — Waggoner was a conservative Democrat appointed to the commission by Reagan — was a leading indicator that the final deal tilted to the left. For the first time, Social Security benefits for higher-income recipients would be taxed. Altogether, the changes favored low-income Americans and ensured the survival of a strong Social Security system.

Chairman Alan Greenspan said that the main reason for the commission's ultimate success had been the care he'd taken to keep the president and the Speaker agreeable to the decisions every step of the way. Still, it could not have been done without the two principals working the issue from both ends. "It was very helpful to have a few giants around them who were willing to put their credibility on the line and take a position," was the way Republican Judd

Gregg, a young Congressman from New Hampshire starting his second term, saw it. Their sheer weight guaranteed the deal, and even Gregg, new to the game, understood how critical it had been.

Greenspan also told me that, in the final twelve hours of negotiation that Saturday, the White House gang — Jim Baker, his deputy Richard Darman, David Stockman, and Ken Duberstein — was on full alert. It fell to them to carry up-to-the-minute reports and their boss's subsequent responses back and forth between the White House and Blair House (directly across Pennsylvania Avenue), where the commission was meeting.

Robert Ball, for so long both an overseer and champion of the Social Security system, called his work on the commission the most important of his life. "More than any other event in recent times, the Social Security compromise demonstrated that there is a political center in America that can govern for the benefit of the country even when there are extremely difficult problems to be faced and strongly held differences of opinion about solutions. This bill demonstrates for all time our nation's ironclad commitment to Social Security."

That Monday, Reagan, seeing blue skies

ahead, made phone calls all around to congratulate Tip, Rosty, Howard Baker, and a couple of commission members themselves. The deal was, indeed, an "all together" mutual solution. The policy and the politics were a tight match to both Social Security necessity and electoral expedience.

What's important to me — with my own strong feelings about the role of Social Security in America's common life — is that the man for whom I worked had given up the issue politically in order to get a better deal for the people he sought to champion. A cynic could say he'd made splendid political capital of the issue in the 1982 election and now figured on diminishing returns, even a downside, to continuing the fight through 1984. Equally, had the system failed in any way, he and the Democrats, as its traditional defenders, would surely have been blamed. What's important is that what might have happened, didn't.

Staffers in politics tend to mimic their bosses. You take your key from them. Tip's staff had good relations with Reagan's, and I give a lot of credit to the Reagan people. They always took our calls and were incredibly — by later standards — collegial. There was a sense, on a certain level, of working together in service of the country. What's strange is that I can claim such a thing even though the rivalry was so often ferocious.

It's easy, from the vantage point of today, to mock all those Irish jokes and the swapping of stories between the president and the Speaker. But I was there, and the plain truth is, they kept the conversation going when no progress seemed possible otherwise.

I arrived home from Africa just in time for President Reagan's second State of the Union address, on January 25. Meeting him once again, as he waited for his cue in the Speaker's ceremonial office, this time he struck me as more on-guard, more James Cagney than Jimmy Stewart. Now he had a bottle of Perrier on hand. As he waited, he greeted an old California political associate, Democratic congressman Don Edwards, who came in the room. The president seemed stunned to see Edwards already holding a copy of his speech in hand. I explained that the White House traditionally let out an early copy for use by the East Coast papers in their early-morning editions.

What no one told him — and I wasn't about to — was what the Democrats had up their sleeve, once his speech was under way. In the draft, which we'd now seen, one of the themes was the responsibility of job creation. As soon as President Reagan got to the part where he was planning to say, "We in government must take the lead" in putting people to work, our plan was for everyone on the Democratic side of the aisle to stand up and applaud loudly, dramatically — and triumphantly.

The point behind all the noise was to make sure the entire country grasped the nature of the very large milestone occurring. Here, for the first time, the current White House occupant — famed as an unyielding ideological conservative — was admitting to government's obligation when it came to jobs. With the unemployment rate at 10.8 percent in December, it was news. Big news. And we wanted to make sure both the American people — and the press — didn't miss it.

When the moment arrived, I saw those on the Democratic side still in their seats, hesitant to make such a brazen display of themselves. Then, just as it appeared no one would have the guts to do it, Congressman Ed Markey of Massachusetts bolted to his feet, cheering. With that, he opened the floodgates as dozens of others rose and joined him.

Reagan, seeing and hearing the commotion, was taken aback, but only for an instant. After executing a true Hollywood double take, he said, "And here all the time, I thought you were reading the paper."

The Democrats laughed appreciatively. But I sensed that Reagan actually managed to score off them more effectively than they realized. His quip about "reading the paper" slyly directed the people listening at home to see in their mind's eye a bunch of lazy pols dozing over the afternoon newspapers. As usual, Ronald Reagan was playing not to the room he was in, but to the camera.

(Not long after, at his seventy-second birthday party, he let loose with another crafty ad-lib that hit its mark. As he handed out slices of cake — a surprise treat brought by Nancy to the press conference that day — one of those present was ABC's Sam Donaldson. "But you understand we won't sell out for a piece of cake!" he yelled. "No deals!" It was a perfect setup for Reagan. "Oh, you've sold out for less than that," the president cheerily stung Donaldson on national television as his colleagues cracked up. It was hard to steal a march on a man who could fire off a comeback like that.)

Was Ronald Reagan serious in what he'd

said about the government's duty to create jobs? Here was a man who, previously, had been unwavering in his long-held belief that free-market forces were the solution to the unemployment problem. Now he was saying otherwise. "He spoke of creating jobs but opposes jobs *legislation,*" said a skeptical Tip O'Neill. "The government has a responsibility not simply to admit a problem but to take action in meeting that problem."

It was a pointed comment. At stake was a $5 billion public works bill the House had passed in December. It was a narrow vote, however, just 204 to 200. Even if it were to pass the Senate, which it hadn't, that wasn't enough to survive a presidential veto — an important detail.

The day after the State of the Union, Reagan was scheduled for a quick trip to Boston. One of his stops was the Eire Pub, a traditional Irish bar in the blue-collar neighborhood of Dorchester. There, with an open trench coat over his suit, he raised a mug, posing next to a local fellow wearing a plaid shirt and watch cap. The idea was to show his solidarity with the country's workers, those fellow citizens unhappily stuck in a slough of 10 percent unemployment. For this brief moment, at least, the "new" Reagan was convincing enough.

But not for long. An event in the suburban town of Bedford, Massachusetts, called for him to sit down with a clutch of high-tech executives. There he managed to quickly ring down the curtain on the excellent scene staged earlier in Dorchester. "I realize that there will be a great stirring and I will probably kick myself for having said this," he explained to the businessmen listening, "but when are we all going to have the courage to point out that . . . the corporate tax is very hard to justify?" Here was Reagan reverting to those out-of-office years when he could freely express, through columns and speeches to businessmen, his view of the universe. It was an old argument believed by businessmen that corporate taxes were double taxation.

Back in Washington, the president's incursion onto his home turf got Tip's attention. After the cozy photo op in the pub, his adversary had morphed back from kindly Dr. Jekyll into the more familiar Mr. Hyde. And Tip was quick to note the transformation. "On the same day the president sat down to drink with the workingmen of Boston — and I have no complaints about that — he showed his heart was still in the corporate boardroom."

Reagan had known it was coming: "Well,

I said yesterday I'd be kicking myself. I have." A few days later it was O'Neill doing the kicking. The top leaders of both parties in both houses had been invited to the White House — the president was preparing to deliver his new budget to them — and Tip chose the moment to go on the attack. In a verbal brawl that lasted nearly forty-five minutes, the Speaker attacked the president for failing to take action to deal with the country's highest unemployment since before World War II.

Reagan: God damn it, Tip, we *do* care about those people.
O'Neill: It's easy to say that you care but you aren't willing to do anything *about* it.

In his diary that night, the president narrated the fight. "Tip & I got into a donny brook — I really had my dander up. The worst of it was Tip didn't have the facts of what is in the budget — besides he doesn't listen." Jim Wright, who was in the room, called it "the toughest going-over I've ever heard a president subjected to."
Yet fifteen minutes after the tense meeting in the West Wing, the president and the Speaker found themselves together again, reunited in a different corner of the White

House. Reagan had invited Senate and House committee chairmen to be briefed in the State Dining Room on his annual budget. As the administration officials put on their dog and pony show, Reagan approached O'Neill. He'd just spoken to Budget Director Stockman, he told him, and wanted Tip to know that working jointly on a jobs bill with him wasn't out of the question. "Dave tells me we're really not that far apart," the president offered reassuringly. When asked later what the two had been whispering about, Reagan replied they were "just two Irishmen plotting."

Back at the Capitol, O'Neill reflected on his conversation with the president. "Whether this means a ray of hope, I don't know." He said they remained "very far apart" on a jobs bill.

Clearly, Reagan hoped to smooth matters between them. He quickly gave permission to Stockman and a group of other staffers to meet with O'Neill with an eye to working through their differences. "We stand ready to compromise," Tip said. "We are Americans first and Democrats second. I truly believe that we have to stimulate the economy. We are interested in getting people back to work as quickly as possible. Next to Social Security, that is our No. 1 agenda.

You can't stimulate the economy if you can't put people back to work. That is how we've gotten out of every recession."

But even as the first working session with Tip was about to take place, Stockman had a more pressing concern. Joked the Speaker, "I understand he's getting married Saturday . . . When he goes on his honeymoon, he won't be thinking about Tip O'Neill."

Stockman got to the church on time — but not before first getting to the meeting with the Speaker. That very same day, after Tip had made reference to his impending nuptials, Stockman accompanied Jim Baker, Dick Darman, and Ken Duberstein to Tip's office. There they reached agreement with O'Neill and his lieutenants on a $4 billion bill to create 125,000 jobs. While this made only a minimal dent in the unemployment rate, it allowed the Democrats to claim they'd made progress with the president, while at the same time giving Reagan and the Republicans a way to show they were sensitive to the country's pain.

"When I met with President Reagan on January thirty-first, he promised that he would direct David Stockman to find areas where government spending could create more jobs," the Speaker said on February 10. "The president has kept his promise.

Today, Jim Baker and David Stockman brought me a number of immediate approaches for creating jobs and relieving the human suffering caused by the current economic situation."

The week after coming to a deal with the White House on the jobs bill, Tip O'Neill got a new — temporary — job of his own. His cameo on an episode of *Cheers,* which would become one of the country's best-loved and most popular TV series, propelled him to a new level of celebrity. When he agreed to lend local verisimilitude by strolling into that iconic Boston bar "where everybody knows your name," it helped turn him into a household name.

Doing battle with Ronald Reagan on behalf of his fellow Americans, many of whom had no other champion, was helping to make him a folk hero. But folk hero or not, he still had to run for reelection himself in 1984, and in March he threw his hat into the ring for the seventeenth time. On the following day, the House passed that hard-fought-for jobs bill he and the president had managed to bring into being.

Reagan Diary: March 17

St. Patrick's day. A shamrock tie from Margaret Heckler & one from Tip O'Neill. Lunch on Capitol hill as Tips guest. About 30 people including F.M. Barry & Ambas. O'Sullivan of Ireland. Tip is a true pol. He can really like you personally & be a friend while politically trying to beat your head in.

For Tip's part, for the good of the country — especially its workers — he would wish Reagan the best with his economic program. "I always figured that — listen, I'm an American. I hope that it'll work, like everybody hopes that it'll work."

Tip O'Neill suspected to the end that Reagan had launched the invasion of
Grenada to distract from the terrorist attack on the marine barracks in Lebanon.

CHAPTER SEVENTEEN: LEBANON AND GRENADA

> "If I had an hour to solve a problem, I would spend 55 minutes thinking about the problem and five minutes thinking about solutions."
>
> — ALBERT EINSTEIN

As leaders often do, Ronald Reagan saw the world as a board game, where the winning side was the one gaining territory. In the post–World War II years, anyone could see the communists were the biggest winners in Eastern Europe, North Korea, then China, then in North Vietnam. If they weren't stopped as they'd been in South Korea, or challenged bloodily as in South Vietnam, there was no saying they wouldn't be at our very borders next. (After all, what about Cuba?) Those who subscribed to this thinking — I certainly did — had reason for a troubling worldview.

For a solid explanation, you need only

look back to what Adolf Hitler tried to do and wound up perilously close to achieving. Yet there'd been a pivotal moment, an opportunity to put a check to his intentions. At the Munich Conference in 1938, when England and France lacked the resolve to stop the German chancellor from seizing the German-speaking part of Czechoslovakia, known as the Sudetenland, their weakness turned into Hitler's mandate. The global horror of Axis aggression proceeded from there. For Reagan, for his contemporaries, and for many in the generations after them, the word *Munich* was understood as code for any nation's stepping back from the necessary toughness.

Ronald Reagan's zealous anticommunism had been an integral part of his political makeup since the days when, as Screen Actors Guild president, he'd first encountered the hard left's bullying ways and treacherous practices. During those postwar years in Hollywood, he'd gone head to head with hard-left union bosses, some of whom had direct Soviet ties. In the end he could only regard them as spreading *evil,* and from then on, he refused ever to regard any communists as trustworthy, on any level whatsoever.

He came to the presidency with views that

had only grown harder over the decades. Yet that antagonism, born out of his personal experience with communism, had another side — one linked to the reverence in which he held his ideal of democracy. The American Way was the bulwark against the communist threat here in this country, he felt, and the truth of that was undeniable. As the 1950s began, he made his political odyssey past a fading acting career. Then with *General Electric Theater* he grew in determination as he traveled across time and geography to that extraordinary prize, the White House. All the while he saw the rising tide of global communism and spent his second career bucking it.

In the mind of Ronald Reagan, the Soviet system itself was *through*. America would prevail, of that he had no doubt. We win. They lose. Born of personal witness, his anticommunist narrative never faltered. Reagan was a man who knew exactly what he believed and was willing to trumpet it wherever there were listeners.

Speaking to members of the British parliament in London in June 1982, he appropriated a turn of phrase that had been first employed sixty-five years earlier by Leon Trotsky for the Russian revolutionary's own, opposite purposes. His confident American tones resounding through the Royal Gallery at the Palace of Westminster, Reagan declared, "What I am describing now is a plan and a hope for the long term — the march of freedom and democracy which will leave Marxism-Leninism on the ash heap of history as it has left other tyrannies which stifle the freedom and muzzle the self-expression of the people."

Tip O'Neill was similarly a Cold Warrior, though without Reagan's sense of ideology — meaning, *his* own ideology — as destiny. Equally repelled by the notion of communism, the Speaker regarded as key the unity inherent in our country's very name: the United States of America. He resolutely held to the civic wisdom that reminds, "Politics ends at the water's edge." It had actually been a Republican senator, Michigan's Arthur Vandenberg, who'd first put these words into the political phrasebook. "To me," Vandenberg wrote in the early 1950s, " 'bipartisan foreign policy' means a mutual effort, under our indispensable two-party system, to unite our official voice at the water's edge so that America speaks with maximum authority against those who would divide and conquer us and the free world."

Tip O'Neill had come up in politics during an era very different, of course, from the one in which he now was a senior figure. During his formative Washington years, he'd watched Speaker Sam Rayburn and Senate majority leader Lyndon Johnson follow the foreign policy line taken by President Eisenhower and his advisors at the same time as those men, in turn, were willing to accept the Democrats' hegemony when it came to domestic affairs. However, like many Democrats, O'Neill had broken with "water's edge" bipartisanship when it came to Vietnam.

After opposing the escalating U.S. involvement there, he was left, once we withdrew our forces, in an understandable quandary. For him, the possibility of "another Vietnam" now joined a tug-of-war with the prospect of "another Munich." Even before Reagan attained the presidency or he the Speakership, Tip had worried Vietnam might wind up the operative model should the United States ever find itself tempted to engage in anticommunist excursions in our own hemisphere.

When it came to Central America, Tip had his own personal reasons to believe we'd end up fighting on the wrong side. In the mind of a man who'd grown up in working-class North Cambridge, U.S. involvement during the first half of the twentieth century in places like Panama, Honduras, Guatemala, Costa Rica, and Nicaragua had its origins in the arrogant might exerted by the United Fruit Company, at one time a Boston-based import giant with vast Central American interests. Tip blamed United Fruit's internal meddling in the affairs of these countries for our military interventions in them in the 1920s.

"Why are we there?" the young O'Neill had asked Eddie Kelly, a marine who returned from Nicaragua in a wheelchair. "We're taking care of the property and rights of United Fruit," he recalled the young man's answer. "Gunboat diplomacy," to Tip O'Neill, was only another variant on the rich calling the shots and he wanted no part of it. "A few people made a great amount of money," he said of the early-century troubles in Central America, "and we are responsible for it."

In the first third of the twentieth century the United States had intervened in Nicaragua militarily. An occupation by American marines that began in 1912 didn't end until twenty-one years later. It was then that a guerrilla group led by Augusto César Sandino successfully confronted both the local regime and the U.S. troops. But only three years later, Sandino himself was killed, and for the next four decades Nicaragua was ruled by the corrupt, authoritarian Somoza family. In 1979, a rebel group calling itself the Sandinistas forced out the Somozas.

Upon taking office in January 1981, Ronald Reagan decided to make his anticommunist stand in Nicaragua. Accusing the Sandinistas of collaborating with the Soviets and Cuba in efforts to overthrow the rightwing government in El Salvador — a nearby country separated from Nicaragua by a chunk of Honduras — the White House terminated U.S. financial aid to the country's government. By year's end, the president had escalated the battle, signing an order that gave arms, equipment, and money to an anti-Sandinista rebel group, known as the Contras because they were waging a *contrarrevolución.* Made up of several anti-Sandinista factions, the Contras had unified with the approval of the United States and had suddenly emerged to launch military attacks against the Nicaraguan government.

Angry Democratic reaction to the Reagan administration's backing of the Contras led to the passage of the first Boland Amendment in December 1982. This was a measure sponsored by Congressman Edward

Boland, O'Neill's former roommate whom he had named chairman of the Permanent Select Committee on Intelligence. It banned military support "for the purpose of over-throwing the Government of Nicaragua." The Speaker said the White House's backing of the Nicaraguan rebels would eventually lead to American troops going into that country.

In June 1982, Israel invaded Lebanon. Its goals were to eliminate the Palestine Liberation Organization's base of operations in southern Lebanon, eliminate Syrian influence there, and establish an alliance with a Christian-led government. The task at hand, forcing the PLO to leave the country, was accomplished quickly. President Reagan now agreed to send in U.S. troops as part of a multinational force, its purpose being to safeguard the Palestinians' evacuation. Once this mission had been achieved, the American troops were sent back to their ships.

Then came a pair of horrors.

First, on September 14, Bashir Gemayel, the Lebanese president-elect, was assassinated in his party's East Beirut office. Two days later, approximately seven hundred Muslim civilians — many women, children, and elderly men — were massacred between September 16 and 18 in Palestinian refugee camps in Beirut. The attacks were linked to the Phalangist party of Bashir Gemayel; and revenge for his death was the obvious motivation. In the aftermath of these acts of violence, President Reagan made the decision to summon the marines back into the country to help maintain order with their presence.

The dangers inherent in this second deployment should have been obvious. These members of the American military were dispatched originally as a symbol to a region where symbols were synonymous with targets. They went in as peacekeepers where there was no existing peace to keep. Summoned to serve as the "linchpin" of a diplomatic effort to rebuild the Lebanese government, the marines' presence quickly became a pretext for further violence.

Tip O'Neill gave President Reagan his backing on Lebanon policy from the outset. When talk first arose of sending the marines — for their initial appearance on the scene, to help oversee the evacuation of the PLO — he was openly positive. "If he asks my views," he said, responding to a reporter's question just before a White House briefing he was attending, "I will be happy to tell him through the years that I've always felt that if we had a bipartisan foreign policy the nation would be better off. I wait to see what the president has in mind." He had the same reaction on hearing that Reagan intended the second deployment of the marines. "I would hope that the leadership on both sides could be unanimous," he told the press.

As might have been anticipated, the return of the U.S. marines to Lebanon triggered a violent reaction. On April 18, 1983, the United States Embassy in Beirut was car-bombed. Sixty-three people were killed, including seventeen Americans. Afterward, the attackers were defiantly open about their motivation: *Americans, get out!* had been the message.

On August 29, the Lebanese civil war reignited. U.S. marines were drawn into firefights, with two killed and fourteen wounded. Democrats began demanding that the 1973 War Powers Act — which gave Congress the right to set constraints on a president's ability to make war, a law that remains subject to dispute to this day — be invoked.

By September, it was obvious that the American military role in Lebanon had grown beyond its stated mission as a peacekeeping force. Increasingly, our marines there were seen as belligerents on the side of Israel and the Lebanese Christians, and thus as enemies of the Muslim communities. By October, Secretary of Defense Caspar Weinberger was warning Reagan that the Syrians and other enemies of the Christian-led government regarded the Americans in their midst as combatants. From offshore, American ships were pounding Muslim positions in the mountains, with U.S. marines in forward positions acting as spotters. Worse yet, they had been assigned to what essentially was guard duty at Beirut International Airport. This placed them in close proximity to a radical Muslim neighborhood, which the marines had nicknamed "Khomeiniville."

The clock was ticking until the next wave of retaliation.

What was now clear was that the deployment to Lebanon fell under the provision in the War Powers Act's category of troops placed in a situation "where imminent involvement in hostilities is clearly indicated." That provision requires that the Congress approve any continued U.S. military involvement where U.S. forces face active hostilities. It is quite specific. Troops must be withdrawn within sixty days —

ninety, if the president asserts he needs more time — unless Congress specifically authorizes them to remain in the war zone. The marines' circumstances in Beirut clearly met the act's standards of "imminent involvement in hostilities." As Tip O'Neill put it, "The marines are being shot at and are firing back."

However, despite the ongoing September fighting, the Democrats in Congress, led by O'Neill, refused to use the War Powers Act as a way to order the marines to leave. "We discussed showing a united front," he reported after a phone conversation with Jim Baker. "We are in there with three other nations. . . . we want to work together for the betterment of world relations and peace. And if Syria, for any reason, thinks the parties of America are divided and they can just hang around till we pull out, I would say they are wrong."

The Speaker was taking his cues from the House Foreign Affairs Committee. Key members of that panel, unfortunately, lacked his wariness of foreign entanglements, his "no more Vietnams" mind-set. One member of the Democratic leadership who called it as he saw it was Tom Foley. "That country is coming apart," he said at one backroom meeting I attended over the

Lebanon resolution. "The only difference in whether we put those troops in is how many casualties we're going to take."

At this point, the Speaker pushed for a resolution that gave the president what amounted to a grace period of a year and a half before he'd have to go back again for further congressional approval to keep Americans on the ground in Lebanon. He was putting his leadership behind a committee-made policy, including the trade-offs and compromises that involved. Here was Tip's defense of the time limit, just as I recall hearing it at the time: "If it were for six months, the Syrians would sit it out. If it were a year, it would be in the political sphere and at the height of the presidential campaign. So, eighteen months was the most favorable time."

But O'Neill was clearly counting upon Reagan, not the eighteen-month time frame, to ensure "a Vietnam-type escalation is avoided." "I believe the president when he says he has no plans to change the peace-keeping role of our Marines. I believe he is expending every possible effort to see that differences in Lebanon are settled through negotiations, not through force of arms."

It was Democratic congressman Sam Gibbons of Florida who made a speech that offered the compelling case *against* accepting the troop deployment. "If we are there to fight, we are far too few. If we are there to die, we are far too many." It's difficult for me to explain what was going through Tip's mind on Lebanon, how it ran so differently from his general fear of "another Vietnam," but in the end it was he and he alone who managed to sway enough Democrats to win. Even so, it was a close vote. The resolution to allow the U.S. marines to remain in Lebanon for another eighteen months passed the House 270 to 161, with 130 of Tip's Democrats voting "Yea" and 134 voting "Nay."

Right after the vote, President Reagan phoned the Speaker to thank him for his critical support. "He was grateful," O'Neill said, describing the call. "He thinks it was in the best interests of the nation. My response was that I hoped we could get the marines out as quickly as we possibly can and get the whole thing completed."

In truth, the Speaker was uncomfortable in the role he'd just stepped into. "I was doing my duty as a leader of the party and as an American. There will be plenty of things along the line that the president will not be happy with me," he told reporters. He hated being separated from his party's liberal, antiwar base, and that is precisely where he now was.

Reagan also thanked Tip publicly. "I want to thank the House of Representatives for its strong, bipartisan vote today supporting our policies in Lebanon and the continued presence of the U.S. peacekeeping force," said a Reagan statement. "This vote would not have been possible without the strong leadership of Speaker O'Neill."

One last detail remained. In order to solicit and win the bipartisan support Tip had supplied, Ronald Reagan had agreed to sign the resolution, thereby meeting the terms of the War Powers Act. He was, in O'Neill's view, doing no more than accepting the constitutional separation of powers between the executive and legislative branches of government, which required that he do so. "The important thing is not what the president said today but what he did," I told the New York Times . . . after the ink had dried.

In the early morning of October 22, 1983, Ronald Reagan was given the news that six island nations — Jamaica, Barbados, Dominica, Antigua, St. Lucia, and St. Vincent — in the eastern Caribbean were asking the United States to intervene in neighboring

Grenada. A British colony until 1974, Grenada lay about a hundred miles off the coast of Venezuela. With a population at the time of around ninety thousand, and a tropical climate, it was home to an offshore American medical school that would soon take on historic importance.

Two weeks earlier, the country's socialist leader, Maurice Bishop, had been placed under house arrest in a Cuban-supported Marxist coup d'état. Demonstrations and counterdemonstrations occurred. Bishop, briefly, was freed. Escalating violence brought civilian deaths. General confusion, not surprisingly, reigned. The unfortunate Bishop, along with members of his cabinet, quickly found himself put to death before a firing squad. At this, the island descended into chaos, without any formal government to speak of.

What's interesting is the way this small, little-known Caribbean island — its area roughly 133 square miles — became, along with Nicaragua, "an obsession," as one White House official put it at the time, for President Reagan. In a speech to the Organization of American States in February 1982, he'd noted specifically "the tightening grip of the totalitarian left in Grenada and Nicaragua." He'd viewed both places in the reflected light of Cuba, as Soviet beach-heads in the hemisphere. Those same half dozen neighbors of Grenada now calling for U.S. intervention had shared their concerns with Reagan the year before. This had occurred during a visit he and Nancy had paid to old Hollywood chum Claudette Colbert, who kept a second home on Barbados. The president had done a round of meetings with officials there that weekend.

At the time the Reagans had traveled to the Caribbean, Cuban workers on Grenada were building a ten-thousand-foot airstrip. Hearing of this project, Reagan worried it would be able to serve Soviet long-range bombers, as well as large Russian transport planes landing with arms for Central American insurgents. The one bit of news offsetting these disturbing revelations was that Bishop, the Grenadian prime minister, was not at all gung ho in turning his country socialist. He'd been encouraging private investment in hopes of making Grenada a popular tourist destination, and had made a ten-day visit to the United States to try to allay fears about his political intentions. Unfortunately, after Bishop's death at the hands of his rivals for power, that moderating factor was gone.

Adding to the impetus for action was the

presence of a thousand Americans on the island, six hundred of whom were students at the St. George's University School of Medicine, established seven years earlier. It was not unreasonable to think Americans studying there might be taken hostage or harmed in what looked to be such an unstable situation. "The cost of not doing Grenada," Reagan's defense chief, Cap Weinberger, said later, "was obviously greater than the cost of doing it. We didn't want students held 440 days as hostages." The memory of what had happened in Tehran, the incident that made Reagan's 1980 victory possible, was never far from the administration's mind.

"I've OK'd an outright invasion in response to a request by 6 other Caribbean nations including Jamaica & Barbados," Reagan jots in his diary.

On Sunday, October 23, he was once more wakened in the middle of the night, this time with news that the U.S. marine barracks in Beirut had been hit — catastrophically. A suicide bomber had driven into the barracks, where his vehicle exploded with enormous power, killing 241 marines.

In the language of the official report, "The truck drove over the barbed and concertina wire obstacle, passed between two Marine guard posts without being engaged by fire, entered an open gate, passed around one sewer pipe barrier and between two others, flattened the Sergeant of the Guard's sandbagged booth at the building's entrance, penetrated the lobby of the building and detonated while the majority of the occupants slept. The force of the explosion ripped the building from its foundation. The building then imploded upon itself. Almost all the occupants were crushed or trapped inside the wreckage." The FBI described it as the biggest non-nuclear blast on record.

Even under these terrible circumstances, the Speaker continued to stand by the American mission in Lebanon. It was painful to have American fighting men robbed of their lives on an assignment hard to reconcile with even an expanded notion of American security. Even so, he felt, to pull out the marines now "would be the worst possible thing we could do."

Years after, O'Neill would look back to a briefing he'd gotten from the president's top national security advisor, Robert Mc-Farlane.

He spoke of an agreement under which the Israelis and the Syrians would remove their troops, and the prime minister of Lebanon would put together a new, broader cabinet. As part of the new arrangement, we would keep our marines in Beirut as the symbol of American power and prestige. Put that way, the presence of the marines made sense. But at the time, nobody mentioned that their real mission was to protect the highly exposed Beirut airport. When neither the Syrians nor the Israelis withdrew, our boys became increasingly vulnerable. Not knowing the real purpose they would be serving, I supported the president's decision to keep the marines in Beirut. In the House, I delivered enough Democratic votes to give us a bipartisan policy with regard to Lebanon.

There's an expression, "mission creep," that I think applies here. The sad fact was, the administration had engaged in a maneuver changing the terms of the marines' assignment without being up front about what it was doing. They had committed troops to a diplomatic role — one that ended up with them patrolling the Beirut airport, often with unloaded guns — that was, or should have been, wholly unacceptable. Cast officially as peacekeepers, they were regarded in the region not merely as unwanted interlopers but as imported allies of the Lebanese Christians and, even more dangerously, as foreigners secretly answering to Israel.

That Monday morning, the day after the barracks was hit, Reagan called O'Neill and Senate leader Howard Baker for assurances. "Phoned Tip & Howard B. to express hope they'd stay firm on keeping the Marines in Lebanon — both said yes." At his daily press conference that morning, the Speaker grappled with what had happened as best he could. When asked if he had any "second thoughts" about backing the War Powers resolution on Lebanon, he fell back on the argument that none of the options before the House, even the six-month limitation of the troop deployment, would have gotten the marines out in time.

Question: Should we pull out?

Speaker: In my opinion, that would be the worst possible thing we could do. We are committed to the Middle East. I think it would be a victory for our adversaries, particularly Russia, and, I think, Syria, who is acting as a satellite of Russia. . . . What would happen to free Europe in the event they would lose the oil fields to Russia?

Question: Do you think the U.S. has an obligation to stay in the Middle East?

Speaker: We are committed to the Middle East regardless. That is the policy of the U.S. The troops were there when the bloodshed happened when the Israelis were pulling out, as a peacekeeping force, to see if we could keep foreign nations out, and, thirdly, to see if we could help stabilize the government. I think, personally, to pick up and run would send a terrible message, particularly to moderate Arabs of that area who are depending on us, and to the terrorists of the world who have said they could drive us out. I don't see this as a political issue. I hope my party . . . believes that we are Americans first and Democrats second.

Question: Did you tell Reagan you thought the marines should be on ships?

Speaker: No.

Question: Did he raise that with you?

Speaker: Our discussion was about the grief that both of us have about the tragedy that has happened to America.

Question: Do you think you can succeed in dealing with your party so that it won't become a partisan issue?

Speaker: I certainly hope so. There has been no bigger adversary of the president than the Speaker of the House — both on domestic and foreign policy. Throughout the years I have tried to support the President on foreign policy because I think it's in the best interests of the country. I split with Johnson over Vietnam policy. I try to make a solid judgment as to when the country is right. I think we are wrong in Central America, but I think this is in the best interests of America.

Asked if he trusted President Reagan, O'Neill said he wouldn't have voted for the Lebanon resolution if he didn't. Then he added: "But no one thought there would be terrorists." The one responsible — and accurate — defense of such a statement is that he and Reagan both retained a mind-set that saw wars fought on battlefields between national armies. Despite all recent history saying otherwise, what still, for him, made the most sense — even in a senseless world — was the idea of trained soldier against soldier, not a smiling suicidal car-bomber raging forward in the dead of night.

It was a tough time for the Speaker. It was especially hard that morning, knowing that he'd pushed for the resolution giving the president a year and a half to continue his operation in Lebanon. Thus, he found himself in an excruciating position: one he recognized as only bound to get more so, of backing Reagan against his own Democratic base, which would be pushing hard for a pullout.

Now came the U.S. action that would focus Ronald Reagan — and the American people — once again on the familiar East-West rivalry. Later that Monday, after the president had phoned both Tip O'Neill and Senate leader Howard Baker, White House Chief of Staff Jim Baker met with the Speaker in his Capitol back office. He told Tip that the president needed to see him that night for a hush-hush meeting. A Secret Service car would pick him up. Resisting the cloak-and-dagger, O'Neill said he'd have his own driver bring him to the White House.

That night, O'Neill and the other congressional leaders, for the first time, were informed that the United States was in the process of invading Grenada. In a ninety-minute briefing they were given the full rationale: the assassination of Bishop, the ten-thousand-foot airport strip being built that would allow the landing of heavy military aircraft, the call by the neighboring Caribbean countries to intervene, the American medical students at risk of turning into sitting ducks.

"You are informing us, not asking us," O'Neill told Reagan after hearing the decision to invade had been made, that the action was under way. According to Ken Duberstein, who was there, Reagan acknowledged that Tip was right, but that he had taken an executive action. Duberstein also recalled that the Speaker, from time to time, reached over and reassuringly touched the president on the arm. At the end of the meeting they shook hands, and Tip touched Reagan's elbow and said, "God bless you, Mr. President."

Then, after he'd finished laying out the Grenada plan, Reagan changed topics. Acknowledging that there were calls in Congress for the administration to build a better public case for staying in Lebanon, he suggested the possibility of his addressing a joint session of Congress. The Speaker endorsed this option, admitting, "I need some help."

As far as the invasion of tiny Grenada went, O'Neill wasn't yet ready to share his views. He "kept his own counsel," Duberstein recalled. The following morning, O'Neill continued to reserve judgment. "This is no time for the press, or we in public life, to be critical of our government," he said at his regular morning press conference back in the Capitol. "We are the opposition. They don't ask for my advice; they just tell me."

But while staying off the record on Grenada, the Speaker now gave an impassioned plea to stick with the president on Lebanon. When asked what he thought of those Democrats seeking a new resolution to shorten the marines' mission in Lebanon, he was brutal. "I am bitterly disappointed. When you are talking about America, you forget the party issue. I am acting as an American. I think it's the wrong thing to pick up and leave at this particular time."

It would, he voiced, signal American weakness. "The resolution would be to cut off funding as of January 1. But I think it is wrong. I think the fanatics and terrorists of the world . . . it would show they have accomplished what they have set out to do." What was important now was for President Reagan to make his own case, in his own words, as clearly as possible. "The people of America don't appreciate the fact of why the marines are there, and it's time for the president to explain it — and explain it better than his administration has." It would be to his advantage as well. He'd stuck his neck out for the Lebanon mission and now very much needed the president to give him protection with his own restless Democrats.

Yet, addressing a caucus of his fellow Democrats, he swung into a memorable declaration of "water's edge" foreign policy. "As the leader of our party, elected by you, I am not talking as a Democrat. Yes, I love partisans. They say I am the toughest partisan that has ever been in the House. I love politics. They say I am one of the toughest politicians in America, and I am proud of people like that." However, a different allegiance now called. "I am an American, and at a time of patriotism, I think what is in the best interest of this nation, and I try to lead my party down that road. I don't look to the next election. I don't look to the fear of being defeated in the ballot box."

On Wednesday, the day after the Grenada invasion, he was still not commenting on it. "I will have plenty to say when the action has stopped and our boys are secure." He was also waiting to hear what the president would say the next night, speaking simultaneously to the Congress and the American people, about both situations, Lebanon and Grenada.

What he heard was a Reagan defense of U.S. actions in Lebanon and Grenada, ending with a *cri de guerre* to resist Soviet aggression. "Not only has Moscow assisted and encouraged the violence in both countries, but it provides direct support through a network of surrogates and terrorists." The president was addressing both countries in the only terms he fully grasped, the Cold War, downplayed the swirl of confessional rivalries in Lebanon, ignoring the ongoing history of resentment against U.S. imperialism in the Americas.

If Lebanon and Grenada were worth us fighting for, as Reagan argued, then, by extension, so was Nicaragua. He was exploiting the absolute horror in Lebanon, along with the more troubling excursion into Grenada, and, out of both, building a case for what he and his advisors saw as justifiable aggressive action against Nicaragua. He was, at the same time, exploiting Tip O'Neill's backing for his policy in Lebanon and to-date silent acquiescence on Grenada to win the same bipartisan backing on what he might choose further to do in Central America. He was using Tip's old-fashioned patriotism to push a Nicaraguan policy that he was fully aware the Speaker could not abide. Essentially, he was tucking an unwilling Speaker into bed with him.

When he met with reporters the next morning, all the instinctive antagonism

O'Neill felt toward Reagan's Central American policy came bursting forth. He began by explaining why he'd remained silent as long as there was actual fighting in Grenada. He'd learned, he said, from former presidents what effect such political rifts on the home front do to the morale of those putting their lives on the line.

Then, what about the American medical students on Grenada? Were they truly in danger? "The question I asked the president was, 'Will we put them in danger by sending the marines in?' " What seemed obvious to the Speaker — and he was no longer reluctant to say so — was that, unless the military action off the Venezuelan coast was truly to protect students, the United States had no right to invade.

"He broke international law. I don't like that. I think he is wrong. To be perfectly truthful, he frightens me. I think he was looking for a reason to go there, and he found the opportunity last week. Whether it was right or wrong depends on the safety of our people. We can't go with gunboat diplomacy. The marines did a tremendous job down there, but we can't continue that route — going into Nicaragua and places like that. His policy is wrong and frightening. I sat silently by when it was going on, because I thought it was in the best interests of the men fighting down there."

Nonetheless, he avoided taking any jabs when it came to Reagan policy on Lebanon. "Nobody wants to cut and run. They want the safety of the marines. I think the average Member of Congress knows what our policy is in the Middle East. We fight for the protection of the people in that part of the world, and that means so much that there be peace over there."

The following week he announced the formation of a bipartisan fact-finding committee that he would send to Grenada. It would be cochaired by Tom Foley, the Democratic whip, and Wyoming's Dick Cheney from the Republican leadership. Kirk and I were to go along. I was entrusted specifically with ensuring that California congressman Ron Dellums didn't commandeer the headlines with his opposition to the invasion. The very last thing the Speaker wanted was to give the Republicans a chance to spin "the Democrats" as discrediting the president's success in saving American lives.

My recollection of St. George's, the capital, is of a lagoon city straight out of Errol Flynn swashbucklers. British, quiet, and quaintly colonial, it appeared at the moment an unlikely hotbed of Marxist revolutionary sentiment. Clearly, the Grenadians had been glad to see the Americans. We overnighted at the Calabash, a grouping of small cottages stretched along a tree-lined beach. For dinner, we ate K rations and drank a very good white wine. And, given all the hype about the cache of weapons, I was unimpressed. The only guns on display were a pile of old rifles that could have been collected from any shed in Pennsylvania's deer hunter country. As for the Cuban construction workers I saw squatting in an outdoor stockade, I felt only embarrassment for my country. What right did the United States have to mount an invasion and take those men prisoner? Was our incursion truly justifiable as a rescue mission?

When I put that question to an American consular official over dinner in Barbados the next night, he was unequivocal. The issue was not about getting the medical students off the island. The coup leaders had made it clear every one of them was free to go. (The White House press room confirmed that two days before the invasion the Grenadian leaders had offered to allow the United States to come and retrieve them.) When I asked my dinner companion to explain the invasion, his answer was unforgettable. "There were other factors," he said, poker-faced.

Thinking what I'd just heard important information to return to Washington with, I approached Tom Foley and his cochair. My mistake was to believe this "fact-finding" mission actually involved finding facts, especially any that contradicted the intended salute to the U.S. invasion. When Cheney heard me question the Reagan administration contention that the students' safety was its driving concern, he struck me as irritated and certainly dismissive. Looking back, it should not have surprised me. The mission was to support the president's action, not assemble a bill of particulars opposing it.

Whatever the Speaker thought at the time, the fix was in. When it came to Grenada, nobody wanted to fight a fight that was already won. After hearing from the Foley-Cheney committee, the Speaker went along with its finding that Reagan's invasion of Grenada was justified. "But he better not try this again," he added. (That is, the president had better not take my grudging okay for this strike into a communist-leaning country as license to repeat the show in Nicaragua.)

Years later, Tip O'Neill would offer his own lasting verdict on the Reagan action of

October 25, 1983. "Today I feel even more strongly that we should not have invaded Grenada. Despite what the administration claimed, the students were never in danger. None of the students trapped in the second campus of the medical school for nearly two days after the invasion were harmed, and neither were any of the American residents on the island. But over a hundred American troops were killed or wounded in that operation. And as far as I can see, it was all because the White House wanted the country to forget about the tragedy in Beirut."

It's consistent with what I remember him feeling at the time. But Grenada was one thing, Lebanon another. The continued presence of American marines in Lebanon — a deployment he was on record as supporting — steadily grieved him. Tip was like a burn victim, and any touching of the wound was excruciating. I remember one day when Kirk and I were sitting in front of his desk and he suddenly asked if anyone on the Democratic leadership team had been against the sending of our troops into Beirut. "Chris was," Kirk said, cutting through the powerful silence. He was being loyal to me, respectful of my opposition to the misconceived campaign — but I don't

445

think it made the Speaker all that happy to hear it.

The Speaker was, quite simply, in a bad mood. In a conversation with James Reston — one Tip and I both had believed was for "background" use only — he'd been frank about a number of issues. And particularly rough on the president, expressing his opinion that he didn't think he'd seek a second term in 1984. Anyway, Nancy Reagan, he cracked to Reston, wanted to go back home and become "Queen of Beverly Hills." It was this last comment that convinced me Tip, authentically, had believed his exchange with the veteran Reston was not for publication. That's because he never ever, as long as I worked for him, took a shot at any member of any person's family. And it was especially true of the First Lady, about whom he would never ever say a negative word. He was stricken.

The moment he saw the quote in the *Times,* he immediately telephoned Mike Deaver, asking what he might do to make amends. Deaver's advice was to send a handwritten letter, which he did. The Speaker understood that the bleak misery he felt over Beirut and the fix he'd gotten himself into by backing Reagan had nothing to do with the man's wife, whom he admired. The trouble was, as David Rogers wrote in the *Boston Globe*, quoting a friend of the Speaker's in the House, "Lebanon is eating his heart out."

Within a month of the Beirut attack, the unity of the Reagan team was in shambles. "President Reagan is facing growing political and military sentiment within his administration to remove U.S. Marines from Lebanon or to redeploy them soon to safer positions, officials said yesterday." This lead in the *Washington Post*, reported by long-time Reagan-watcher Lou Cannon, revealed deepening discontent with the policy for which Reagan continued to cheerlead. One top presidential adviser, quoted by Cannon, identified Lebanon now as the administration's "Achilles' heel." Chief of Staff Jim Baker and defense chief Cap Weinberger had both joined the let's-get-them-out-of-there chorus.

With the arrival of 1984, Tip O'Neill warned Reagan either to produce diplomatic gains in Lebanon soon or else face the consequences. The "status quo," the Speaker insisted, had become unacceptable. By the end of January, Reagan himself was envisioning a shift. "We're going to study a possible move of the Marines to the ships off shore," he wrote in his diary, "but an Army force on shore to train the Lebanese army in anti-terrorist tactics."

Yet for the time being, Reagan stuck strictly, in public, to the administration line: the marines must stay. Three days after committing the shift in plans to his diary, there were news reports of a "hot" fight with the Speaker, during the course of which the president had insisted he would not let terrorists drive the United States out of Lebanon. "I tried to tell him the facts of life as I saw them," O'Neill said afterward.

Reagan was getting increasingly angry about the way he was being covered by the media. "Dropped in for a minute on the T.V. anchor men & women who were being briefed on tonites St. of The Union address. I cannot conjure up 1 iota of respect for just about all of them." When he went on to deliver the State of the Union, he carefully tried to brush off the subject of Lebanon. But the Speaker wasn't letting him off the hook. "In a ten page speech," Tip said, "he devoted only one paragraph, buried on page eight, to this vital subject. The president can try to bury the issue of Lebanon in his speech. But he cannot bury it in the minds and hearts of the American people."

The very next day, Reagan again addressed more fully in his diary what he'd neglected to deal with in his speech to Congress and the nation. "We took up the business of Beirut again with a plan for redeployment of the Marines but only after sending in Army training units who specialize in anti-terrorist measures." His plan was to get the Lebanese president ". . . to ask for this change." Meeting with Republican House members the next day for breakfast, he held to the administration position that removing the marines would be defeat. "I gave a little lecture on why we can't bug out," he wrote. "We're trying to get the Israeli lobby which is very effective in the Cong. to go to work on how much Israel has to lose if Congress forces a withdrawal of our troops."

He was also giving thought to Lebanon's effect on his reelection. "Campaign time is coming closer even though I have not actually said the words to anyone (except Maureen and Nancy) that I'll run."

At this point, Tip was starting to get wind of Reagan's actual intentions in the matter of the marines in Beirut. "One night, at a social event, I ran into a White House official who said, 'Isn't it great that the president is planning to bring home the marines?' He must have assumed that I knew the decision had already been made, but it was news to me." He certainly knew *now*! Still, it was an advantage he knew how to run with. "The next day I seized the initiative and came out with a statement demanding once and for all that the president bring the boys home. The president's response was to try to make me the villain."

Which is to say that when the Democrats passed a resolution on February 1 that called for a withdrawal of the marines, Reagan spokesman Larry Speakes instantly went on the attack. The Democrats' proposal, he sneered, "aids and abets" the enemy in the Middle East. I recognized an old communist-baiting phrase even if the guy who'd said it didn't. The instant I heard Speakes's comment, I called reporters at the White House. "Aiding and abetting is legal language for being a traitor," I told ABC's Sam Donaldson. I said that Speakes was engaging in "a new form of McCarthyism . . . Charlie McCarthyism." Puppetlike, Reagan's spokesman was speaking in Reagan's idiom.

Reagan himself now went straight for the Speaker, attacking Tip for refusing to defend a policy even the president had quietly abandoned. "He may be ready to surrender," the president told the *Wall Street*

Journal, "but I'm not."

Soon, however, the administration plan to pull out the marines was no longer a secret. Within the week, the White House announced they were being redeployed to the sea. The *Journal* itself chronicled the now public switch: "Only five days later, the president announced he would do just what he had so harshly criticized the speaker for advocating. Some observers believe the disarray may give the Democrats a potent election-year issue by damaging the president's credibility just as he's gearing up for his reelection effort." Even more damningly, a former defense secretary was quoted as saying of Reagan's team, "They are cutting and running . . . but they don't want to admit it. They want to have it both ways."

Congressman Lee Hamilton, a Foreign Affairs Committee member who had supported the Lebanon policy, offered its best epitaph. "I don't think there is much evidence that the military power we deployed off the coast of Lebanon had any effect on events, on the way political events were developing. I don't find much evidence that military power helped accomplish our goals. As events wore on, they were not able to carry out a peacekeeping function. They were no longer perceived as neutral. Their only function had become one of defending themselves."

But the politics of the Lebanon disaster weren't finished. Reagan continued to claim that Democratic opposition to his Lebanon policy had encouraged the terrorists. O'Neill was nastier still. "The deaths lie on him, and defeat in Lebanon lies on him and him alone."

It's not hard to deny the bad blood that came out of it. Reagan was angry because O'Neill failed to stick with his policy. O'Neill was angry he'd been led to join it at the outset. Both were bitter, deeply and understandably so, that history — and their consciences — now marked them for the deaths of young patriots, all killed on a mission to which smarter, better leaders would have never sent them.

Tip O'Neill joins ABC's Charles Gibson on election night 1984 to see how correspondents get their early results. Gibson would later become the network's top anchor. On the far right is O'Neill aide Jack Lew, the future secretary of the treasury.

Chapter Eighteen:
Victory and Survival

"I don't need you when I'm right."
— Tip O'Neill

In February 1984, Tip O'Neill told Martin Tolchin, a reporter for the *New York Times* whom he'd long known, that he might retire at the end of the year if Reagan was defeated for reelection. He explained to Marty that he had wondered how it would be to serve as ambassador to Ireland for a Democratic president. However, if Reagan was reelected, the Speaker said, then he'd run for one more term.

He would later dutifully list his reasons. First, there was the fear of hanging around too long, as he believed previous Speakers Sam Rayburn and John McCormack had done. Second, he was starting to think about spending more time with his family, whom he felt he'd shortchanged during his three decades of Washington politics. Finally, his sense of fairness to Jim Wright, waiting around for his job, came into play. Wright, after all, had been loyal and deserved his "day in the sun."

Separately and together, these were the seventy-one-year-old's true emotions. "I could have stayed on indefinitely," he would later remark, "but I had no great desire to end up as a tottering old congressman." However, the Speaker realized almost immediately — soon after the *Times* photographer arrived at the office, to take a picture to run with the piece — that he'd made a pronouncement he might quickly regret. "See what happens when you make a casual statement when you think you are talking to a friend?" he confessed at that morning's press session. "My wife said to me this morning, 'We have been married for 43 years and have known each other for 50 years, and you have never had enough sense to keep your mouth shut.' So I can't say anything more than that. I love Jim Wright. He is a beautiful man. When I do leave, I would be very much disappointed if he were not elected Speaker."

Knowing from experience the justified ambition of a man elected majority leader, his words to us that same morning were less flowery. "I intend to be Speaker right up to the last day. If Jim Wright tries anything, I'll cut his balls off." He knew better than anyone how a majority leader can promote himself to de facto party chief while another man still sits in the Speaker's chair. Nevertheless, he called Wright and apologized for the whole thing.

O'Neill's true rival, of course, was still sitting in the Oval Office. For both seasoned pols, 1984 would offer trials neither could have seen coming. What makes politics a learning profession is the need to master situations that elude prediction. That aspect of the game is precisely what makes politics so fascinating to the observer, so treacherous to the ungifted. Fortunately for Tip and the Gipper, their capabilities were perfectly matched to the tests ahead.

O'Neill was a political retailer. His strengths were of the one-on-one sort: making and maneuvering friends, intimidating, bluffing, outnumbering — or outlasting — challengers. He knew *everyone,* knew their children, knew their problems, and, more often than humanly imaginable, *cared.* He would show he did by calling upon what seemed an encyclopedic stock of information he maintained about so many of the people he knew. He would remember the relative who was sick, which kid had gone to which college. It was a skill he'd finely tuned, and it was one based, as far as I could see, on the fact he simply thought such matters were important.

Reagan was the wholesaler of the two. He had few friends, and saw his associates as largely interchangeable, if not outright dispensable. At one White House reception, he greeted one guest as "Mr. Mayor" only to discover he was a member of his cabinet. His son Michael had been treated to the same experience at his high school graduation. "Dad, it's me," he'd found himself saying.

But if he focused on few individuals in particular, he was superb when it came to addressing the mass audience. That was the connection he never got wrong. When reaching out to his fellow citizens, he had no rival.

Above all, he was convincing. The average guy out there had no way to grasp the craft this man brought to the presidency. Though Reagan was the fellow charged with running the U.S. government, when he belly-ached about "the deficits," he sounded just like your next-door neighbor. The country went for it. Again and again, speaking as the occupant of the White House, Reagan, adopting a scolding tone, would censure not just "deficits" but the government itself, as if he and it had no connection to each other. He could speak and act as if "Washington" — always a villain in his vocabulary — was a place where he only rarely, and then just by necessity, spent any time.

In March 1984, as he was in the fourth year as the nation's chief executive, I wrote an essay on Reagan for *The New Republic*. I argued that the role affected by the man now in the White House was very little different from that of the man who'd once hosted *General Electric Theater*. His great achievement, in both instances, was to position himself as existing in a previously unidentified space. As president, where he looked out from was a "unique point — previously uncharted — *between* us and government."

If you thought about it, the Ronald Reagan we were getting in the 1980s strangely resembled the 1950s version. Back then, just as now, he was handsome, upbeat, and, above all, persuasive. "Here at General Electric," he would declare convincingly as we sat there in our living rooms, "progress is our most important product."

Yet that "here" didn't mean a factory somewhere, one of those buildings where assembly lines turned out GE products. "Here" was the "host's" chair, located in a mysterious dimension between not just his listeners and the actual corporation, but also between it and him. I'd grown up with that Ronald Reagan, and I came to recognize that if the old one and the new one blurred together for me, there was a reason. On occasions such as when he stood on the West Front of the Capitol beseeching the Congress to produce a constitutionally mandated "balanced budget" — an accounting reality that he, Ronald Reagan, president of the United States, had never once felt the need to send to the Congress — I couldn't help feeling a bit of déjà vu.

Tip O'Neill gloried in being a man of government, believing he could do good for people because that's what he'd chosen to be. The downside was that he'd never match Reagan's ability to connect with the American public at large, and, unfortunately, in the election year of 1984, neither did his preferred candidate for president.

Like Tip, Walter Mondale — a former two-term Minnesota senator and then for four years Jimmy Carter's vice president — was quite capable of connecting to individuals. He was even better, though, with groups.

When speaking in public, he'd developed a knack for appealing to agglomerations of people by homing in on the parts that made up the whole. For example, he would reach out to a packed fund-raising dinner with such comforting embraces as "standing shoulder to shoulder with labor," or "giving teachers the resources they need and then getting out of the way," or a strong applause line backing the State of Israel. As he went warmly and knowingly on, cycling through the familiar litany of Democratic interests, different clusters of tables would loudly applaud. The folks sitting at them knew he was talking *straight* to them.

The problem was, rarely did he ever manage to hit a note in 1984 that caused an entire banquet hall to roar in excitement. As the candidate anointed by the Democratic establishment to run against Ronald Reagan, he operated under a severe handicap. Unlike the man he hoped to dethrone, he was able to offer neither a fresh message nor a manner that could thrill his entire party, much less a majority of the American electorate. He simply didn't operate like that. What he operated like was the steward of various interest groups that he was, tending to each according to each's wants. When urged to display independence, his response

461

was instinctive: "Why would I want to fight with our friends?"

This isn't to say he wasn't popular. The elected Democrats in Congress and around the country saw him as their brother in arms, a guy who'd worked his way up "through the chairs" as they had. In his case, he'd worked in the 1948 Senate campaign of Hubert Humphrey, served in the army, then attended law school on the G.I. Bill, stayed active in home-state politics, and wound up himself a senator, arriving in Washington in 1965. A native of tiny Ceylon, Minnesota, he'd been loyal to every mentor and patron along the way, including Jimmy Carter. He would be equally faithful to the Democratic interest groups, especially the big labor unions, if elected president. His problem was that the world at large knew this, including those who thought the interest groups had enjoyed too much clout for too long already. The same world at large believed it was time for the Democrats to have a candidate free of the musty rooms where candidates swore fealty to the groups before they cut their deal with the voter.

Senator Gary Hart — born Gary Hartpence, he'd shortened his name in his twenties — was such a candidate. Eight years younger than Mondale, but also more stylistically youthful in manner and appearance, he hailed from Colorado. That made him a man of the West, an idea that carried a certain romantic resonance in American public life, and though he'd managed the presidential campaign of leftish George McGovern, he carried the brand of a moderate independent. He was the fresh, outdoorsy breeze that could just possibly blow the septuagenarian Republican out of the White House. Where Mondale would be asking the voter to retrace his or her steps and admit they'd taken the wrong path in 1980, this less familiar face could say it was simply time, once again, to move forward.

In full candor, that's how I looked at the Democrats running in 1984. But it was not the way my boss did. Tip O'Neill liked political *regulars*. And it would cost him. When the big upset arrived, it came early. Even though it only involved Hart's coming in a distant second in the Iowa caucuses, the Coloradan suddenly was in position as the Mondale alternative, which is precisely what many Democrats were looking for. In the buzzword of the day, he then "slingshot" himself from Iowa to a convincing victory over the former veep in New Hampshire.

Now came the big test, on 1984's Super Tuesday, March 13, when nine states held contests. Going in, the Mondale people understood their man was hovering, politically, at death's door. Fortunately, the not-quite-deceased had Bob Beckel, a clever troubleshooter, working on strategy. Beckel, writing the story his way, put out word to the media that if his candidate, who was Jimmy Carter's vice president, tanked in Jimmy Carter's home state of Georgia, he was finished. Now, on that Tuesday, there were, as I said, nine states voting, including large ones like Florida and Massachusetts. Beckel's genius was to make it seem, just as he intended, that it was all about *that one southern state.* Losing Georgia would be the knockout punch Mondale dealt to Hart.

Beckel then filled Washington's Capitol Hilton ballroom to the rafters for the Mondale victory party. Calling in every chit he had out, he instructed lobbyists, contributors, and job-seekers alike that it was "show up, or else." To make the crowd appear even bigger, he used the old Kennedy advance man's tactic of shrinking the room itself. "We threw up a partition that made the room a third the size of the ballroom. You couldn't move in the fuckin' place." He wanted that crowd of meal tickets already in position at ten o'clock when NBC began its hourlong network special coverage of

Super Tuesday.

Beckel's ruse worked. Though Mondale lost six of the nine contests that day — Florida, Massachusetts, Nevada, Oklahoma, Rhode Island, and Washington — and won only in Alabama, Georgia, and Hawaii (also in American Samoa), he hogged the coverage. Hart's actual dominance mattered little. Mondale's ace operator had spun it so brilliantly. If losing Georgia spelled defeat, then winning it spelled victory. It was that simple. And so, a few minutes after 10 p.m. Eastern Standard Time, Bob Beckel announced the great news to a crowded ballroom on live NBC television. To the viewers at home, what they saw was indistinguishable from a Mondale victory party. The next morning, when Beckel appeared on *Today*, host Bryant Gumbel congratulated him. "Yup," Bob beamed, "it's the comeback of the year."

But the old tricks went only so far. They couldn't make Walter Mondale the candidate to beat Ronald Reagan in 1984. The main issue wasn't that he came across, as he put it, as "official" that spring, as he warded off the lanky, mop-haired Hart, but that the economy was turning itself around. From its height in late 1982, the country's unemployment rate had cascaded three points. And as the numbers were going down, the country's mood was heading up. Things were looking brighter and people were beginning to feel it. All it would take now would be a Reagan campaign that seized the advantage of that percolating national feeling. All the Mondale people could rely upon, thematically, was the invocation of past eras and past pain.

As the primary season wore on, Mondale's electioneering — a slog if ever there was one — demanded that Democrats wear a happy face. But it was hard. Especially for such staunch old liberal Democrats as the Speaker. Young voters, in particular, weren't buying his candidate. Tip could see this and didn't like it a bit. He'd observed how, at home in Massachusetts, Hart had been the one drawing the younger crowds. "I think it will be right down to the wire. Hart is the frontrunner, and he will have to make sure there are no soft spots in his armor, because he will be attacked from every angle. I had hoped we could get everything out of the way . . . so we could go for the common enemy — the fitness of the president to run the government . . . his complete lack of knowledge with regard to foreign affairs."

Tip was not a happy man. The economy was now working on behalf of the Republicans. The Democrats lacked both a coherent message and a charismatic candidate able to forge one. "We have the Boston Marathon and there is a place called 'Heartbreak Hill.' Mr. Mondale is going up that hill." The Speaker could see that the odds of limiting Ronald Reagan to a single term were beginning to lengthen.

O'Neill's resentment toward Reagan was growing, no doubt increased by the president's enhanced election-year standing. There'd been the usual niceties, like the House singing "Happy Birthday" after Reagan had finished delivering the State of the Union. "Well, he still calls me on the telephone, and we talk," O'Neill told a reporter in January who asked about their relations. "That is the way it should be. Our party is the adversaries of those who run the government. We are expected to criticize. Some of us do and there are others out there who should do it more often."

In late February, he tried a different sort of explanation for the often seesawing relationship. "On St. Patrick's Day, I will probably have lunch with him. That is how democracy works. I go to France and Italy, and the majority never speaks to the minority. I can argue with Bob Michel and he can say severe things about me — and we play golf on the weekend. I go with Silvio Conte and play bridge with him. You can disagree, but still be friendly. I don't see anything wrong with that."

What didn't go away, and what only got worse as time passed, was the way O'Neill remained haunted by Beirut. In April, when Reagan took unfair partisan aim at the Democrats by citing the deployment they'd agreed to, O'Neill ripped back with a hay-maker, saying only one person bore responsibility for the dead marines, and that was "the president of the United States."

After this exchange, a hard-line Reagan supporter sent a letter of complaint to the White House. "I must not be too bright," it began. "You and Speaker of the House Tip O'Neill have a few disagreements — but when you are shown together whether on TV or in a photo there is always a feeling of camaraderie, arms around each other, smiling faces. Yet this man O'Neill (and I realize you both are of Irish extraction) holds you responsible for the deaths of 260 of my people — Americans!"

The writer went on to add a postscript. "I think what I'm trying to say, Mr. President, is I can't stand seeing Speaker O'Neill continually do what he does to you and you turning the other cheek."

Reagan's handwritten response was attuned to the writer's keen partisanship. "I don't think you've seen me embracing or being embraced by Speaker O'Neill recently. And yes I find some of his personal attacks hard to forgive. He's an old line politico. Earlier in my term and before recent events he explained away some of his partisan attacks as politics and that after 6 p.m. we were friends. Well that's more than a little difficult for me to accept lately."

May was not a good month for O'Neill. Depressed by the Democrats' divisive primary battles, dismayed by the Reagan comeback, he now faced an assault from across the aisle in the House. Led by Newt Gingrich, a firebrand from Georgia, Republican backbenchers had organized a sly series of daily assaults on the Democratic Party foreign policy record. Each evening, after the House's official business was completed, Gingrich's merry band of ideologues took the floor to make use of a legislative time slot known as "Special Orders."

Previously, what went on in these "Special Orders" involved less-than-scintillating readings-into-the-record having little to do with issues any broader than, say, showing support for a chrysanthemum festival back home. However, Newt Gingrich's insurrectionist zeal had led him to see opportunity where others registered only tedium. The new, insidious use he made of the previously snoozeworthy "Special Orders" was simple: get in there and dump on the Democrats. And since there were members remaining on the floor to speechify, the C-SPAN cameras, as always, were recording their monologues as if they were normal House debate. What the viewers at home couldn't see, however, was the row after vacant row of seats in the chamber. Everyone had gone home. It was truly an empty House.

You had to hand it to Gingrich. The escapade was simple, diabolical, and for his revolutionary purposes, effective. Tip, of course, was incensed. What got to him more than anything else was that Gingrich was playing to those unoccupied benches while vigorously attacking the national security records of a host of Democrats, including Massachusetts congressman Edward Boland, Tip's career-long pal. "The camera focused on Gingrich, and anybody watching at home would have thought that Eddie was sitting there, listening to all of this," O'Neill would later recall. "Periodically, Gingrich would challenge Boland on some point and then would step back, waiting for Eddie to answer. But Boland had left hours ago, along with everybody else in the chamber."

Fed up with the fact that this phony-baloney theater currently under way in his own front yard, Tip O'Neill decided to take action. The solution was as simple as the original inspiration. He directed that the House television cameras, which were under his control, begin panning the chamber. It was a true "gotcha" moment, and one of Gingrich's guys, Robert Walker of Pennsylvania, having been passed a note, suddenly understood they'd been unmasked. He now faced the ignominy of admitting right there on live television that the audience at home could now see there was no one in the House chamber but him. The contrivance of using the "Special Orders" to assault the Democrats' foreign policy record was being exposed in real time.

Naturally, the Republicans were testy. Yet, in the ensuing floor debate over the episode, it was the Speaker who, truly furious, lost control of his temper. Dropping his gavel, he left the Speaker's chair and ran down to the floor. He had something he wanted to say to Newt Gingrich, in particular, in defense of his fellow Democrats, and nothing was going to stop him. "You challenged their patriotism, and it is the lowest thing that I have ever seen in my thirty-two years in Congress."

Alerted by his floor assistant Billy Pitts that the Speaker had just ignored the House rules on personal attacks, Minority Whip Trent Lott of Mississippi demanded that what O'Neill had just said be "taken down." In House-speak, that meant that Tip's righteous blast be struck from the *Congressional Record.* Of course, he'd meant every word of it. "I was expressing my views very mildly, because I think much worse than what I actually said."

O'Neill's street-corner response to Gingrich had larger consequences. The Speaker of the House, provoked beyond what he could bear, had done the little-known Georgia congressman an immeasurable favor. Suddenly Gingrich had a startlingly higher profile. As Billy Pitts would point out, Tip had just made Gingrich a "household name."

Also around this time, the Speaker found he had another unanticipated problem on his hands: me. For whatever reason — ego, career restlessness, whatever — I began causing him trouble he didn't need. I mentioned that article I'd written for the

New Republic in which I described what I saw as Ronald Reagan's enduring identity as America's "national host." Not content to stop there, I then contributed a Sunday piece to the *Washington Post* in which I discussed the president's fondness for cinematic imagery, and also his playing to the hilt the Mr.-Reagan-Goes-to-Washington bit. As I earlier pointed out, too, he'd snatched Spencer Tracy's "Don't you shut me off; I'm paying for this broadcast" from *State of the Union,* transforming it to "I am paying for this microphone" in the 1980 New Hampshire primary debate.

I had a lot of fun putting the article together — since I am, as anyone who knows me will attest, a passionate movie buff — but I should have had the basic common sense to withdraw it the very second a *Post* editor told me that, when it ran, it'd be paired with one from a writer holding political views quite different from my own. As it turned out, the contribution that appeared in counterpoint to mine was a brutally satiric attack on Tip comparing him to — it still hurts to remember, I admit — W. C. Fields.

On Monday morning, Kirk alerted me that he'd heard from the Speaker's son Kip. Not surprisingly, the dueling pieces in the

473

Sunday *Post* had not gone over well with the family. Here's my journal entry that night.

Monday, May 7 —

Worst day. TPO mad as hell, tear ass at me for setting him up W Post.

"A half dozen people called me & asked me how I could let some guy . . . Just to get your name in the paper you let them humiliate me, just for a few bucks. If you want to do that, we don't want you here. The next time you write something like that clear it with us."

But the true *worst* was yet to come. For reasons that are easy to understand but difficult to defend, I'd allowed a number of magazines to write about my role with the Speaker. Initially, they had no effect, seeming not to cause a bother.

Then they did.

"You running for something?" Tip wanted to know after a small profile ran in the *Washingtonian,* the city's glossy monthly. But that was just a preview. The true blowup came when a new national men's magazine, *M,* featured yours truly as the one calling the shots in the Speaker's office. "Everyone in Washington who is anyone knows how Christopher Matthews guides the Speaker of the House."

"Guides." Where was I going to hide? And for how long? What's more, it quoted me saying the Speaker "hates" Reagan, a choice of word I recalled having self-corrected instantly to "resents." I'd merely been trying to temper the writer's over-the-top notions of the pair's collegiality. I believed that anyone reading the piece needed to know that the differences between O'Neill and Reagan were both real and heartfelt. However, such a convoluted excuse would have done me no good with O'Neill, even if I tried to offer it. The whole episode was a brutal lesson in excessive hubris. As Richard Nixon's speechwriter William Safire, later a columnist of the *New York Times,* put it, "I've been right and I've been paranoid, and *it's better being paranoid.*"

Wednesday May 30

- Worst day —
- TPO attacks me for the M article
- Said I made him look bad
- " 'Hated!' When did you ever hear me say I hated Reagan?
- "Do you think you came up with

Social Security issue?

- "I've got more political sense in half my ass than you have in your whole body. Do it again and I'll get rid of you."

And so went my attempts to win publicity and start a writing career while still on the job with the Speaker of the House. Forced to look back on these days, I can only wonder at my brashness and the man's forbearance. Nobody's perfect but, with all his anger, Tip O'Neill had the capacity to understand and let it go. A short while later, I managed to get a better expression of Tip's view of Reagan in a *Post* "Style" section column.

Speaker Tip O'Neill and President Reagan are Irishmen of a different green. Their running battles have not exactly been brawls, but they have been testy affairs at times. O'Neill likes to explain to Europeans that American political anger subsides at 6 p.m. When O'Neill was in Ireland on April 29, he publicly stated he would be opposed to any demonstrations against Reagan on the president's recent trip to the home sod. Or as his press aide Chris

476

Matthews puts it, "Tip believes in condemning the sin, not the sinner."

When I brought that item into the Speaker's back office and sat there alongside him, waiting for his reaction, I was glad to hear and see him laugh. "Penance," I said by way of explanation. He shook his head. No — he made clear in an instant — everything was already okay between us. A year later, Martin Tolchin would deliver a major piece about my role. "Whether or not Mr. O'Neill is the most partisan member of Congress, as many believe, Mr. Matthews is just about the most partisan of Congressional aides," his piece in the *New York Times* asserted. "The speaker acknowledges, moreover, that he has had to reign him in on occasion." The Speaker had no trouble at all with it. "It's all about the timing," was Kirk's verdict.

For President Reagan, the 40th anniversary of the Allied landings in Normandy would serve as an important symbol for his reelection campaign. In a speech broadcast from France and timed to be seen live on *Today, Good Morning America,* and the other TV morning shows, the president paid glorious tribute to the men, many now seated before him, who'd landed beneath the Normandy cliffs on June 6, 1944. Like millions of others, Kathleen and I watched the intensely moving broadcast. Though I was engaged full-time in a heated contest against the political Reagan, I once again was witnessing his special magic.

Refusing to act the warrior himself, his admiring and evocative praise of those who *had* been warriors now set him in a special place. He seemed to me at that moment the one person I knew of who could so convincingly conjure up the spirit of such a harrowing, glorious historical challenge that his own countrymen had met so perfectly.

Now it was time to take him on. The Democrats, led by Walter Mondale, were headed to their convention in San Francisco. What the ticket needed was what the nominee needed but didn't have. Buzz. Sizzle. *Pizzazz.* Tip O'Neill, who would be chairing the convention, knew just where to find it. "Sure I have a candidate," he said early in May. "Her name is Geraldine Ferraro, she's from New York, she's a Catholic, she's been an effective member of the House, and she's very smart."

Tip had been grooming the congresswoman from Queens for years, pushing her for top jobs in the House leadership. When other members complained about her ambition, O'Neill had his quick answer. "Sure she's pushy. That's what it takes in this business." When reporters called, I figured he wanted me to trumpet his endorsement of the Queens congresswoman.

"She has a lot of political moxie," I told the Associated Press. "The Speaker feels she would add to the ticket dramatically." With the *Times,* I went further, saying Ferraro would be the perfect foil in debate with Reagan's vice president and running mate, George Herbert Walker Bush. "She looks very classy, very familiar, whereas he's a red-and-green belt type guy who's a bit aloof." I pitched her as representing the populist, ethnic, big-city values of the crucial blue-collar voters who, four years earlier, had turned away from the party. Just possibly, Geraldine Ferraro could bring back the Reagan Democrats — the Notre Dame subway alumni — to the party of their roots.

After acquiescing to O'Neill's call for him to select Ferraro, Mondale turned and asked the Speaker for a favor. He wanted him to agree to stand down as the Democrats' leading spokesman. Otherwise, every day that Tip was featured on the evening news attacking Reagan, *he,* Fritz Mondale

— the actual candidate — wouldn't be. That's what he told him. The former vice president very clearly felt himself in the position of attempting to command the spotlight from underneath Tip's extralarge shadow. Unfortunately, any spotlight can be dangerous if and when you happen to make a mistake.

Conventions are always chaotic and exhausting, yet also exhilarating, and this one was no different. Also, I sometimes think that political parties are the most energized, the most galvanized, and have the best times when the going is roughest. However, in the end, the sole unforgettable moment came when Mondale called for a tax increase. "I was sitting in a broadcast booth with Dan Rather," the Speaker would recall, "and I couldn't believe my ears. It was a terrible mistake, which played right into the hands of the Republicans. It gave Reagan the opening he was looking for, and allowed him to use his favorite line on the Democrats: 'There they go again, tax and spend, tax and spend.' "

After Labor Day, after the campaign began in earnest, Tip started to show publicly his concern at the Democratic nominee's passivity. He called on Mondale to stop letting himself "be punched around" by the president, to "stop acting like a gentleman and come out fighting, to come out slugging." And Mondale did seem to start showing his teeth. In the first debate that fall, in Louisville, Kentucky, he in fact scored a clear victory over Reagan — and the public couldn't fail to miss what had happened.

"People in the White House tend to get old mighty quickly," O'Neill rubbed it in a few days later. Worse was the *Wall Street Journal* headline: IS OLDEST U.S. PRESIDENT NOW SHOWING HIS AGE? REAGAN DEBATE PERFORMANCE INVITES OPEN SPECULATION ON HIS ABILITY TO SERVE. Jim Baker, obviously shaken, felt worried enough to release copies of his boss's most recent medical report. If tests were any measure, the man sitting in the Oval Office remained "mentally alert."

Far more telling was this on-the-record observation by Howard Baker, the Senate Republican leader. "If the point of this is to get an inside view, you got more of that tonight than I've ever seen in public with Ronald Reagan."

Having watched Mondale attack his administration's record with such relish, Reagan, now the incumbent, was forced to take stock. "I never realized how easy it is to be

481

on the other side," he'd later admit. "Well, the debate took place & I have to say I lost. I guess I'd crammed so hard on facts & figures," he confessed in his diary. "I guess I flattened out — anyway I didn't feel good about myself."

But the lurking age issue was the serious question, and it wasn't going to go away. "Another disastrous performance," Reagan later wrote to himself, "could send Nancy and me packing, headed back to the ranch for good." He'd even heard one television correspondent refer to the matter of the seventeen years he had on his Democratic rival as the "senility factor."

But, from the start of the next debate, held in Kansas City, Reagan came prepared with one of those easy utterances he seemed to have been born to let fly. He'd used it before, had been counseled by debate advisor Roger Ailes to ready it now, and so had only to await his cue. When the chance to say it arrived, it came as a question directed to him about his ability to deal with suddenly escalating situations, say, the Cuban Missile Crisis, for example. After assuring the reporter who'd asked — and, of course, the tens of millions watching — that he felt up to the job, Reagan offered his beaut of a reply. "I want you to know that I will not make age an issue of this campaign. I am not going to exploit, for political purposes, my opponent's youth and inexperience."

Even Mondale chuckled. I have to think he knew his campaign's one brief, shining moment — that first debate, when he'd been able to overpower his opponent — would be forgotten in the cascades of laughter at what Ronald Reagan had just said.

Soon after, the course of the election stopped being in real doubt. The GOP ticket was going to walk away with the big chunk of the Democratic vote Tip O'Neill knew it needed to prevail. Out on the campaign trail, where the president was in his element — he'd perfected the whistle stop during those years of crisscrossing the country for GE — Reagan was thrilled to have the loyalty of blue-collar workers, "voters traditionally allied with my former associates in the Democratic party."

The Speaker, too, was leaving Washington regularly, to do his part supporting both Mondale-Ferraro, along with other embattled Democratic candidates. But when away from the Capitol, he'd encounter, though far less happily, the same voters the president had. One day, while in New Jersey campaigning for Mondale, he met a woman employee at a sausage factory. "I love Mr. Reagan," she informed the Speaker. And then, with some indignation, asked, "Why don't you leave him alone?"

Closer to home, but unknown to Tip — as well as to those of us looking out for him — trouble now was brewing. A group of those Watergate babies elected to Congress a decade earlier had started to get restless, and, foreseeing the Democratic losses facing them — including a large number of seats in the House — they were meeting secretly. They'd begun discussing what had previously been unthinkable — a change at the top. The talk tended toward a coup d'état, one that would challenge the leadership if November went as disastrously as feared. Whether that would include the Speaker himself was never spelled out.

My first inkling of what was up came by way of a hometown guy, Philadelphia congressman William Gray. I was at my desk in the Speaker's rooms when he found me and laid it on the line. There were members plotting against the leadership, and Bill, concerned, named several names. I refused to believe it. It came out of nowhere, as far as I was concerned, and seemed unthinkable. It marked the one, rare time when we, the people around him, whom the Speaker relied upon for intelligence, let him down. All those days of asking, "Anything I ought to know?" — and we'd failed to catch any telltale signs of a rebellion in the ranks.

It was the voters themselves who wound up saving the day. While the president won forty-nine states — carrying a quarter of the Democrats who voted — his party gained just fourteen seats in the House, losing two in the Senate. The American public had reembraced Ronald Reagan but held back when it came to his policies. "Well 49 states, 59% of the vote & 525 electoral votes," a defiant Reagan noted. "The press is now trying to prove it wasn't a landslide or should I say a mandate?"

But while the mixed message delivered by the electoral results dampened the confidence of the congressional plotters, it didn't stop them. The Speaker had put his weight behind Walter Mondale — an old-fashioned liberal of his own stripe — for the party nomination, and now he had to pay a price. Who's to say that a younger, lesser-known westerner like Gary Hart might not have given the aging Californian in the White House a real fight? Mondale had failed to, and that was what mattered. The defeat meant that Tip would now have to fight and win the battle his candidate had lost.

It turned out that two camps were arraying themselves against the Speaker that November. First, there were the conservative Democrats. Led by Texas congressman Charlie Stenholm, the guys on "Redneck Row" had been joined by moderates in the party from other regions of the country. The usual crew of twenty-nine had grown to seventy-five.

The second camp was this crowd elected in 1974 and 1976, drawn into politics by the drama of the Watergate era and the promise of a different Washington. From either the suburbs or urban middle-class areas, these members weren't part of the old Democratic machines. They were more likely to flaunt their independence. While the old breed, like Tip, Rosty, and New York's Charlie Rangel, was bonded to the folks back home by tribe and tradition, this crowd was more into change and reform. What they loved most was hanging out to discuss *policy*, especially "new ideas."

However, the characteristic they shared dearly with the old breed was a desire for more influence. They knew they'd have to wait decades to get the prized chairmanships. But that was the old way, and it wasn't good enough. What they wanted was to be *heard* — and heard *now*.

For Tip, this meant waging a war on two fronts. The first call I got from him was an instruction to keep him out of the newspapers. There'd been a moment, when he'd been out there fighting Reagan — after we'd talked him into accepting the spotlight — that he'd decided he might have been occupying too much of it. "I don't have to be on the front page every day," he'd kidded me back then.

This time around, he was deadly serious. If the hopes of those taking aim at him were so focused on his "image," Tip O'Neill was determined that it be a nonissue as he now went about the business of destroying those hopes.

The assault he planned on the first faction, the party conservatives, accomplished in true backroom style, was artful and old-school perfect. Its initial stage involved skillfully taking on those previously nonaligned individuals who'd joined up with the conservatives; he intended to peel them away, one at a time. He went to a member from Alabama who immediately swore his allegiance, and then, from that guy, heard of a Georgian who didn't feel he was getting enough attention. Next, he learned that a congresswoman from Maryland hadn't been allotted even a single slot to appoint a youth from her district to the minor but desirable patronage position of House page. Having won reelection several times, she wondered why her rising seniority hadn't been recognized. Tip saw to it she was immediately satisfied on this score. And so forth.

Tip and Leo Diehl went about the task at hand systematically, discovering each member's beef, and then figuring out the best method to resolve it. Charlie Stenholm saw what was happening and backpedaled, abandoning the rebellion he'd begun. "I found out that even some of my friends would not support it."

That left the other malcontents to deal with. But their yearning for regime change all of a sudden seemed to have lost steam. One day, Dick Gephardt of Missouri, its recognized leader, requested a sit-down with the Speaker. When Tip asked him just what it was he and his crowd wanted, his visitor explained that it was a matter of *process*. They didn't want Tip's head; they just wanted his attention. That's all.

So much for the revolution. The demands of the new-breed cabal now came down to all the various factions of the House joining together in a "Speaker's Cabinet," which would meet with the leadership and top committee chairmen on a regular basis to share in the big decisions of the day. Fine, O'Neill agreed. However, he set a giant condition. He, the Speaker, would get to select the members who'd be representing the various factions — the Young Turk crowd, the more conservatively inclined southerners, African-Americans, etc.

Each and every one he picked was, naturally, a trusted Tip ally.

Thus, the Speaker's Cabinet started its weekly sessions. For the spot, Tip chose his Capitol hideaway down the hall from his working office. It was a room without windows, encased in the thick marble of the Capitol's East Front. We met there on Wednesdays for breakfast, sitting around a square made up of several tables. The fare was heavy: eggs, bacon, sausages, fried potatoes, hot biscuits. What I recall about those mornings, more than anything else, was the mass fatigue of that bunch of well-fed politicians, up early and now wondering what, exactly, they were doing there. Dan Rostenkowski and Energy and Commerce chairman John Dingell were the outliers when it came to that very question: *why do I have to sit through this?*

They didn't have to wait for long. I think it was the third week of this peculiar exercise that the electricity went off in the Capitol, right in the middle of the eggs and bacon. Sitting together, there in the total darkness, surrounded by all that marble, the full absurdity of the occasion sunk in. While someone went for candles, the Speaker, Rosty, Dingell, and the other old-line chairmen just sat there. They might have muttered under their breath a bit, but they didn't have to. Their refusal to stand up and leave was their response. This wasn't *our* idea, they were signaling, but we're being good soldiers. You wanted us; here we are. Now what?

Eventually, the lights came back on, but the Speaker's Cabinet never met again.

When Inauguration Day arrived, on Monday, January 21, 1985, it was far too wintry, with the temperature hovering near to zero, to hold the oath-taking outside. The decision was made to move the swearing-in to the Rotunda of the Capitol. It proved a cozy ceremony. Though I'm six foot three, I remember having to stretch to see over people's shoulders as, once again, Ronald Reagan took the oath.

"In my fifty years in public life," Tip O'Neill said in salute to the president at lunch afterward, "I've never seen a man more popular than you are with the American people." O'Neill, himself, had won a measure of similarly genuine recognition from the other side. "For Republicans," said Congressman Bob Walker, a Republican firebreather, "he has become a polarizing figure, seen as an old-fashioned liberal wielding power dictatorially. But some Democrats see him as a kind of folksy figure who is making certain that the Democratic Party philosophy gets a fair hearing within government."

Neither Ronald Reagan nor Tip O'Neill would ever again have their names on a ballot. At ages seventy-four and seventy-two, they knew, despite their victory and survival, this was right and fair. They had both been visited by their political mortality.

It was Tip O'Neill who hand-delivered Reagan's letter asking Mikhail Gorbachev for a meeting. He told the new Soviet leader that the American president was sincere about negotiating a nuclear arms agreement and that he spoke for all the American people, not just the Republicans.

CHAPTER NINETEEN: MIKHAIL GORBACHEV

"Blessed are the peacemakers: for they
shall be called the Children of God."
— MATTHEW 5:9

Ronald Reagan had always fought a Cold
War he believed in winning. Not for him
the ambiguities of détente! In the classic
Hollywood ending he envisioned a day
when the Soviet Union fell and the West
stood alone in triumph. Where others were
resigned to what Jack Kennedy had called
in his inaugural address the "long twilight
struggle," Reagan looked to the morning.

He stood apart in another regard. Fellow
Cold Warriors held faith with nuclear weapons and the idea of the "balance of terror."
British prime minister Margaret Thatcher,
for one, believed that the existence of
nuclear deterrents had saved the planet
from World War III, from the end of World
War II in 1945 all the way through until the

1980s. The fact that total war between the United States and the Soviet Union could mean launching their huge stockpiles of intercontinental ballistic missiles against each other was sufficient to keep either side from pushing the other too far. For the West, it was also a way of offsetting the mighty on-the-ground edge of the Red Army in Europe.

The fortieth American president found little comfort in this strategic reliance on nuclear arsenals. According to Ron Reagan, his father's greatest nightmare was "that through misunderstanding, unforeseen circumstance, or some bizarre technical glitch, he would be compelled to launch our nuclear missiles." Though he understood the doctrine of "mutual assured destruction," he questioned the morality of it. "I have to believe," the elder Reagan had told his son, "the Russian people are no different from Americans. Hell, they're victims of their own government. Why should millions of them have to die, along with millions of our people, because leaders on both sides couldn't work things out?"

Secretary of State George Shultz would recall Reagan asking more than once: "What's so good about a peace kept by the threat of destroying each other?" Like John

494

F. Kennedy, he'd seen in human history the rule that once a weapon is devised, it is only a matter of time before it is used.

The president's own goal, as he'd explained in an "Address to the Nation on Defense and National Security" in March 1983, was the establishment of a land- and space-based system of strategic defense.

When I took office in January 1981, I was appalled by what I found: American planes that couldn't fly and American ships that couldn't sail for lack of spare parts and trained personnel and insufficient fuel and ammunition for essential training. The inevitable result of all this was poor morale in our Armed Forces, difficulty in recruiting the brightest young Americans to wear the uniform, and difficulty in convincing our most experienced military personnel to stay on.

There was a real question then about how well we could meet a crisis. And it was obvious that we had to begin a major modernization program to ensure we could deter aggression and preserve the peace in the years ahead.

He then went on to say, "I've become

more and more deeply convinced that the human spirit must be capable of rising above dealing with other nations and human beings by threatening their existence. Feeling this way, I believe we must thoroughly examine every opportunity for reducing tensions and for introducing greater stability into the strategic calculus on both sides." Now came the point he was building toward: "What if free people could live secure in the knowledge that their security did not rest upon the threat of instant U.S. retaliation to deter a Soviet attack, that we could intercept and destroy strategic ballistic missiles before they reached our own soil or that of our allies?" Describing the basis of this favored scheme as "defensive technologies," he'd crossed into the seemingly futuristic realm of vast invisible missile shields soon to become popularly known — to Reagan critics, at least — as "Star Wars."

He then concluded with what amounted to a vow: "I am directing a comprehensive and intensive effort to define a long-term research and development program to begin to achieve our ultimate goal of eliminating the threat posed by strategic nuclear missiles. . . . We seek neither military superiority nor political advantage. Our only purpose — one all people share — is to search for ways to reduce the danger of nuclear war."

Out of President Reagan's triple ambition to win the Cold War, create a missile shield, and eliminate nuclear weapons altogether came his distinctive approach to the Soviet Union. What he had decided to do, essentially, was outgun them. What he and key advisors recognized was that the opportunity seemed to be at hand to exploit emerging U.S. advances in strategic weaponry as a way to drive the Kremlin to the bargaining table.

There was a sense of personal destiny at work — he'd followed his own path to the White House, arriving there when others had doubted — but there was also that instinctive patriotic positivism that so often informed the Reagan outlook. By exploiting two great American strengths — its innovative ingenuity and its economic dynamism — he, Ronald Reagan, might bring the Cold War to an end by finally convincing the other side of that which it most hated and feared: the possibility of our actual superiority. To his thinking, a shrewd Soviet leader might be convinced to see that.

At the same time, obvious obstacles presented themselves, not the least of which was his own historic hatred of the Soviet Union, a well-documented hostility he'd never softened on, had never been shy about. Why would he trust any leader who rose up to represent the communist system he so despised? Why, too, would any such person trust him?

Even if you got beyond the problem of mutual suspicion — well justified as it was — the issue was still whether anyone in Moscow could be found who'd consider listening to what he had to say. They keep dying on me, Reagan would complain.

Meanwhile, closer by, the president had a different set of historic antagonists with whom to contend — the Democrats. Among them, the idea of a nuclear "freeze" — stopping the nuclear arms race at the status quo, letting both countries keep current stockpiles but build no more — had numerous adherents, particularly on the liberal left. Back in the spring of 1983, the House had passed — with Tip O'Neill's backing — a nonbinding "freeze" resolution by a vote of 278 to 149. Reagan had termed it "not an answer to arms control that I can responsibly support." Such an approach would, among other consequences, kill deployment of the MX missile, also known as the Peacekeeper, which could carry up to ten warheads, each with twenty times the explosive power of the bomb dropped on Hiroshima. Just two weeks before his televised speech to the nation on national security, the president had traveled to Orlando to address the annual convention of the National Association of Evangelicals. There he'd added to the lexicon of immortal political phrases by referring to the Soviet Union as an "evil empire," declaring its "totalitarian darkness" and "aggressive impulses" as justification for the nuclear arms race. "I would agree to a freeze," he said to applause and laughter, "if only we could freeze the Soviets' global desires." Yet, just minutes later, he assured the ministers listening to him in that Sheraton ballroom of this country's commitment to negotiations toward "real and verifiable reductions in the world's nuclear arsenals and one day, with God's help, their total elimination."

That he planned to "win" the Cold War by flashing our most lethal weapons at Moscow, as well as by developing and deploying a strategic defense shield against all incoming, presumably Soviet, nuclear missiles, was only part of the equation. He was also hoping for the happy ending.

Despite his deep antipathy to Moscow, Reagan had entered the White House back in 1981 with a keen personal interest in establishing a one-to-one relationship with Leonid Brezhnev, the tough and toughly enduring Soviet leader. As general secretary of the Central Committee of the Communist Party, succeeding Nikita Khrushchev, Brezhnev had held on to the position over a formidable seventeen-year span. Still recovering from the attempt on his life, Ronald Reagan, in the spring of his inaugural year, had joined in a quiet exchange of letters with his Russian counterpart. In one correspondence, he'd included a request that Brezhnev release dissident Natan Sharansky, a well-known figure in the campaign to permit Jewish emigration to Israel. "If you could find it in your heart to do this," Reagan said, "the matter would be strictly between us which is why I'm writing this letter by hand."

Early the following year, Reagan was urged by West German chancellor Helmut Schmidt to hold a meeting with Brezhnev. "He says he is very curious about me & doesn't know what to expect," was his journal entry for January 5. "Also says B. truly fears war. Maybe our disarmament talks might work after all."

But by year's end, Brezhnev was dead.

Reagan turned down the State Department's suggestion he go to Moscow for the funeral. After being briefed by George Shultz upon his return, the president noted in his diary that the secretary of state had agreed "I was right not to go."

Leonid Brezhnev was succeeded in November 1982 by Yuri Andropov, former chairman of the KGB. Very quickly, there was talk of setting up a personal back channel between the two heads of state. To this end, "Geo. Shultz sneaked Ambassador Dobrynin (Soviet) into the W.H. We talked for 2 hours. Sometimes we got pretty nose to nose. I told him I wanted George to be a channel for direct contact with Andropov — no bureaucracy involved. Geo. tells me that after they left, the ambas. said 'this could be an historic moment.' " That unofficial but obviously lively conversation between the president and the Russian diplomat took place on February 15.

Three months later, the idea of a personal meeting between Reagan and Andropov once again became a topic for discussion, this time during a National Security Council meeting. "There is possibility Andropov might come to the U.N. If so we should invite him to Wash. & will," recorded Reagan. In the end, the new Soviet leader stayed home, though Andropov himself gave encouragement to the president after another handwritten note was sent from the White House. "Expressed a desire to continue communicating on private basis and wants to talk about main issues," Reagan jotted that summer.

Unfortunately, in October, the American ambassador in Moscow, Arthur Hartman, confirmed what had been previously reported, that Andropov had dropped out of view. In fact, General Secretary Andropov had apparently been seriously ill since the moment of assuming the Soviet leadership; by February 1984, he, too, was being given a state funeral and laid to rest in the Kremlin.

This time, Reagan wasn't waiting around. He was ready to talk to the new Soviet leader, Konstantin Chernenko, from the start. Having sent Vice President George Bush to represent him at the Andropov funeral, he discussed the report he brought back with Secretary of State Shultz: "George S. & I met and discussed mainly the Soviets & how we should react to Chernenko's mild sounding talk with George B. I have a gut feeling I'd like to talk to him about our problems man to man & see if I could convince him there would be a material benefit to the Soviets if they'd join the family of nations etc. We don't want to appear anxious which would tempt them to play games & possibly snub us. I have our team considering an invitation to him to be my guest at the opening of the Olympics — July in L.A. Then he & I could have a session together in which we could start the ball rolling for outright summit on arms reductions, human rights, trade etc. We'll see."

Over the next months, President Reagan wrote three times in his diary about having a "gut feeling" that it was time for him to meet personally with the new Russian chairman. Talking to the new West German leader, Helmut Kohl, further convinced him. "He confirmed my belief that Soviets are motivated, at least in part by insecurity & a suspicion that we & our allies mean them harm. They still preserve the tank traps & barb wire that show how close the Germans got to Moscow before they were stopped. He too thinks I should meet Chernenko."

Later that month, though, the picture shifted once again when intelligence reports from Moscow revealed that the newest Soviet boss, Chernenko, was not truly in charge, that Foreign Minister Andrei Gromyko was the one calling the shots. By the summer, President François Mitterrand of France had informed Reagan of his own recent encounter with Chernenko, saying the Russian had given every "evidence of not being well & doesn't say a word without a script in front of him."

As November rolled around, Reagan continued to hold out hope for the appearance of a figure of authority in Moscow with whom he could meet and come to an accord. But, in March 1985, Konstantin Chernenko, too, joined the roll call of the recent Kremlin dead, and was succeeded by the relatively young — certainly in Soviet leadership terms — Mikhail Gorbachev, a Politburo member trained as a lawyer.

President Reagan now came to a shrewd realization. Before trying to establish contact in Moscow, he first needed to deal with the Democratic opposition in Washington. When he approached Gorbachev on matters of strategic policy, he could not afford to find himself undercut by Congress. He needed, as much as possible, to be speaking for a united America.

In the same way as Ronald Reagan, Tip O'Neill had his own complex set of motivations and goals. He wished to keep faith with his party, which was strongly pro-nuclear "freeze" and very much against production of the MX missile — Reagan's "peacekeeper." In the eyes of the Democrats, such a weapon — with its vast potential for destruction — could have *no* upside. Because the MX itself held so many missiles, it would be vital for any enemy to strike it before it ever left its silo. For the identical reason, it was equally vital for the country that possessed it to launch it before it was hit.

A secondary concern was jobs. Pulling the plug on the MX meant a serious economic loss to locales like Seattle, Washington (Boeing), and Lexington, Massachusetts (Raytheon). The Speaker understood this.

A further warring set of elements in Tip's mind pitted his Democratic loyalties against his hierarchical feeling toward the president — any president — when it came to superpower negotiations. Well aware that he was no strategic policy expert, he, even more crucially, believed the United States needed to speak, in such instances, with a single voice.

These different pressures explain, perhaps, the Speaker's changing positions in the long debate over the MX. When we staffers expressed our opposition to the proposed missile system and were eager to fight it, Tip himself held back.

Two decades later, Max Kampelman, a major figure in the Democratic Party, would recall his time as U.S. nuclear arms negotiator. Here he recounts what happened when the administration asked him to return for the arms negotiations in Geneva to try and persuade House Democrats to vote for the MX:

I was not and never have been a lobbyist, but I agreed to return to Washington. I wanted my first meeting to be with the Speaker of the House, Tip O'Neill, who, I was informed, was the leader of the opposition to the appropriation. . . .

At the end of the day, I met alone with the president and told him that O'Neill said we were about 30 votes short. I told the president of my conversation with the speaker and shared with him my sense that O'Neill was quietly helping us, suggesting to his fellow Democrats that he would not be unhappy if they voted against his amendment.

Without a moment's hesitation, the president telephoned O'Neill, and I had the privilege of hearing one side of this conversation between two tough Irishmen, cussing each other out, but obviously friendly and respectful.

I recall that the president's first words went something like this: "Max tells me that you may really be a patriot. It's about time!" Suffice it to say that soon after I returned to Geneva I learned that the House had authorized the MX missiles.

An event that undoubtedly affected the outcome was the shooting of an American army major outside an East German military installation. The two sides could come to no agreement about the details: whether or not the major had entered an actual "restricted area," or if Major Arthur Nicholson, stationed at Potsdam, was fired upon by a Soviet sentry. But there was no question that a U.S. officer's death under such circumstances rekindled Cold War anger at the very moment President Reagan was seeking approval for a weapon he intended to use as a negotiating wedge with the Soviets.

Major Nicholson was killed on Sunday, March 24. The House voted to authorize money for 21 additional MX missiles by the narrow vote of 219 to 213 on Tuesday the twenty-sixth, and voted again to appropriate that money by a vote of 217 to 210 on Thursday the twenty-eighth. In his diary entry, Reagan confirmed the Speaker's commitment as Kampelman described it. But he added, "But right down to the wire he twisted arms, threatened punishment of the 61 Dems. who went with us — in short he was playing pure partisan politics all the way."

He was, I contend, missing the nuances of Tip O'Neill's inside game. Knowing the Speaker — and observing this one from up close — I could see he was doing pretty much what he'd promised the president he would do. I'd watched Tip O'Neill fight hard on those issues he cared deeply about — Social Security, programs for the sick and poor, opposition to Reagan's Central American policy, to name important ones. I saw none of that passion when it came to the MX issue. I could tell, though, how taken he was with the administration lobbying effort. "In thirty-two years," he told the press, "I haven't seen such an all-out effort. I have to admire it." Bringing in Max Kampelman — who was, after all, a respected Democrat — to push for the MX, said Tip, may have been the key. "If the president will fight as hard for the START [Strategic Arms Reduction Talks] as he has for the MX, it will do the nation good."

In early April, Speaker O'Neill was set to

lead a thirteen-member bipartisan congressional delegation to Moscow. Republican leader Bob Michel would join him. Before departing, they visited the president at the White House. "Just wanted a last min. briefing & our blessing," Reagan jotted in his diary. "Gave them both." But, along with his blessing, he also gave O'Neill a letter to hand personally to Soviet general secretary Gorbachev. He asked also that Tip convey with it a simple message. He wanted him to assure the new man at the top in the Kremlin on two accounts: one, the degree to which Americans *were* united; two, the sincerity of *Ronald Reagan* in his desire for meaningful negotiations. As O'Neill biographer John Aloysius Farrell wrote, the Speaker made for "a particularly credible messenger," given the frequency with which he'd shown himself at odds over Reagan's policies and his criticism of his past opposition to nuclear arms treaties.

When O'Neill was asked what he intended to tell Mikhail Gorbachev, if the Soviet leader inquired about President Reagan, he answered without even an instant's hesitation. "I'm going to tell him that he got fifty-nine percent of the vote and he whaled my party!"

■ ■ ■ ■

"We have a mutual friend," the new Soviet leader, networking from the start, said as he greeted his guest that April day in Moscow. He was referring to Archer Daniels Midland's Dwayne Andreas. It had been Andreas who'd passed word to O'Neill four years earlier how impressed the Soviet leaders had been by Reagan's decisive handling of the air traffic controllers' strike. Though at first, drumming his fingers and checking his watch before his visitors entered the room, Gorbachev seemed intent on a brisk meeting, he quickly turned into a man with questions and plenty of time on hand to get them answered. Bob Michel, the top Republican on the trip, saw that Gorbachev had his notes marked in different colors for the main points he intended to make. In the end, his session with the O'Neill delegation lasted nearly four hours.

Because O'Neill was carrying a letter from the president, a Republican, he was quick to clarify his role in the American political system. "I'm part of the opposition," he explained. "We're trying to understand what the position of the opposition is," Gorbachev shot back, intrigued, "as well as the position of those in power." "There's a big difference," Tip replied. "On some questions, we don't agree on *everything.*"

Later, Tip recounted his Kremlin experience this way:

I remember when I went in first to meet with him, face-to-face, just the two of us, he spoke to me in English. He said, "You are the leader of the opposition." He said, "I do not know what the opposition means, Democrat, Republican, you all oppose Communism."

I said, "Mr. Gorbachev, let me say this to you: At home, on the domestic front, we have issues and we have opposition philosophically, oftentimes on foreign affairs. But when the President of the United States goes to Geneva with you, he is representing our country, and we talk as one. So yes, you may say you do not know what the opposition is because both Democrats and Republicans are opposed to communism. But we stand together in support of the President of the United States, not only Tip O'Neill, but the party that I stand for, and the party that I represent, and the Congress of the United States."

After the encounter, he'd been impressed if not completely overwhelmed. What he found familiar was that Gorbachev reminded him of a "New York lawyer." He was, Tip said, "a master of words and a master in the art of politics and diplomacy." Also, he "had a flair about him. He had charisma about him. He had a Western style."

The letter O'Neill brought with him confirmed Ronald Reagan's desire — relayed originally by George Bush when attending the Chernenko funeral — to meet with the new Soviet leader. Tip praised Gorbachev's positive reaction. "I think it augurs well for world peace when the two dominant nations of the world can get at the table and sit down. . . . If they only keep talking that's the most important thing." He had no worries, he added, about the possibility of Gorbachev outmatching Reagan. ". . . The president will be able to handle himself," he told the press. "Don't you worry about the president."

"It was hard to be impressed by what I saw of the Soviet Union's economic development," Tip later noted. "I'll never forget the ride into Moscow from the airport: the countryside seemed unbelievably dismal. We stayed in a government-owned hotel where the beds were so small that I had to put two of them together — and it still wasn't big enough. Inside the Kremlin walls, however, the buildings were fantastic. And although the Russians are officially atheists, I've never seen so many carefully preserved paintings of the saints."

And when he and others in the delegation met afterward with President Reagan to report on their trip, Tip had a striking revelation to share that had come of the conversation with the new Soviet leader. The single thing that seemed most to bother Mikhail Gorbachev had been the American president's characterization of the Soviet Union as an "evil empire."

The plan was for Reagan and Gorbachev to hold their first summit in Geneva, site of the ongoing nuclear arms talks. Trying to ensure that the president arrived in Switzerland with a politically united Congress behind him, Tip O'Neill called for a ceasefire in the two parties' current disputes over government spending. Above all, this meant the question of appropriations for national defense. A short-term agreement between the Democrats and Republicans on Capitol Hill would permit Reagan to enter talks free of simmering partisan debate back home. "We need to clear the decks for the President in Geneva," the Speaker said on the eve of the leaders' meeting.

When President Reagan meets with Mr. Gorbachev next week he deserves the support of all Americans regardless of party or philosophy. In Geneva, there will be only one American spokesman. There will be only one American having both the authority and the mandate to build a secure peace. That man is the president of the United States.

We Americans know the awesome stakes of this summit. We also know the difficulties. The United States and the Soviet Union have major disagreements. Some of our differences may simply be insurmountable, regardless of the wisdom and good will that is shown next week. But we also believe there are encouraging signs that progress can be made in Geneva. The greatest challenge, and the highest priority in Geneva, must be to reduce the risk of nuclear war.

O'Neill was guarding his party as well as

his country. He was giving Reagan no opportunity to blame the Democrats if the summit went badly. He wanted all the authority — and, with it, all the responsibility — in Reagan's hands alone. "I don't want to send the president to meet Mr. Gorbachev in a position where he doesn't dare pick up the check."

Reagan, for his part, clearly hoped to forge an ongoing personal connection with the new Soviet leader. To this end, he even made a special point of scoping out ahead of time the room where he'd meet with him, "where I hope to get Gorbachev aside for a one on one." The president would later write that he'd headed off to Geneva convinced that the new leader of the Soviet Union *wanted* a deal for the very basic reason that he *needed* one. "He had to know we could outspend the Soviets on weapons as long as we wanted to." Not all that long ago, Gorbachev had been complaining openly — more like a small businessman than a world leader — to Tip and his delegation about the "gold rubles" he was spending that year to keep his arms negotiators in place at the Geneva bargaining table. If he had to worry about the per diem costs of his diplomats, how could he match Reagan's challenge on futuristic missile defense?

Once they'd opened their discussions, the two men's real differences, especially over Reagan's proposed missile shield system, soon came to the fore. The American president argued that "Star Wars" was intended to serve defensively only; the Soviet leader saw it differently. In his mind, it would allow the United States to deliver not just a first strike but one made with impunity. This is despite Reagan's offer to share the technology with the Soviets once it had been developed. "It's not convincing," Gorbachev challenged him. "It opens up an arms race in space."

Yet progress was being made, and much of it was personal. Here's Reagan's account. "That evening it was our turn to host dinner and I saw, as I had the night before when the Soviets had entertained us, that Gorbachev could be warm and outgoing in a social setting even though several hours earlier we'd had sharp differences of opinion; maybe there was a little of Tip O'Neill in him. He could tell jokes about himself and even about his country, and I grew to like him more."

The Geneva summit, at its close, was pronounced a success, yielding as it did agreements for similar future meetings in both Washington and Moscow, as well as a pledge to cut the two countries' nuclear weapons stockpiles in half.

To trumpet the president's success and bring home to the American public this historic first thawing of the Cold War, the White House decided, once again, to go for its own version of street theater. The scenario called for the president to arrive back from Geneva onto the very steps of the Capitol — there to report, with full silver-screen drama, to a joint session of Congress.

But that wasn't all. "In an unusual procedure," the Speaker announced on the morning of the Reagan return, "I have been asked by the White House to go with Bob Dole to greet the president of the United States and to fly by helicopter back here with him. And Mrs. O'Neill has been asked to be seated with Mrs. Reagan, which is an unusual circumstance.

"I expect a full report, a true report of what happened. It will not be partisan whatsoever. I am more than delighted that there will be continued talks with Gorbachev coming here next year and our president going over there the year after. As long as we are sitting at the table, although we might not always get along, there is the possibility that something can be agreed upon."

That night, introduced by the Speaker, President Reagan expressed his gratitude. "You can't imagine how much it means in dealing with the Soviets to have the Congress, the allies and the American people firmly behind you." After five hours of one-on-one meetings with Gorbachev, he obviously was feeling positive, saluting his Soviet counterpart for, among other attributes, being a "good listener." As for more substantial aspects of the exchange now placed on the table, Reagan cited a proposed 50 percent cut in nuclear arms and a plan to eliminate *all* intermediate-range missiles in Europe. "The summit itself was a good start," he concluded, "and now our byword must be: steady as we go."

Both as theatrics and as politics, the president's appearance counted as a hit. "I haven't gotten such a reception since I was shot," he wrote. "The gallerys were full & members wouldn't stop clapping & cheering."

A date for a second Reagan-Gorbachev meeting was eventually set for the fall of the following year in Iceland. In the run-up, Tip O'Neill found himself playing a quiet but consequential role. The nuclear "freeze" faction of the Democrat membership had by then revved itself up and, no longer willing to wait, was demanding action. Indeed, the time had come for an up-or-down call on the whole panoply of nuclear arms issues. Congressmen Ron Dellums and Edward Markey believed they stood at a great moment in history, one in which they could frame clearly the grand goal of global nuclear disarmament.

The Speaker summoned a meeting in his office. Bluntly, he warned what would happen if Reagan failed at Reykjavik. They and the other Democratic doves would bring the weight of the blame upon the entire party. Tip prevailed. It was better to wait, as both Dellums and Markey accepted, even though having to delay their crusade against nuclear arms proliferation was "heartbreaking," as Dellums put it. Yet not even the freeze leaders themselves could have predicted that Reagan and Gorbachev would themselves talk of eliminating all nuclear weapons.

For those of us who'd spent our early youth hiding beneath our fragile wooden school desks imagining a nuclear air raid, a seismic change was occurring. Despite the roadblock at Reykjavik — Reagan's insistence on strategic defense — the scene of two superpowers headed toward Armageddon had evanesced. Suddenly, the world might no longer be the one we'd known since the early 1950s. Mikhail Gorbachev understood what was happening. "This," he told Steingrímur Hermannsson, the Icelandic prime minister, as they stood together on the tarmac in the sleeting rain, "is the beginning of the end of the Cold War."

Tip O'Neill secretly begged Reagan to win Margaret Thatcher's backing for a new British policy toward Northern Ireland. It began the process toward reconciliation between Protestant and Catholic in Ulster.

CHAPTER TWENTY: HURRAH!

"What matters most about political ideas is the underlying emotions, the music to which ideas are a mere libretto, often of very inferior quality."
— SIR LEWIS NAMIER

Both Ronald Reagan and Tip O'Neill were American Irish, but different kinds. One was the corner buddy, staying close to home, holding fast to his tribal identity. The other was the rambling boy, making his name and fame elsewhere. It explains why they shared their Irish stories differently. Reagan offered his, theatrically, with a brogue, just as he'd done for that Vegas revue he'd once briefly emceed. Tip's anecdotes came with his DNA, I'd say. But he'd also accumulated a useful collection over the years, heard at weddings and christenings and a thousand political dinners.

Reagan, raised Protestant by his Scots-

English mother, over the years was in danger of forgetting the other half of his bloodline. His heavy-drinking Catholic father was a beloved, if embarrassing, connection to the religion Reagan would refer to, without animus, as "Bells and smells." Pat O'Brien was another reminder of the old sod when he welcomed the young man starting to make his way in Hollywood into the clan at the Warner Bros. commissary.

"I knew I was Irish even before I knew I was American," wrote Tip when he sat down to look back on his life. At the age of seven, he'd been enrolled in a Gaelic language school. Around him was a world of families that closely resembled his, yet as he grew up, signs in shopwindows still warned: NINA. NO IRISH NEED APPLY. For the likes of Tip and his peers, they mirrored the anti-Catholic bigotry across the Atlantic that kept Northern Ireland a battle zone. Tip also remembered other signs from those days — I GAVE TO THE ARMY being one. It meant a contribution had been made to the Irish Republican Army.

Like so many in his community, O'Neill had loyally supported the IRA up through the late 1950s. However, as the situation changed, so did his thinking. With the eruption of the bloody violence — "the

Troubles" — in the era that followed, he began to question the conventional Irish-American habits of mind he'd previously taken for granted. What now became apparent to him was that the struggle between nationalist and loyalist in Northern Ireland would not, in the end, be decided by gun and bomb.

Influenced by John Hume, a Northern Ireland nationalist leader pressing for a nonviolent approach to the rights of the Catholic minority, Tip and three other well-respected Irish-American politicians — Senator Edward Kennedy, Senator Daniel Patrick Moynihan, and New York governor Hugh Carey — had joined forces in 1977. All four men recognized the truth of what Hume urged, that the continuous flow of Irish-American dollars funding the IRA arms stockpile had to stop. They also understood that the Protestant majority was never going to give up its loyalty to Britain, while, at the same time, the minority Catholics should never have to accept second-class status. Any agreement arrived at, they knew, would need to be based upon democratic principles, and if Northern Ireland were ever to join the Republic of Ireland, it would have to be by majority vote.

Dubbed the "Four Horsemen" in honor

of the famed Notre Dame backfield of 1924, Tip and his cohort made themselves first heard on St. Patrick's Day of 1977 in a statement that called for an end to the sectarian killing and encouraged the possibility of dialogue. While the new approach stirred anger by the hard-liners, it began to show results. Tip, speaking for the other "Horsemen," found a key ally in Jimmy Carter. Always an advocate for human rights, President Carter now tried pushing the British government for a settlement in Northern Ireland, and promised U.S. aid as a way of sweetening the initiative.

As I've shown, from the moment they met, Tip O'Neill accepted Ronald Reagan as a fellow Irish-American, sharing jokes and stories. He made an annual ritual of hosting a St. Patrick's Day lunch in the Speaker's dining room, with the president always the guest of honor. When Tip visited Ireland in April 1984, just prior to a Reagan arrival there that June, he set about smoothing the way for the president, wanting to be sure he was treated properly. (The Speaker, I should add, loved noting that the name of the president's ancestral village, Ballyporeen — to which Reagan intended paying the expected pilgrimage — was Gaelic for "valley of the small potatoes.")

Upon arrival, Reagan was delighted with his reception and repaid Tip's courtesy by calling his Democratic rival "a great son of Ireland and America." Their shared heritage was, he joked, "part of our blood. . . . That's what I keep telling myself every time I try to iron out my differences with the speaker of our House of Representatives, a lad by the name of Tip O'Neill."

In Dublin, Reagan addressed the lower house of the Irish national parliament on June 4, and opened by describing how, when he'd landed at Shannon a few days earlier, "something deep inside began to stir." He then reminded his listeners that the first Washington embassy he'd officially visited, upon becoming president, had been Ireland's. "I'm proud that our administration is blessed by so many cabinet members of Irish extraction." Pause. "Indeed, I had to fight them off Air Force One or there wouldn't be anyone tending the store while we're gone." Then, quickly, he got serious.

Although the bulk of his speech looked beyond Irish borders to larger East-West issues — the spread of "democratic development," and U.S. efforts at ensuring global security — Reagan first spoke forcefully of the need for peace in Ireland, north and south. "All sides should have one goal

527

before them," he said, "and let us state it simply and directly: to end the violence, to end it completely, and to end it now." Yet he made clear the United States' position was only one of solidarity. "We must not and will not interfere in Irish matters nor prescribe to you solutions or formulas. But I want you to know that we pledge to you our goodwill and support, and we're with you as you work toward peace."

Three months earlier, in March, back in Washington, Irish prime minister Garret FitzGerald — his own family home was, as it turns out, less than seven miles from Ballyporeen — had traveled to America and lunched at the White House. Naturally, also on hand for the event was Tip O'Neill — giving Reagan the chance to quip during his welcoming toast, "In fact, the secret wish disclosed the other day by my friend, Tip O'Neill, is an indication of the hold that Ireland has on all of us here in the States. This is a nation where the Speaker of the U.S. House of Representatives aspires someday to be Ambassador to Ireland. 'Tip, what about day after tomorrow?' "

Now, in Ireland and standing before its parliament, President Reagan referred back to that earlier event. "When he was in America in March," he said, "your Prime

Minister courageously denounced the support that a tiny number of misguided Americans give to these terrorist groups. I joined him in that denunciation, as did the vast majority of Irish-Americans."

Tip and others committed to changing the situation in Northern Ireland recognized the necessity of shifting the American approach to Great Britain. They saw that the elusive key to peace in Northern Ireland was to be found only in London. However, in October 1984, that vital piece of the puzzle became more elusive still, as Margaret Thatcher, the British prime minister, only narrowly escaped harm when the IRA bombed a Conservative Party conference. Even before, her Tory loyalties had allied her to Protestant Unionists. In the aftermath she was even more hardened, opposing the very notion of a Catholic and Protestant power-sharing in Northern Ireland.

In November 1984, of course, President Reagan was re-elected. The following month, just before Christmas, Prime Minister Thatcher crossed the Atlantic to attend a roughly three-hour meeting at Camp David with the president and his senior advisors. The primary reason for the trip was to discuss with Reagan her own recent session with Mikhail Gorbachev. But other subjects were covered, including the current situation in Ireland.

Anticipating American interest, Mrs. Thatcher herself raised the matter. She emphasized that, with regard to Ireland, despite reports to the contrary, she and Garret FitzGerald were on good terms and . . . making progress on the difficult question. In reply, President Reagan told her that in Washington there was great congressional interest in the issue, adding that he'd had a personal letter from Tip O'Neill asking him to appeal to Mrs. Thatcher to be reasonable and forthcoming. The president followed through, writing Tip later to assure him that he'd done as he asked.

On November 15, 1985, Thatcher and FitzGerald signed the historic Anglo-Irish Agreement, which established two critical principles for future talks. The first was that their two countries now agreed on their equal interest in Northern Ireland. Second, both London and Dublin also accepted the fact that any change in Northern Ireland's status would have to be made by the popular vote of its citizens, Protestant and Catholic alike. The agreement ushered in an era of genuine negotiation between Great Britain and the Republic of Ireland, but even beyond that, it made it possible for John

Hume, the visionary nationalist from Derry, to help bring the IRA openly to the bargaining table. It was the beginning of the end to the Troubles. Both Tip O'Neill and Ronald Reagan had played roles they could take pride in.

The episode warmed the Speaker's heart toward Reagan as never before. "His feelings changed to one of appreciation and respect for Reagan when he let the Four Horsemen and him personally change the public posture of the United States from viewing Northern Ireland through the prism of Great Britain," his son Tom would say with his own warm recollection. "He knew it put the president and Thatcher in an awkward position. They were close, the two of them. But Reagan never resented it and she did."

President Reagan's State of the Union address for 1986 was scheduled for January 28. However, at 11:39 that morning, the *Challenger* exploded less than two minutes after takeoff. Six astronauts were killed, along with thirty-seven-year-old Christa McAuliffe, a New Hampshire high school teacher chosen from more than eleven thousand applicants for the coveted primary slot in NASA's Teacher in Space Project.

The State of the Union address was postponed, the first and only time to date that that has happened. Instead, at five o'clock, sitting in the Oval Office, the president went on television — with far different matters on his mind and in his heart. "Ladies and gentlemen," he began, "I'd planned to speak to you tonight to report on the State of the Union, but the events of earlier today have led me to change those plans. Today is a day for mourning and remembering."

He was plainspoken, and all the more eloquent for it. "We've grown used to wonders in this century. It's hard to dazzle us. But for twenty-five years the United States space program has been doing just that. We've grown used to the idea of space, and perhaps we forget that we've only just begun. We're still pioneers. They, the members of the *Challenger* crew, were pioneers."

Millions of young schoolchildren, he told his country, had been watching with special interest, excited that a teacher, just like the ones they saw every day, would be riding into space with astronauts. "I know it is hard to understand," he said, addressing them specifically, "but sometimes painful things like this happen. It's all part of the process of exploration and discovery. It's all part of taking a chance and expanding man's horizons. The future doesn't belong to the fainthearted; it belongs to the brave. The *Challenger* crew was pulling us into the future, and we'll continue to follow them."

His conclusion, for me, was the most memorable, quoting as he did the haunting phrases of the heroic poet-aviator John Gillespie Magee, Jr., who died in a Spitfire over England in 1941. "The crew of the space shuttle *Challenger* honored us by the manner in which they lived their lives. We will never forget them, nor the last time we saw them, this morning, as they prepared for their journey and waved goodbye and 'slipped the surly bonds of earth' to 'touch the face of God.' "

I watched the president's speech, sitting next to the Speaker. He was as moved as anyone could have been, and I think the tragedy was particularly hard for those whose lives, as Tip's was, had been for so long inextricably linked to serving their country. I think what probably added a dimension, too, was his awareness that Christa McAuliffe was a New Englander born in Boston. "As I listened to him," Tip would later write, "I had a tear in my eye and a lump in my throat. It was a trying day for all Americans, and Ronald Reagan spoke to our highest ideals."

The next morning, still extremely affected by what he'd heard, the Speaker quietly put in a call to the White House to learn who'd written the address for the president. He then called Peggy Noonan to thank her on behalf of the country for her achievement. In O'Neill's opinion, Ronald Reagan, with a prepared text, was simply the best public speaker he'd ever known, and that included FDR and Jack Kennedy. It was a seasoned man's assessment. In the case of the *Challenger* speech, he'd found himself personally moved and personally grateful, and, for Tip O'Neill, that meant a lot.

Tip would call the tax reform bill of 1986 a prime example of what can be accomplished when the two political sides work together. Along with saving Social Security, it was their finest achievement in domestic policy. Reagan "brought down the house" at Tip's good-bye party that March.

CHAPTER TWENTY-ONE:
COMMON GROUND

"There is no limit to the amount of good you can do if you don't care who gets the credit."
— A SIGN ON PRESIDENT REAGAN'S DESK

Tip O'Neill made no secret of his worry that the revelation, made two years earlier in that conversation with Martin Tolchin, that he wouldn't be running for reelection in 1986 had been a mistake of timing. The cat — or, in this case, you might say the lion — was out of the bag, and nothing could be the same as the clock began to tick away his remaining hours and days up on Capitol Hill. "Still, after half a century in politics," he later admitted, "I should have done a better job at stage-managing my own retirement." No politician enjoys being a lame duck, and, after sixteen terms in the House of Representatives, Tip — who'd first sought elective office back in 1935, running for Cambridge City Council, the only contest he ever lost — was no different.

But this time, his impulse to candor worked to his advantage. His declaration of his plans to finish out his career at the end of 1986 created just the right tone for his last term in office. Doors opened that would have remained otherwise shut.

His retirement season climaxed, appropriately, on the evening of March 17, when the O'Neill family staged a grand dinner at the Washington Hilton to honor him, the proceeds of which would benefit Tip's alma mater, Boston College. Among the 2,200 gathered to celebrate the Speaker and his accomplishments were former president Gerald Ford, Irish prime minister Garret FitzGerald, Senator Edward M. Kennedy, and legendary entertainer Bob Hope. Yet, in the words of Thomas P. O'Neill III, Tip's oldest son, the occasion's "centerpiece" was President Ronald Reagan. It escaped no one that evening that they were listening to an admiring and affectionate tribute by an old pro at the top of his game. There he stood in the ballroom of the very hotel where five years earlier he'd been shot.

"But to be honest, I've always known that Tip was behind me," he joked, "even if it was only at the State of the Union Address."

It was an opener the crowd loved, hearing Reagan turn the seating arrangement for his annual speech, traditionally delivered in the House of Representatives, into such a sharp gag. "As I made each proposal," Reagan went on, still summoning up that familiar yearly scene, "I could hear Tip whispering to George Bush, 'Forget it. No way. Fat chance.' "

Over the preceding five years, the two men had alternated between cooperation and consternation. It had not been easy, and both knew it. Their exchanges had often been harsh. But they had also frequently shared celebrations. This moment was the valedictory culmination of the good times. "And Mr. Speaker," Reagan now went on, "I'm grateful you have permitted me in the past, and I hope in the future, that singular honor, the honor of calling you my friend. I think the fact of our friendship is testimony to the political system that we're part of and the country we live in, a country which permits two not-so-shy and not-so-retiring Irishmen to have it out on the issues rather than on each other or their countrymen."

When it came Tip's turn to respond, he was equally gracious, praising their across-the-aisle efforts by acknowledging how unusual they were. "I have traveled the nations of the world. You see on one side of the hall the leadership and on the other side the minority and they don't talk." His personal view of Reagan had always comprised a complicated mix of emotions. Less than two years apart in age, they had managed, over the course of the relationship thrust upon them, to find common ground. Even as each remained an exotic figure to the other, each managed to appreciate the other's differences.

"Mr. President," he continued, "we have differing philosophies, but I want to tell you how much I admire your ability, your talent, the way you handle the American people, the love the American people have for you and your leadership — even though I'm opposed to it," he said, to unrestrained laughter.

"You're a beautiful individual, Mr. President," he said. "Thank you for being here. I think of your charm, your humor, your wit. You know, sometimes when I get up in the morning, I say, 'Don't let it get to you, old boy.' " Again, the room exploded. The contest had gone on for five crisis-packed years, and, in the end, both team captains had survived to score memorable home runs.

■ ■ ■

A few weeks later, on schedule, the Speaker left Washington for his regular Easter trip overseas, accompanied by the usual eager gang of legislators. The congressional delegation he led, ably cochaired by Ways and Means chairman Dan Rostenkowski, this time had an itinerary pointed southward, to Venezuela, Brazil, and Argentina. After that, it was back up through the Dominican Republic.

But since Kirk O'Donnell, his accustomed foreign policy hand, couldn't make the trip, I was asked to accompany the group as Tip's chief traveling staffer. The assignment quickly turned into a two-week blur of meetings and lavish dinners, often hosted by American corporate lobbyists. There were definitely no K rations, as there'd been the last time I'd accompanied a group of congressmen to the region. Back then, I'd landed on the recently invaded island of Grenada, off the coast of Venezuela; now I found myself in roaring Rio de Janeiro. One morning we were awoken for a flight along the beaches of Ipanema and Copacabana, and above Sugarloaf and the Christ statue. Through a friend of mine, Gabriel Guerra,

I'd gotten use of the Governor of Rio's helicopter. What a ride it was! That night I recall a line of tall, dark, spectacular-looking Brazilian women high-stepping onstage before us. Tip O'Neill leaned over and whispered: "See, I told you if you stuck with me you'd have a great time!"

But there were duties more critical than junketing to occupy the Speaker during his final months in office and to keep all of us busy as we wound down. The historic tax reform bill of 1986 was one such challenge on the near horizon, and its milestone success had much to do with Tip's closeness to his traveling buddy from Chicago. Rosty, or "Danny," as the Speaker inevitably referred to him, was not just his ally but also a real pal of many years' standing, both men having entered the Congress back in the 1950s. And though I always suspected a bit of envy on the Chicagoan's part due to his having narrowly missed election to the Speakership, that's not how Tip saw it. Or else, he just had a different way of dealing with his friend's possible sensitivity.

A good example of that is how Tip insisted that fellow Democrat Rosty — and not the more obvious candidate, Republican leader Bob Michel — have the distinction of being listed as "cochairman" on all the protocol lists, each Easter, of that traveling congressional delegation, the one that caused such embarassment during the big Reagan fight in 1981. Their habitual giant duffel bags, too, were clearly labeled the "O'Neill-Rostenkowski" trip to wherever. Those trips were always bipartisan in makeup, yet the Speaker always made a point of honoring Rosty as his partner on the road. He loved the guy and never wanted to let him down, especially when he knew how much his old friend's heart was in it.

For his part, from early 1985 on, Dan Rostenkowski regarded the passage of an important tax reform bill as a way, truly, to make his mark as an historic Ways and Means chairman. The measure he advanced, with Reagan's blessing, would end up reducing the number of brackets to two, 15 and 28 percent, allowing these lower rates by sharply cutting the number of deductions, limiting even those for business meals and entertainment. Most impressive, it raised the rate for capital gains to the same as ordinary income. Money made *from* money would now be taxed as high as money made from work.

All in all, it created a more transparent tax system — one that both Reagan and

O'Neill, each for his separate reasons, wanted passed. The president believed high marginal rates were a brake on enterprise and risk-taking, while the Speaker liked the progressive features of the bill. Reagan had himself campaigned on a promise to make "the whole system more fair and simple for everyone." Neither of the two men, certainly, wished to be blamed for the defeat of a good bill.

For several nervous days and nights in November 1985, it was touch-and-go, with the odds shifting briefly against success. A vote late in 1985 to bring the bill to the House floor was defeated when the bulk of the Republican caucus failed to back it. According to Tip O'Neill, the GOP congressmen had, disloyally, "voted to humiliate the man who had led them to victory." The Speaker agreed to give it a second try only if the Republicans would now guarantee they'd be able to rally a minimum fifty GOP votes in favor. He knew well the truth in the adage of Louisiana's Senator Russell Long, the veteran chairman of the Senate Finance Committee. "Don't tax you; don't tax me; tax that fellow behind that tree." He wanted the president's party to suffer a few degrees of the heat the Democrats would face from the wealthy and the corporate world.

The night that the White House managed to come up with the required number of Republican ayes, the Speaker was having dinner at the Phoenix Park Hotel, a Capitol Hill spot he favored, enjoying its traditional Irish ambiance. As the agreed-upon deadline of 8 p.m. came and went, he still had not returned Reagan's call. On tenterhooks because of Tip's silence, James Baker, now treasury secretary — the former White House chief of staff had switched jobs the previous year with Reagan's first-term secretary of the treasury, Donald Regan — would later recall his side's uncertain wait. "Four frustrating hours passed before the men talked. Why so long? I suspect the Speaker just wanted to play us a bit before he closed the deal."

He was right. That's precisely what my boss was doing, letting the Republicans dangle just enough to sweat. "Three times he called," Tip would later confess, "and they tell me at the White House he was in a *dither.*" But then, when the time came for the vote itself, the Speaker came through with what Baker rated as "an excellent speech in support of the bill." The much-anticipated tax reform bill passed with a strong Democratic vote that was joined by seventy Republicans. Tip O'Neill had helped

Ronald Reagan achieve what would prove to be his major second-term triumph.

Another bipartisan effort that fall dealt, if not as effectively, with immigration. The measure was two-pronged. It offered citizenship to those who had entered the country illegally in the past while punishing employers for hiring them in the present. The measure angered both those opposed to "amnesty" for illegal immigrants, and Hispanic organizations that argued the sanctions on employers would encourage discrimination. Tip O'Neill and Ronald Reagan both took considerable heat for endorsing the dual provisions. Though it took a balanced approach and provided citizenship to millions of immigrants, the Immigration Reform and Control Act of 1986 lacked the "teeth" to stop illegal hiring. The best that could be said is that the measure offered future reformers a road map on the kind of immigration law that was still needed.

If you have had a difficult time fathoming the Speaker's actual view of the other man, join the club. When he wrote about Reagan, he would offer up comments that ran from deeply impressed — "as beloved a leader as this nation has ever seen" — to grumpy, calling him "the worst" president he had served under. He called him "out of touch" but also possessing "tremendous powers of friendly persuasion." He'd talk about what an "agreeable man" Reagan was and speak of the "pretty good friendship" they kept up despite the disharmony of their philosophies.

To me, their personal agreeability was as natural as their political antagonism. Had Tip and the Gipper been on the same side, meeting at fund-raisers and after-hours dinners, they would have gotten along swimmingly. Where they did meet was on the fighting line between liberal and conservative, Democrat and Republican, and that made all the difference.

What makes my case is how proud Tip was to work with Ronald Reagan when the two could find common ground — like on Social Security and bringing peace to Northern Ireland and on this historic 1986 tax reform bill.

Yes, it was a victory he could proudly share. "After the vote, I was struck by how much could be accomplished when the president and the Speaker, coming from opposing parties but working together, could agree on specific legislation," Tip explained. "Only a few months earlier, none of the lobbyists had given tax reform a chance. . . .

This was one case where leadership made all the difference."

Reagan and O'Neill saw the fight in Nicaragua from different histories. For the president it was the Cold War, pure and simple— the Soviets and their Cuban allies were trying to expand the communist presence in the hemisphere. For the Speaker, the U.S. support for the Contras was yet another example of "gunboat diplomacy," of the United States trying to impose its will on the weaker countries to the south.

CHAPTER TWENTY-TWO: LAST BATTLE

"There are two kinds of success: initial and ultimate."

— WINSTON CHURCHILL

Back in the 1980s, when you entered the members' dining room of the Capitol on Tuesday through Thursday mornings, you were invariably greeted by a familiar quartet of faces. First, at the table nearest the door you'd see Bob Griffin, Tip O'Neill's Boston College buddy, employed by the Chrysler Corporation as a lobbyist. His breakfast companion, as predictable as the dawn, was Leo Diehl, indispensable to the Speaker as an ally since their early days together in the Massachusetts legislature.

At a table closer to the swinging kitchen doors would be the second predictable morning duo I remember so well. One of them was Eddie Boland, who for twenty-four years had roomed with Tip before he stopped his weekly commutes back and forth from Cambridge and brought Millie to Washington to live. Boland's tablemate was fellow Bay State congressman Joe Early, of Worcester. Years later I would be reminded of these two Black Irishmen mumbling grimly to each other when I overheard two Old Gaelic speakers in the rural Cork bar where Michael Collins had his last meal.

Tip's ex-roommate was more substantial than he seemed. The son of Irish immigrants who'd settled in Springfield, Massachusetts, Edward Patrick Boland never in his political life had lost an election and would eventually represent his district for thirty-six years before retiring. A World War II vet, he'd marched in Selma, Alabama, with Martin Luther King. A bachelor until the age of sixty-one, he then married Mary Egan, the president of the Springfield City Council, with whom he had four children. He and Tip had entered Congress the same year, 1953, and Boland's long friendship with the now Speaker — as the *New York Times* put it in his obituary when he died in 2001 — was "a touchstone of his career."

Tip knew Boland as well as he knew any man and trusted him enough to make him chairman of the new Permanent Select Committee on Intelligence. The main mission of this committee was to keep a congressional eye and ear on what the Central Intelligence Agency and the rest of the intelligence community were up to, at which point it would then decide, discreetly, what to do with that information. When forming the committee, the Speaker had explained that he, himself, hated those occasions when he'd needed to be briefed by the Agency. It placed him, he said, in the position of being either accomplice or whistle-blower, and the truth was, he wished to be neither. Instead, with this new committee up and running, his good friend Eddie could take on the responsibility he preferred to abdicate — and thus Boland found himself joined in the last great partisan debate of the Cold War.

Ronald Reagan had, as I explained earlier, revealed an early interest in Central America. Seeking an edge as he sought the Republican presidential nomination back in 1976, he'd decided to make a battle cry of his opposition to ceding U.S. ownership of the Panama Canal. "We bought it, we paid for it, it's ours, and we're going to keep it." It was the simple truth, at least as he saw it, and he repeated it again and again to wild cheers while on the stump across the country. Beginning with his upset victory in that year's North Carolina primary, his Canal *cri de guerre* was nearly enough to steal the GOP nomination that year from incumbent President Gerald Ford.

When he took office in January 1981, Reagan looked to what he saw as U.S. vulnerabilities in Central America and quickly moved to put his muscle where his rhetoric had been. The newly elected President Ronald Reagan's first target for action was Nicaragua, where the leftist Sandinista regime had grabbed power in 1979. President Carter had given the new government financial aid to discourage it from forging ties with Moscow. The aid continued even when the Sandinistas began supporting left-wing rebels in neighboring El Salvador. Upon taking office, Reagan signaled an abrupt change in this existing U.S. policy, cutting off every dollar going from Washington to Managua.

By year's end and still not satisfied with the punishment he was meting out, the president ordered arms, equipment, and money sent to the Contra forces opposing the Sandinistas. However, it was only a matter of time before the presidential action provoked a response from the Democratic-controlled Congress. The result was that in December 1982 the Congress passed the first Boland Amendment, which prohibited the use of U.S. funds "for the purpose of overthrowing the Government of Nicaragua."

In October 1983, the United States invaded Grenada. At the same time, the White House, despite the Boland Amendment, continued, covertly, to provide support for the Contras fighting in Nicaragua. Reagan's lieutenants managed to justify it with a pair of loopholes they'd spotted in the bill's language. For one, there was nothing in it specifically preventing wealthy U.S. allies — ones especially reliant on our goodwill and security support — from demonstrating their gratitude. Once hints had been dropped revealing how important the Contras were to the Reagan administration's worldview, Saudi Arabia, for example, could be especially generous.

The second loophole spotted by the Reagan people dealt with the phrasing of the Boland Amendment. It proscribed using funds for the purpose of "overthrowing the government of Nicaragua." They simply denied this was their purpose even if it was the purpose of the Contras themselves. While it could be seen as hairsplitting of the worst kind, it was justification enough in the anticommunist cause.

In January and February 1984, shockingly, the Nicaraguan harbors were mined, damaging local fishing boats, a Dutch dredger, and a Soviet tanker, among other vessels. Initially the Contras took credit. Two months later, David Rogers of the *Wall Street Journal* broke the story that it was the Central Intelligence Agency that had masterminded it. More stunning was the fact that the operation had been run out of Reagan's National Security Council. A young marine lieutenant colonel, Oliver North, had encouraged the use of the mines. Later, one of the planners would be quoted as saying, "The whole thing was a fiasco."

The exposure of the CIA's embarrassing role in the incident was no deterrent for the president, whose commitment to getting rid of the Ortega government was unswerving. "There is a totalitarian government now in Nicaragua. And the Nicaraguan government is supporting and providing ammunition and weapons to the guerrillas in El Salvador, who are trying to overthrow a government that was duly elected by the people," he said at a luncheon of prominent Republican women. "Well, we're supporting people who are fighting for democracy and freedom and those people who shut off that aid are supporting a totalitarian dictatorship in Nicaragua." It was now the company line. "Man, if you weren't hard enough in your support for the Contras," a senior aide said, "you were a commie."

Equally strong in his feelings on the subject, Tip O'Neill labeled the president's phrasemaking on the subject of Nicaragua "demagoguery." Here was Tip, without irony, sizzling Reagan with the same branding iron his rival had used at the outbreak of their ideological range war.

Jim Baker was starting to worry. "If Congress says you can't give aid to the contras," he pointed out at a national security briefing that summer, "you'd better be careful about going out and getting it from third countries." But while he and Mike Deaver were nervous about the administration's Central American excursions, the instigators remained gung ho.

In October 1984, a second Boland Amendment became law. It was designed to plug the loophole, banning the U.S. intelligence agencies from funding the Contras for whatever purpose. It stated that "during fiscal year 1985, no funds available to the Central Intelligence Agency, the Department of Defense or any other agency or entity involved in intelligence activities may be obligated or expended for the purpose of which would have the effect of supporting, directly or indirectly, military or paramilitary operations in Nicaragua by any nation, group, organization, movement or individual."

Then, a week later, the story broke that the CIA had passed on to the Contras a handbook on assassinations. "It is possible," it instructed, "to neutralize carefully selected and planned targets, such as court judges . . . police and State Security officials." The CIA-authored manual also advocated the triggering of Sandinista violence against antigovernment critics. In this way, "martyrs" useful for purposes of Contra propaganda would be created.

According to a White House aide, Reagan knew nothing of the manual. O'Neill, however, went right for the source. "It is nothing short of outrageous that the C.I.A. should do this," the Speaker declared at his press conference the next day. He called for Reagan's CIA director, William J. Casey — the man who'd chaired his presidential campaign — to quit. "I say it's time Mr. Casey should leave his job. I want him out of there." He pointed out that if the CIA chief remained agency head, "then it shows the president condones his actions."

After November, Ronald Reagan was flush with the forty-nine-state victory that had affirmed his personal popularity. And so, buoyed with new confidence, he began early in 1985 to push for $14 million in "humanitarian" aid to the Contras in the form of food, medicine, and clothing. Framed as part of what was called a "Central American Peace Proposal," this initiative pitted him against the Speaker once again. "Have learned Tip is asking Demos to vote against aid to the Contras," he had jotted in his diary, "as a farewell gift to him since he's retiring in 86."

On the day of the speech, Reagan recorded that O'Neill was "bad mouthing" the proposal. "Indeed Tip sounds irrational." *Passionate* is the word I'd have used for Tip's efforts at this time to thwart Reagan. "The president of the United States, and I hate to say this," the Speaker charged, "but I don't think he's going to be happy until he has troops, our boys, in Central America." Tip tried hard to change Reagan's thinking, going so far as to suggest he look at a gruesome recent *Newsweek* photo of a man, his throat slit, lying in an open grave, ostensibly the victim of a Contra death squad. The president would not be swayed. "I saw that picture and I'm told that after it was taken, the so-called victim got up and walked away."

But this round went to the Democratic opposition. Despite determined White House lobbying, Reagan's idea for aid to the Contras met with enough resistance that it was beaten — narrowly — in the House. The failure drove Reagan to new heights of indignation. "Tip has engineered a partisan campaign to hand me a defeat," he committed to his diary, "never mind if it helps make another Cuba on the American mainland."

President Daniel Ortega now made a startling gesture that upped the stakes. After watching Reagan fail in his dramatic effort to support the antigovernment rebels violently attempting to depose him, the Nicaraguan set off on a pilgrimage to Moscow. There he hoped to secure a promise of significant economic aid. It was a way of thumbing his nose at Reagan — and the United States, generally. And by acting the supplicant in this way, he handed the White House ample reinforcement for its vision of his country's status as an all-out Soviet client. When Ortega got to the Soviet Union, however, Gorbachev greeted him warmly, but didn't agree to a specific amount of aid. Moreover, he appeared to deride his guest for continuing to believe in an imminent

U.S. invasion of his country, which he saw as crying wolf.

Thanks in large part to Ortega's poorly timed mission, the House reversed itself on Contra aid that June. Where it had voted to give *no* aid in the spring — not even the requested "humanitarian" kind — it now followed the Republican-led Senate in approving $27 million for food, medicine, and clothing to the Contras. It was roughly double what it had rejected just two months earlier.

Tip blamed Daniel Ortega's blatant play for Moscow's patronage for the House's change of mind. "When that happened it was only a matter of time before the House would rally behind President Reagan and vote with him to fund the Contras," he would write. But what he saw was the United States on a slippery slope to another Vietnam. "He is not going to be happy until he has our Marines and our Rangers down there for a complete victory. He can see himself heading a contingent down Broadway with paper flying out of the windows and a big smile on his face, kind of a grade-B motion picture actor, coming home the conquering hero."

The national debate over Nicaragua was heating up. The media had begun reporting stories of Contra acts of violence clearly at odds with the White House version of their patriotic activities. Earlier in the year, Reagan had paid tribute to the Nicaraguan rebels as national heroes who might well be deemed "the moral equal of our Founding Fathers."

The final struggle in the Reagan-O'Neill battle over Nicaragua came in 1986. It was ignited when the president asked Congress for $100 million in *largely military aid* to the Contras. "We send money and material now so we'll never have to send our own American boys," he told a group of Jewish leaders invited to the White House. "If we don't want to see the map of Central America covered in a sea of red, eventually lapping at our own borders, we must act now." In equally inflammatory language, up on Capitol Hill, Tip O'Neill made the case against this escalation in U.S. military involvement. "Tomorrow, we face another Tonkin Gulf vote," he said, referring to the 1964 resolution in which Congress had approved greater American expansion into Vietnam. "I don't want our kids dragged in."

O'Neill's concern was based on fact. The week before that vote, *Time* described how U.S. troops had been conducting maneuvers in Nicaragua's neighbor Honduras. "A $30 million network of air bases, intelligence posts, radar stations and other installations has been built." The story went on to say that engineers from Fort Bragg had parachuted into the country to construct a 4,700-foot landing field less than twenty-five miles from the Nicaraguan border.

After closing the floor debate on Contra aid with a powerful rebuttal, O'Neill broke with tradition — the Speaker of the House ordinarily doesn't vote — and cast a dramatic "Nay." So did the House majority. "You can appreciate how hard I'm working against the President's program," he wrote to a friend well before the White House proposal for military aid to Nicaragua was defeated. "I believe his policies are absolutely immoral. It appears he won't be happy until American troops are in Central America fighting for what he believes is the ultimate testing ground between the Soviets and our government."

The statement released by President Reagan described the loss as a "dark day for freedom." He continued to argue that his fellow citizens must regard the Contras as noble "freedom fighters" committed to beating back the evil communists. "The American people have begun to awaken to the danger emerging on their doorstep. And one day, in the not-too-distant future, that awareness will come home to the House of Representatives. We are gaining ground. We are winning converts. The next battle will bring us the victory this just and good cause rightly deserves."

But Tip O'Neill, too, had his motives for the Nicaragua fight. He had an aunt, his mother's sister Ann, to whom he was especially devoted and who'd been, all her adult life, a nun. Her religious name was Sister Eunice and, as an early member of the Maryknoll order, she was part of a tradition that had sent women overseas for decades, to places ranging from Korea to Bangladesh, from Manchuria to the Sudan. Since the 1950s, the Maryknoll Sisters had established missions in a new region, having become aware of the needs of the Central American poor. Sister Eunice herself had died in 1983, at the age of ninety-one.

Because of his aunt's community and because of the testimonies he heard — often privately, as a result of his openness to her world — Tip O'Neill was attuned to a Nicaraguan reality distinctly at odds with the one Ronald Reagan insisted upon. "Over and above the briefings I get," Tip had explained to his regular press contingent in 1984, "I have nuns and humanitarians who tell us that the people in the villages of Nicaragua do not know what communism is. But they know they are living a better life — with food and health care — for the first time." He could not forget what he'd heard.

Having lost the March vote on military aid to the Contras, Reagan was far from giving up. "You have my solemn determination," he had sworn after his defeat at the hands of the Tip-led Congress, I will "come back, again and again, until this battle is won." His second opportunity arrived in June, and, with an eye to swaying votes with the president's rhetorical fervor, the White House team decided to ask Speaker O'Neill if Reagan could address the House on the Tuesday before the vote.

Chief of Staff Don Regan was the one who made the request, reaching O'Neill at a charity golf match. Tip, enjoying himself after his big Boston College send-off and seeing no reason to hop to, took his time getting back to him. When he finally did, an hour and a half later, the Speaker refused to agree. To have Reagan simply come to the House on the eve of a vote, he said, would be unprecedented and "constitutionally wrong." However, he offered alternative suggestions. If President Reagan wished to meet with the House, he told the importunate Regan, then he'd have "to participate in open dialogue with members of the body." And if he wished to make a formal address, then protocol called for any such presidential speech to be made before a joint session, with the Senate in attendance as well.

O'Neill believed Regan was trying to embarrass him, making and then advertising a proposal he knew in advance the Speaker would have to reject. "There's no question about it," he told reporters. "It's a cheap political trick and I don't think the president of the United States would do it."

White House officials were "stunned" at the rebuff, a staffer who refused to be named told the *Los Angeles Times.* Reagan became as enraged by O'Neill's straight-arm as Tip himself had been by the dark suspicion Regan and others at the White House had been trying to set him up. "Tip refused to let me speak to the House. I'm going to rub his nose in this one," he announced to his diary. In the end, he settled for going on TV and making his case in a noontime broadcast. He realized that O'Neill's denying him the personal appearance before the House had degraded his address dramatically.

But when the House voted in June on the $100 million in Contra aid, Ronald Reagan wound up prevailing. For him, the victory was made doubly sweet by the fact that he'd won it after coming from behind.

Ronald Reagan knew only too well that he'd originally gained the presidency with a strong assist from Jimmy Carter's failure to win release of the American hostages in Tehran. Starting in 1984, with no surer remedy than his predecessor had, President Reagan found himself with an interminable hostage situation of his own. Over a period of months, seven American citizens would be taken as hostages by Hezbollah, a terrorist group based in Lebanon. As time passed, Reagan increasingly took personally the United States' inability to free these captives. He was particularly upset by the knowledge that one of the men, the CIA station chief in Beirut, William Buckley, had undergone severe torture at the hands of his captors.

National Security Advisor Bud McFarlane now went to work selling Reagan on a plan he believed offered the possibility of a deal by which the hostages might be released. Claiming the existence of "moderate" elements in Iran who might be willing to try to influence the hostage-takers in Lebanon was the first part of his pitch. McFarlane's idea was for the United States to sell our superior weapons to those so-called moderates for use in their ongoing war with Iraq. In return for this support, there was the strong possibility, he'd said, they'd be willing to approach Hezbollah.

McFarlane then offered an added inducement for the old Cold Warrior. Those "moderates" could well assume power upon the death of the Ayatollah Khomeini. They might make all the difference when it came to thwarting Soviet intentions in Iran.

"Some strange soundings are coming from the Iranians," Reagan wrote in his diary on July 17, 1985. "Bud M. will be here tomorrow to talk about it. It could be a breakthrough on getting our 7 kidnap victims back. Evidently the Iranian economy is disintegrating fast under the strain of war." The next day, he met with McFarlane. There are, indeed, Iranians "with reasonably good connections," McFarlane told Reagan, who could help get the hostages freed. "Yes, go ahead," Reagan told him. "Open it up."

Yet Reagan recognized the need for the deepest secrecy, as the conspiracy began to wind its way into history. Here's what he confided in his diary, five months later, on December 5, 1985:

NSC Briefing — probably Bud's last. Subject was our undercover effort to free our 5 hostages held by terrorists in Lebanon. It is a complex undertaking with only a few of us in on it. I won't even write in the diary what we're up to.

The plot very definitely was thickening. Having been initially described as an arrangement involving the United States and Iranian "moderates" in the Iranian ruling circle but outside the official Iranian government — by January 1986 it had morphed into a deal between the United States and elements in the Iranian Revolutionary Guard. Reagan's backing of a deal nevertheless remained constant. What this meant was the United States was now shipping arms to the Iranian leadership itself.

What had begun as a deal to establish a back channel with Iranians possibly able to open discussions with the hostage-takers no longer looked like that. Now what we were entering into had become precisely the sort of quid pro quo Ronald Reagan had said he'd never ever stoop to, in this case, an arms-for-hostages arrangement with Iranian generals, who'd repay our support with a command to release the Americans being held in Lebanon.

The American press ran with the story on November 5, with its original news source for the details the Lebanese weekly *Al Shiraa*. The instant the revelations broke, they hit the White House as an all-out scandal.

Having dumped one president — Jimmy Carter — perceived as weak in confronting Iranian hostage-takers, the American public was in no mood to buy this updated version. An ABC poll showed four out of five Americans surveyed opposed delivering arms to Iran to win freedom for the hostages. Nearly as many citizens questioned indicated opposition to providing Iran with weapons as a way to improve relations with Iranian moderates. A majority of those polled believed Reagan had broken not just with American policies but with his own principles, that he'd been caught "negotiating with terrorists." Suddenly Reagan found himself a man mired in Middle Eastern intrigue, far from his Cold War comfort zone.

On November 25, Attorney General Edwin Meese announced that his investigation of the Iranian arms deal had shown that "monies" from the transaction had then been diverted to the Contras in a ploy overseen by Oliver North. (In fact, I'd known North around this time, though only slightly, encountering him at meetings. Initially, I viewed North as a figure involved with Central America. Later, I'd noticed his name connected to the Middle East. Even back then, in real time, he'd struck me as spreading himself around far too thin for his own good.)

The Iranians had paid $30 million for the missiles, Meese learned, more than double what they cost. Most of the profits, according to an April memorandum from North to Admiral John Poindexter, who'd replaced McFarlane the year before as national security advisor, went to the Nicaraguan Democratic Resistance Forces, that is, the Contras, for "critically needed supplies." It was to "bridge the period between now and when Congressionally-approved lethal assistance can be delivered." After the House had, in March, defeated the $100 million in military aid, the enterprising North simply had decided to make up for the loss.

Though he vigorously denied all knowledge of North and Poindexter's action, Reagan nonetheless made clear in his diary where his sympathies in the matter lay. The

571

diversion of the money, he wrote, was "their way of helping the Contras at a time when Congress was refusing aid to the Contras."

Poindexter, who resigned the day Meese delivered the news, had headed the NSC less than a year. Still, it was long enough for him to reflect on what had gone down on his watch. Here's the epitaph he left to Oliver North's disastrous scheme to divert the profits from the arms-for-hostages deal to the rebels in Nicaragua. "I had a feeling," he later admitted to Don Regan, "that something bad was going on, but I didn't investigate it and I didn't do a thing about it. I really didn't want to know. I felt sorry for the Contras. I was so damned mad at Tip O'Neill for the way he was dragging the Contras around that I didn't want to know what, if anything, was going on. I should have, but I didn't."

Tip and the Gipper.
They showed how two conviction politicians, a liberal and a conservative, can make
politics—and democratic government—work for the American people.

CHAPTER TWENTY-THREE:
LEGACY

"Let us endeavor so to live that when we
come to die even the undertaker will be
sorry."

— MARK TWAIN

Ronald Reagan survived the Iran-Contra
scandal, though the fallout caused his job
approval rating to take a deep dive — dropping more than twenty points in late 1986.
The summit meetings with Mikhail Gorbachev — Geneva in 1985, Reykjavik in
1986, Washington in 1987, and Moscow in
1988 — were thrilling. Peace between two
long-standing enemies, they said, might at
last be at hand. Without a shot being fired,
the dread with which every American had
lived ever since news the Soviets had gotten
the "A-bomb" was gone.

For my part, I felt the wonder of its
absence, and, clearly, so did my fellow
citizens. I remember the morning late in

1987 that I found myself standing alongside throngs of other admirers at the corner of Pennsylvania Avenue and Seventeenth Street, all of us cheering the Soviet president who'd helped to change history. I recall, too, that Gorbachev, startled by such a reception, but pleased, had stepped out of his limousine to shake hands with admirers.

Within a year of Reagan's leaving office, the Iron Curtain came crashing down across Eastern Europe — most movingly, when the ugly wall that had divided Berlin for almost three decades was leveled in celebration. The actual end of the Cold War was surprising, however, and played out far differently from what anyone had expected. The T. S. Eliot phrase "Not with a bang but a whimper" is apt. The sad, pinched bureaucrats of East Germany and the other Soviet Bloc capitals simply converted. As a sly government economist in Budapest cynically told me that spring, "The road to Damascus is very crowded these days." An activist university professor I met was more sublime. "Freedom is contagious," he said.

By 1989, George H. W. Bush was the occupant of the Oval Office, and I'd been working for two years as the *San Francisco Examiner*'s Washington bureau chief. Just as I'd loved being in the thick of the action in the Speaker's office, I treasured the chance now to be a journalist during such a time of great events. That autumn, as the world watched the revolutions in Eastern Europe that signaled the downfall of communism, I devoted one of my twice-a-week columns to saying I wished Ronald Reagan were still president in November 1989.

I would have loved to hear the speech he'd have made. I remembered how, at the Berlin Wall, in 1987, he'd looked ahead to the stirrings that were already in the air. "We welcome change and openness," he declared, "for we believe that freedom and security go together, that the advance of human liberty can only strengthen the cause of world peace."

What had occurred, what was *still* then occurring, meant that all Europe would soon be free, just as Roosevelt and Churchill had once hoped. In those exciting years in the late 1980s and early 1990s, I shared in the glorious sense that the many wrongs of the twentieth century were truly being righted.

But what about my boss, the distinguished Speaker of the House, Thomas P. O'Neill, Jr., and the end to his own Washington service? When he stepped down in late 1986, his job approval rating stood at a heartening 67 percent. "I was almost as well-liked as the president," he noted in his memoir, *Man of the House,* and I know how much that notion meant to him. His book, published the year after he retired, gratifyingly, was an instant bestseller.

Ronald Reagan had held office in Washington for eight years, Tip for thirty-four. They'd begun their political careers on opposite sides of the American continent, and would, I'm sure, never have known each other had not each man felt a compelling pull to affect — in great, not small, ways — the world in which he lived. Both knew, too, when to make a fist and when to shake hands.

At the same time, I'd say that, throughout the era during which I closely observed them, neither of these two highly individualistic, greatly determined men ever penetrated the mystery of the other. Nor did they really try. Their way of life comprised an ever-ongoing series of alliances and antagonisms, but did not include personal analysis of themselves or others. They were men born when the more formal nineteenth century remained the cultural backdrop. Tip would jolt his far younger staffers with casual references to "back in the days of high-button shoes" or when he would casually mention "Taft," referring not to the prominent Ohio senator of midcentury but to the man's father, still in the White House at Tip's birth. This may well have explained the restraint that marked both his character and Reagan's. In his own way, each was a true gentleman in a way we don't ask our leaders to be anymore.

When I worked for the Speaker I came to love the rituals and rhythms of the House, especially Thursday nights when the whole body would come together for the closing arguments and final vote. I recall one particular night that warms my heart even now. I'd begun observing a hot debate with two men in the very heat of it. When it was over, the big vote cast, the Republican member crossed the aisle to the other side and stopped before the Democrat with whom he shared the red-faced debate. "What are you doing this weekend?" he inquired warmly. And then, after a moment of chat, "Say hello to your wife."

I seriously contend if Jefferson or Madison or any of the others had been present for those moments — the debate across the aisle and the getting together afterward — they would say, "We did well. This is what we wanted, what we most hoped would endure."

I've now, in writing this book — but also in the decades before, as I *considered* writing it — thought a great deal about their relationship, where they meshed and where they emphatically parted ways. One thing I know: when I marry Reagan's inability to connect personally to the roughness of the budget cuts to Tip's inability to grasp his rival's hold on the country, what's remarkable is the way what needed to get done did — even with those stumbling blocks along the way.

Yet, given their pre–World War I births, Ronald Reagan and Tip O'Neill both lived to see nearly every great advance of the twentieth century. They knew, too, their own century's harrowing wars and its generations of ever grimmer weapons. The span of decades to which they bore personal witness was monumental.

Each man, as I judge his behavior, thought it always preferable to propel the republic forward — even when the will of the people differed from his own. Why is that? Here I'd like to offer what I regard as the best explanations for their behavior, *at its best.*

1. Both had been brought up to show respect for positions of authority. "Reagan took Congress very seri-

ously," as O'Neill once observed. For his part, the Speaker rarely referred to his political rival by his name but, most often, by his full title: "The President of the United States." The lessons taught him at St. John's High School were long-lasting.

2. Both preferred to play by the rules. Tip understood that Reagan had won in 1980 and, as a result, did not delay action of his economic agenda. He gave the new president a "schedule" for votes on his fiscal program and stuck to it. For his part the Gipper recognized that he'd lost in 1982 and so allowed for the repair of Social Security based on the Democrats' chosen approach.

3. Neither acted like the spoiled kid who when he's losing yells, "It's my ball and I'm taking it home!" Both believed in keeping the process going — through the myriad frustrations — and so filibusters, roadblocks, government shutdowns, all were avoided.

4. Each understood the important rule continually preached by my col-

league Kirk O'Donnell: "Always be able to talk." The two of them, Reagan and O'Neill, matched each other in this, and both had truly able staffs that supported them in keeping communication lines open.

5. Each had the confidence to recruit, and take counsel from, strong advisors. This showed a deep sense of personal security on the part of both men.

6. They had one very big thing in common. Not just their Irishness, but their age. Both were growing not just older, but *old,* and they knew it. Tip was facing the fact that Reagan would be his last president, while Reagan understood that this was the only presidency he was going to get. If each were to leave his mark, then he would have to do it, somehow, with the other. In other words — together. The truth of this political reality became clear when, starting with the 1982 election, Ronald Reagan realized he could no longer shove Tip O'Neill aside.

In fact, as it turned out, their matchup over the course of six years was no zero-sum contest. Not at all. Rather, in combat, as gladiators do, each made the other look stronger, bigger. I can see now how Tip brought out the reformer in Reagan, forcing him to make the case for change as president as he had as a candidate. At the same time, I can't deny that Reagan woke Tip up from years of complacency in a Congress the Democrats had dominated for years.

Fighting on many grand issues, they cast each other in brighter colors as they did so, creating for themselves larger parts in history, I believe, by their sharing of the stage. Reagan without Tip would have lacked the frequent pushback that kept him from the abyss of excess. Tip without Reagan would have been a man who'd reached his pinnacle but without a reason to be there. As it was, he could retire, proud of an undeniable accomplishment: he'd helped make Ronald Reagan a conservative president but not a radical one.

However, I worked for Tip, not the other guy. And just as my grandmother had intuited how much my Peace Corps stint in Africa had changed me, so would anyone be right if they remarked changes in me as a result of those intense, shining years spent in the Speaker's office. Most important, I learned that convictions are not a burden but a strength; they are what separate the fighter from the quitter.

And then there were the lighter moments, rare and therefore treasured. Like the time he called me into his back Capitol office just to have me see him strutting across the room in his green top hat with his Blackthorn walking stick — all just for me.

After he retired, our relationship changed only a little. He took an office at his son Kip's law firm near Dupont Circle. We would have long lunches across the street at the Palm, where I'd listen to him ask the old question, the one that had brought me to attention each morning during all those years. "Whaddaya hear, Chris?"

I was very happy he liked the first book I wrote, *Hardball.* It had been, of course, my time with him — and all those thousands of hours next to Kirk O'Donnell, working *for* him — that inspired it and provided many of its stories. He seemed to enjoy my syndicated twice-a-week column, too. What he didn't like, occasionally, was stuff he heard me say on television; he'd call when an opinion didn't sit well with him and let me know. On that score, nothing had changed. He still looked upon me as "his" guy. I'd earned my political spurs working for him, after all.

Certainly, his pals saw me as Tip's satellite for years after I was off doing my own thing. I remember once in the fall of 1988 when I picked up the phone at 8 a.m. — a *Saturday!* — and there he was. He must have been up all night at a card game and had had to endure ribbing from his buddies for the way I'd called the Bentsen-Quayle vice presidential debate that week. (Yes, incredibly, I'd awarded it to Quayle! I'd done it on points, ignoring the game-changing moment when he'd recklessly compared himself to Jack Kennedy.) What was affecting for me to hear, and accept — even though he didn't come out and say it in so many words — was that, at some level, he felt that when I spoke I still spoke for *him.*

Of course, if you worked for Tip O'Neill, there were all those stories he recounted. He never stopped telling them, and even if we'd heard them before, we never stopped listening. We knew he wasn't just one of a kind, but also one of a dying breed. And if Tip wasn't, when you came right down to it, the most articulate of men, he was, as I've repeatedly emphasized, an Irishman through and through. His son Tommy once told me those stories I listened to for so many hours back then were his father's gift to me. His dad, he said, had known one day I'd write about them.

I was, after all, *his* writer.

I remember one of my last conversations with my old boss. He described a recent trip he'd taken and the young flight attendant who'd mentioned to him how she'd heard an important person was going to be aboard. She apparently had no idea who Tip O'Neill was. "Chris, it goes away," he said. And I heard him.

He died in January 1994. Later that year, Ronald Reagan began his fade from public life. In a handwritten letter to the country, he announced he was a victim of Alzheimer's disease.

I only wish there was some way I could spare Nancy from this painful experience. When the time comes, I am confident that with your help she will face it with faith and courage. In closing, let me thank you, the American people, for giving me the great honor of allowing me to serve as your president. When the Lord calls me home, whenever that may be, I will leave with the greatest love for this country of ours and eternal optimism for its future. I now begin the journey that will lead me into the sunset of my life. I know that for America there will always be a bright dawn ahead.

With dignity and courage, his wife, Nancy, would keep alight the Reagan torch through all the years ahead.

The worse things get in Washington — the more threats of shutdown weaken the country's confidence in government; the more eleventh-hour stopgap deals come along to demoralize us; the more personal attacks are performed on cue for the cameras; the more nasty tweets — the more people who care about our republic look back to an idea of when the world worked the way it's supposed to.

At the start of this book, I mentioned George Washington and Pierre L'Enfant riding on horseback up to Jenkins Hill, then looking down on the prospect before them. It must have taken great imagination for those two men — the general who'd won the war against the great British Empire and the immigrant architect — to see this swamp along the Potomac as the seat of a great new Republic. But how much more hope it must have taken to summon up an idea that had never taken root before, of a fresh and rugged country governed by its own citizens with all their passions and differences.

We need a restoration of that confidence and of the standards for public service it demands. An alertness to common ground, an allegiance to united interest. We need leaders able to balance large purpose with equally large awareness of the electorate, what message the voters have sent.

In a worthy contest this goes for those who've won but especially for those who haven't. Both sides in any debate must respect each other. The rules of fair play can't be simply cast aside. You ask if such behavior is possible. I wrote this book to show that it is.

ACKNOWLEDGMENTS

This book could not have been written without the powerful contribution of President Ronald Reagan. I want to thank Nancy Reagan and historian Douglas Brinkley for bringing his diary to publication. It's a wondrous source of daily insight into Reagan's political personality. Without it, I could not have captured the ping and pong of his relations with Speaker O'Neill.

As a companion document, one recording O'Neill's daily thinking, this book benefits from the daily press conferences the Speaker conducted fifteen minutes before each House session. I must thank Eric Schwartz, now a Washington attorney, for recording these events for the Rules Committee. Reading these transcripts today takes me on a trip back to those years when I stood at the side of the Speaker's desk as he spoke with his accustomed candor about the man in the White House.

The great chroniclers of the Reagan-O'Neill contests were the correspondents of the *New York Times, Washington Post, Boston Globe, Wall Street Journal, Time, Newsweek,* the Associated Press, and United Press International. I began this project with piles of their clippings that towered several feet around my desk. It's with their help I was able to isolate and narrate the episodes recounted in this book. What impressed me most was the accuracy and fairness of the reporting for these quality institutions.

I want to thank Hedrick Smith, the celebrated *New York Times* reporter, for sharing the transcripts of the meaty interviews he conducted for his landmark work, *The Power Game.* Because he spoke with Tip O'Neill, Kirk O'Donnell, and myself back in the 1980s, the interviews carry fresh and still-exciting memories of the events discussed.

There is one person who deserves credit above all for this book. People ask me how I can carry out a project like this while hosting *Hardball* on MSNBC each night of the week. The answer is the great Kathleen Matthews, executive vice president for Marriott International. The queen of my life has allowed me the ambition to sit in my home office and work at all hours of the day. I don't know how to weigh the benefits of the work against the loss of relaxed time together but I can only hope it comes out in favor of the effort.

As for the production itself I hereby acknowledge the brilliance of Tina Urbanski. In addition to her always on-the-mark advisory role, she has been chief operating officer of this project, keeping the worksheets filled, the tasks clarified, the deadlines met. Where there could have been chaos, I came face-to-face each day with an associate committed to the work, dead-set on its completion on the date assigned. Tina *is* my organization. More than that, she is a wartime consigliere, forever ready for the day's challenges, calm in the face of danger.

For the literary challenge of this project, I owe all to my longtime editor Michele Slung. She's fabulous. In the case of each of the twenty-three chapters, including the two she made out of one, Michele has taken my draft and Midas-like transformed it, in flow, cadence, and storytelling, to novel-like narrative.

This being a work of history, I have needed a researcher with the academic background and youthful zeal to put in the hard, essential work at critical stages of this project. Michael Banning, a recent Yale graduate, did the crucial job of identifying and cataloging my research, organizing the material into the giant binders that were the genesis of each chapter. It was also his role to challenge and, where necessary, correct me on the facts. It's my great fortune to have had an associate like Michael ready to take the pains to get it right.

I want to thank as well the authors who preceded me in narrating this period of American history. One is my old boss himself. If you want to know what it was like to sit in Tip O'Neill's back office in the Capitol and hear the stories, get a copy of *Man of the House.* It's his book from cover to cover, filled with the color of an incredible life and career.

Next comes John Aloysius Farrell's masterwork, *Tip O'Neill and the Democratic Century.* It captures all the Irish in the guy, from his days in North Cambridge to his fight to end the "Troubles" in Northern Ireland. It is a great work of biography. Another part of the scaffolding for this book comes from the great biographies of Ronald Reagan. They include Lou Cannon's *President Reagan: The Role of a Lifetime,* Richard Reeves's *President Reagan: The Triumph of Imagination,* Edmund Morris's *Dutch,* and Ron Reagan's *My Father at 100.* Cannon is the best and most compressive when it comes to understanding Reagan's political rise to power. Reeves puts the sharp focus on the presidency itself. Morris goes for the elusive man himself. Ron Reagan gets far deeper, writing with love about a father who kept so much secret.

I want to thank the people in the Reagan White House who were helpful in telling my stories in *Tip and the Gipper*. They include former U.S. secretary of state James A. Baker III, former Reagan chief of congressional relations Max Friedersdorf, and Kenneth Duberstein, who was President Reagan's last White House chief of staff. For my account of the Social Security rescue effort I owe Alan Greenspan, who headed the president's bipartisan commission. This great public servant was generous, thoughtful, and penetrating in his recollection of those tricky days when the country's chief retirement program faced an uncertain future. Bob Michel, the Republican leader in the House during the Reagan years, was another positive help. As was my friend Rockwell Schnabel.

I want to thank the surviving children of Tip and Millie O'Neill for helping with this project, especially with the stories of home life during the political turbulence of the 1980s.

For assistance in producing an accurate account of history, I want to thank Steven Weisman, who reported on Reagan and O'Neill for the *New York Times*. His insightful study of my draft and the revisions he suggested added greatly to the finished product. The same is true of my close friend Mark Johnson, who once again contributed his historic sense and close reading to help me get it right.

At the Reagan Library I wish to express my gratitude to Joanne Drake, and also to Nancy Reagan's assistant, Wren Powell. I thank Nancy Reagan herself for her lively, generous friendship of all these years.

Also, William H. Davis of the National Archives; Bruce Kirby of the Library of Congress; Justine Sundaram and Kathleen Williams of the Boston College Library; as well as Rino Landa, Ed Kaplan, and Annelise Anderson.

I would also like to thank our interns at *Hardball* for the key research assistance they have given me in addition to their daily duties: Sara Bovat, Kara Brennan, Josh Cole, Alex Kaplan, Katie Lesser, Stephanie Melson, Hannah Jane Nunez, Joseph Rabinowitz, and Rachel Witkin.

I want to thank MSNBC president Phil Griffin for his support all these years we have worked together, and *Hardball* executive producer John Reiss for being a great partner day in and day out. He is a newsperson of the first order. So, in fact, is the excellent *Hardball* team, both in Washington and New York.

Now to the two people who deserve the world. Jennifer Rudolph Walsh of William Morris Endeavor is quite simply the greatest representative an author could have. Jonathan Karp, publisher of Simon & Schuster, stuns me with his judgment in every conversation. I quickly came to trust his every editorial decision; now I do it instinctively. What a great mind and sensibility to have at the helm! While I'm at it, I certainly want to thank his associates Nicholas Greene, Jonathan Evans, and Larry Hughes, who promises to be the book tour's Natty Bumppo.

NOTES

The primary sources for this book include President Reagan's diaries (RR), transcripts of Speaker O'Neill's daily press conferences (TPO), which he held — and I attended — before each session of the House of Representatives, and the handwritten journal I kept in an old-style ledger book during my tenure as his administrative assistant (CJM). Most vital, I have to suppose, are my own deep, personal memories of those six years working at my Capitol desk outside the Speaker's ceremonial office.

To strengthen this foundation of day-to-day statements by Reagan and O'Neill — and my own memory — I have used the excellent deadline work of correspondents for the *New York Times,* the *Washington Post,* the *Boston Globe,* and the *Wall Street Journal;* also the weekly journalism of *Time, Newsweek,* and the *National Journal.*

Since the events in this book centered on three decades ago, I have relied on two other sources for contemporary accounts. One is Speaker O'Neill's autobiography, *Man of the House (MOH)* (New York: Random House, 1987), which contains all the old stories I heard him tell. Reading its pages reminds me of sitting in his back office of the Capitol when there was time on our hands and he had the generosity to tell me his tales of lore. The other source, which I found invaluable, were the interviews the much-respected Hedrick Smith conducted for his groundbreaking *The Power Game* (HS). Rick sat with Speaker O'Neill, Kirk O'Donnell, and me for lengthy sessions focusing on the political strategies of our long fight with Reagan. To read those transcripts is to replant oneself back into the history of which we were such a feisty part.

I have added to these with fresh interviews with Reagan's senior aides: chief of staff and later secretary of the treasury James A. Baker III; chief of congressional relations Max Friedersdorf, congressional liaison and Reagan's last chief of staff Kenneth Duberstein, and deputy chief of staff Michael Deaver's widow, Carolyn. Added to these are the conversations I have had with the four surviving children of Speaker O'Neill: Rosemary, Thomas, Susan, and Christopher.

Both Reagan and O'Neill have been the subjects of impressive biographies. Lou Cannon has devoted a huge effort covering Reagan back through the time of his California governorship. *President Reagan: Role of a Lifetime* is, indeed, his masterwork. Richard Reeves has produced the impressive *President Reagan: The Triumph of Imagination* (New York: Simon & Schuster, 2005), and Edmund Morris, for all the controversy attached, has given us *Dutch: A Memoir of Ronald Reagan* (New York: Random House, 1999), a work that the president's son Ron has said gets closest to uncovering what he describes as his father's *strangeness*. John A. Farrell has written the excellent *Tip O'Neill and the Democratic Century* (Boston: Little, Brown, 2001).

Preface

since General Washington and Pierre L'Enfant: The Papers of George Washington Digital Edition, ed. Theodore J. Crackel (Charlottesville: University of Virginia Press, Rotunda, 2008), June 28, 1791.

"What both men deplored": Thomas P. O'Neill III, *New York Times,* October 5, 2012.

Chapter One: Death of a Presidency

In the final weeks of the Carter presidency I wrote an account of the campaign's final days. I wanted to show the drama of that short bit of time between the debate, which Reagan clearly won, and the president's desperate scramble to avoid defeat in the election. This provided me with a useful contemporary record of the events described here.

"You will call him an actor": Author conversation with Gerald Rafshoon.

"I am paying for this microphone": Cannon, *President Reagan,* p. 47.

Choosing a new campaign manager: Ibid., pp. 47–48.

It had been in 1940: Ibid., p. 54.

"The president lately has been saying": Reagan speech, Neshoba, Miss., August 3, 1980.

"Can anyone look at the record": Reagan speech, Republican National Convention, July 17, 1980.

"I'm here because": Reagan speech, Liberty State Park, September 1, 1980.

"There you go again": Reagan-Carter presidential debate, October 28, 1980.

"any attack on an embassy": U.S. Department of State.

ramped up his attack on Reagan: Carter speech, Akron, Ohio, November 3, 1980.

"How many of you": Carter speech, Seattle, November 3, 1980.

Chapter Two: Starting Out

This is my personal backstory, the prelude to my involvement with the Reagan-O'Neill rivalry. Because they formed such an important part of my life, they are memories with deep footprints. They are hard examples of how each step a person takes becomes the course set for the next as well as the prerequisite for getting to take it.

Each of the roles I've played since leaving my beloved Chapel Hill — those unforgettable two years in Swaziland, my five years working for the Senate and then four years in the White House — now reside in the public record. It is a salutary benefit of service in the U.S. government.

Most important to me, these early career experiences serve as a sturdy foundation for my daily commentary on American politics and government.

Chapter Three: Starring Ronald Reagan

"If you live in the river, you should make friends with the crocodiles": Indian proverb.

Among its bullet points: Cannon, *President Reagan,* p. 93.

On the eve of: MOH, p. 26.

In 1936, at the age: Farrell, *Tip O'Neill,* pp. 66–69.

So it was in 1949: Ibid., p. 107.

"We find him very": Boston Globe, February 12, 1981.

"the admiral of the ship": TPO, November 12, 1980.

"the proper course": Ibid.

"Tip is a very practical": United Press International, November 6, 1980.

"Hannibal Jerkin": Farrell, *Tip O'Neill,* p. 452.

"I don't intend to allow": TPO, November 12, 1980.

Reagan had been nursing: Reeves, *President Reagan,* p. 11.

"Why should I have done": Gerald and Deborah Hart Strober, *Reagan: The Man and His Presidency* (Boston: Houghton Mifflin, 1998), p. 131.

He and Nancy first: Washington Post, November 19, 1980.

"Like Jimmy Carter": James Baker with Steve Fiffer, *Work Hard, Study . . . and Keep Out*

of Politics! (New York: G. P. Putnam's Sons, 2006), p. 137.

"I knew that President Reagan": James Baker with Thomas M. DeFrank, *The Politics of Diplomacy: Revolution, War, and Peace, 1989–1992* (New York: G. P. Putnam's Sons, 1995), p. 334.

"I've known every speaker": "Transcript: Richard Nixon/Frank Gannon Interview, June 10, 1983," Walter J. Brown Media Archives, University of Georgia Libraries.

"We were particularly": Author interview with James Baker.

"He'd been aware of all that": Author interview with Max Friedersdorf.

Exactly two weeks: TPO, November 18, 1980.

"When President-elect Reagan": MOH, pp. 331–32

"He told me how": Ibid., p. 332.

"The president-elect seemed to": Ibid., p. 333.

" 'Absolutely, Mr. President' ": Ibid.

"Reagan was proud": Ibid., p. 332.

"He seemed genuinely surprised": Ibid.

"My father didn't get": Author conversation with Tom O'Neill.

warmest oath-taking day on record: http://www.inaugural.senate.govswearing-in/event/ronald-reagan-1981.

Later he'd ask: Reeves, *President Reagan,* p. 2.

"the adversary relationships": Reagan Toast at the Inaugural Luncheon, January 20, 1981.

"I look forward to working": Ibid.

"With thanks to Almighty God": Ibid.

Before leaving the Capitol: Farrell, *Tip O'Neill,* p. 547.

"Government is not the solution": Reagan Inaugural Address, January 20, 1981.

Chapter Four: New Kid on the Block

"Civility is not a sign of weakness": John F. Kennedy's Inaugural Address, January 20, 1961.

"It won't be the last time": Christian Science Monitor, November 20, 1980.

By January's end: Cannon, *President Reagan,* p. 83.

"The first fundamental": Ibid., p. 84.

"The second fundamental": Ibid.

For his part: MOH, p. 336.

"so clearly preposterous": Ibid., p. 337.

"Surely everybody could see": Ibid.

In early February: Reagan Address to the Nation on the Economy, February 5, 1981.

"I'm speaking to you tonight": Ibid.

"Last night, he was carefully": Washington Post, February 6, 1981.

"He comes across beautifully": New York Times, February 7, 1981.

Included in a White House: RR, February 6, 1981.

Not long after this: RR, February 16, 1981.

Among the others on hand: Ibid.

"Maybe Tip & I": Ibid.

"There are times when real life": MOH, p. 27.

"He's a terrific storyteller": Ibid., p. 334.

It had, according to: Author interview with Max Friedersdorf.

"We didn't discuss": TPO, February 17, 1981.

That afternoon the Speaker's: RR, February 17, 1981.

"Tip had last word": Ibid.

"by 77 to 17 percent": Washington Post, February 19, 1981.

"I have been up here": TPO, February 17, 1981.

"With a Republican in": MOH, p. 340.

"And with Jimmy Carter": Ibid.

Two nights after: Reagan Address Before a Joint Session of the Congress on the Program for Economic Recovery, February 18, 1981.

"A few weeks ago": Ibid.

"I would direct a question": Ibid.

In the White House meetings: MOH, p. 360.
"You want to talk to him": Author interview
with James Baker.
"How about this?": Author conversation with
Richard Allen.

Chapter Five: Joining the Fight

"I've learned that people only pay attention to
what they discover for themselves": Pretty
Poison, 1968.
When Reagan's top lobbyist: Author conver-
sation with Max Friedersdorf.
"tremendously strong": TPO, February 24,
1981.
"I don't know how many": Ibid.
honeymoon was "wearing thin": Ibid., March
4, 1981.
Asked in early March: TPO, March 4, 1981.
"We are not ready to play": Ibid.
"What I am curious of": Ibid.
"We haven't communicated": Ibid., March
11, 1981.
"He was very persuasive": Author interview
with Susan O'Neill.
"As you know": TPO, January 29, 1980.
"Nobody Knows What Happened to McCarty":
Farrell, Tip O'Neill, pp. 4–5.
"I was convinced": Mott, p. 344.
"You've made my day": Washington Post,

March 6, 1981.
"We have undone": UPI, March 19, 1981.

Chapter Six: The Lord Is My Shepherd

"I do not know that in our time": Senator Daniel Patrick Moynihan, remarks on the Senate floor, April 2, 1981.
The young Jerry Parr: Del Quentin Wilber, *Rawhide Down: The Near Assassination of Ronald Reagan* (New York: Henry Holt, 2011), p. 18.
When he was nine: Ibid.
The nine-year-old: Ibid.
In 1962, at the age of: Ibid.
Over the following years: Ibid., p. 19.
In March 1981: Ibid., p. 21.
Determined to make Foster: Ibid., pp. 36–39, 54–8.
Since a central plotline: Ibid., p. 37.
On March 30, 1981: Ibid., p. 77.
"I hope you'll forgive": Reagan Remarks at the National Conference of the Building and Construction Trades Department, AFL-CIO.
As soon as he'd finished: Wilber, *Rawhide Down,* pp. 76–80.
"Let's get out of here": Ibid., p. 83.
"My day to address": RR, March 30, 1981.
Here's White House detail: Parr FBI report,

March 31, 1981.

Suddenly Agent Parr: Wilber, *Rawhide Down,* p. 90.

"Okay": Ibid., p. 91.

Barely three minutes: Ibid., p. 95.

"Honey, I forgot to": Ibid., p. 138.

Within a week: Reeves, *President Reagan,* p. 48.

Baker learned: Letter to author from Max Friedersdorf.

"Jim called me with": Ibid.

"I was in the room": Ibid.

"The president still seemed groggy": Ibid.

" 'I'd better be going' ": Ibid.

"I suspect that in": MOH, p. 336.

The week before the shooting: RR, March 21, 1981.

"I looked up at the presidential": Reagan, *An American Life,* p. 254.

Chapter Seven: Ronald Reagan's Journey

"Go West, young man": Fred R. Shapiro, ed., *The Yale Book of Quotations* (New Haven: Yale University Press, 2006), p. 322.

in Tampico, Illinois: Marc Eliot, *Reagan: The Hollywood Years* (New York: Crown Archetype, 2008), p. 13.

Over the next seven years the Reagans moved five times in Illinois: Lou Cannon,

Governor Reagan: His Rise to Power (New York: Public Affairs, 2003), p. 12.

nicknamed "Dutch": Eliot, *Reagan,* 13.

was nine: Cannon, *Governor Reagan,* p. 12.

Now they moved again: Ibid.

His father, Jack, a salesman: Ibid., p. 11.

Neil Reagan: Ibid.

Jack Reagan drank too much: Ibid.

"the Irish curse": Cannon, *President Reagan,* p. 176.

Reagan would write: Ronald Reagan, *An American Life: The Autobiography* (New York: Simon & Schuster, 1990), p. 33.

playing varsity football: Eliot, *Reagan,* 21.

enough to be elected: Cannon, *Governor Reagan,* p. 21.

He was also: Eliot, *Reagan,* 21.

Setting out to convince: Cannon, *Governor Reagan,* p. 24.

first for a fraternity: Ibid.

his majors had been economics and sociology: Ibid., pp. 32–33.

Davenport, Iowa: Eliot, *Reagan,* p. 27.

There he landed a slot: Ibid., p. 30.

After Davenport: Ibid., p. 32.

In 1937: Cannon, *Governor Reagan,* p. 49.

five years after saying good-bye: Eliot, *Reagan,* pp. 26–30.

"goodbye sports": Wayne Federman, *The At-*

lantic, November 14, 2011.

twenty-six-year-old: Eliot, *Reagan,* p. 13.

A native New Yorker: Cannon, *Governor Reagan,* p. 75.

Returning after her four years: Nancy Reagan at Smith College 1911–1943, Reagan Foundation website.

He'd gone as: Eliot, *Reagan,* p. 47.

But the chance to take: Morris, *Dutch,* p. 130.

to keep an eye on the Chicago Cubs: Cannon, *Governor Reagan,* p. 48.

In Los Angeles: Eliot, *Reagan,* p. 42.

in the Biltmore Hotel's: Cannon, *Governor Reagan,* p. 48.

One performer was a singer: Ibid.

He sent a note: Eliot, *Reagan,* p. 42.

It was a break: Ibid., p. 48.

he be billed as Ronald, not "Dutch": Cannon, *Governor Reagan,* pp. 49–50.

Reagan's first film: Ibid., p. 53.

Love Is on the Air *was:* Ibid., p. 54.

The reviews: Eliot, *Reagan,* p. 53.

Over the next few years: Ibid., pp. 353–55.

He appeared as a military cadet: Cannon, *Governor Reagan,* p. 54.

and as an army private: Turner Classic Movies.

In a change of pace: Eliot, *Reagan,* pp. 94–96.

1940, the year Knute Rockne: Ibid., p. 356.

On the Warner lot: Ibid., p. 69.

Each day: Ibid., pp. 70–71.

When O'Brien won: Ibid., p. 113.

he soon learned from Reagan: Cannon, *Governor Reagan,* p. 55.

and that he'd grown up worshipping both: Eliot, *Reagan,* p. 116.

died in 1920: Jack Cavanaugh, *Sports Illustrated,* December 30, 1991.

he'd once even started: Reagan, *An American Life,* pp. 90–91.

he brought in: Ibid., p. 91.

"This is a helluva important role": Cannon, *Governor Reagan,* p. 55.

offering to read Rockne's lines: Ibid.

premiered in South Bend: Eliot, *Reagan,* p. 117.

the role he himself considered his best: Cannon, *Governor Reagan,* p. 57.

as he often did in those years: Nicholas Wapshott, *Ronald Reagan and Margaret Thatcher: A Political Marriage* (New York: Sentinel, 2007), p. 49.

Opening in early 1942: Bob Colacello, *Ronnie and Nancy: Their Path to the White House, 1911 to 1980* (New York: Warner Books, 2004), p. 150.

"Where's the rest of me?": Eliot, *Reagan,* p. 142.

what Reagan's character, Drake McHugh, demands to know: Ibid.

the title of his 1965 autobiography: Ibid., p. 4.

Measured by box office: Ibid., p. 357.

with Errol Flynn: Cannon, *Governor Reagan,* p. 66.

Two years earlier they'd appeared together in Santa Fe Trail: Ibid., p. 55.

Desperate Journey *follows the perilous path:* Ibid., p. 154.

On December 8, 1941: Prologue, The National Archives, Winter 2001, Vol. 33, No. 4.

The movie industry: Eliot, *Reagan,* p. 161.

The month before he'd moved: Ronald Reagan Library.

Arriving in Hollywood, he was appointed: Ibid.

two months after Kings Row: Colacello, *Ronnie and Nancy,* p. 150.

kept him from assignment to a combat unit: Ronald Reagan Library.

Transferring from the cavalry: Ibid.

then to the just-created First Motion Picture Unit: Eliot, p. 161.

Never before had a military unit: Ibid.

It was this unit: Ibid., p. 162.

now dubbed Fort Roach: Ibid., p. 162.

In 1943: The Academy of Motion Picture Arts and Sciences.

he'd narrated: Cannon, *Governor Reagan,* p. 68

won the Oscar: The Academy of Motion Picture Art and Sciences.

Though he both appeared in and voiced-over numerous movies: Eliot, p. 166.

he was also: Ronald Reagan Library.

at the end of his active duty: Eliot, *Reagan,* p. 176.

and Burbank: Ibid., p. 163.

wife of eight years: Ibid., p. 7.

She'd become a Warner: Cannon, *Governor Reagan,* p. 63.

though often as an uncredited: Internet Movie Database.

chorus girl: Cannon, *Governor Reagan,* p. 63.

thirty or so pictures: Internet Movie Database.

A native Missourian: Cannon, *Governor Reagan,* p. 63.

her showbiz start in radio, as a singer: Eliot, *Reagan,* p. 81.

She'd also been twice married: Ibid., pp. 81–82.

But by 1948: Ibid., p. 179.

She'd been nominated: Ibid., p. 194.

the Hollywood gossip mills went to town:

Ibid., p. 213.

"Don't ask Ronnie": Wapshott, *Ronald Reagan and Margaret Thatcher*, p. 43.

"You bore me . . . Leave!": Eliot, *Reagan*, p. 210.

By his own account: Reagan, *An American Life*, p. 47.

would shut down the campus: Ibid.

Reagan was the one picked: Ibid., p. 48.

"When I came to actually": Cannon, *Governor Reagan*, pp. 25–26.

Robert Cummings, his Kings Row *costar:* Eliot, *Reagan*, p. 145.

Nancy, whom Ronald married in 1952: Ibid., p. 253.

One, he wrote, was the "public": Ron Reagan, *My Father at 100* (New York: Viking Penguin, 2011), p. 13.

he wasn't being considered for parts: Eliot, *Reagan*, pp. 176–77.

He shot a few: Ibid., pp. 357–59.

a young actress ten years his junior: Ibid., p. 7.

she'd dated Clark Gable: Ibid., p. 230.

"My life really began": Nancy Reagan Biography, White House Historical Association.

who'd voted for FDR: Cannon, *Governor Reagan*, p. 37.

had backed Helen Gahagan Douglas: Ibid., p. 101.

would remain a registered: Morris, *Dutch,* p. 326.

In 1937 Reagan had joined: Cannon, *Governor Reagan,* p. 85.

In 1946 he became: Ibid., p. 86.

Ugly violence: Eliot, *Reagan,* p.190.

In the weeks that followed: Ibid., pp. 188–91.

"Ronnie Reagan has turned": Ibid., p. 192.

Reagan would go on to serve: Reagan Biography, SAG-AFTRA.

"citizen-politician": Cannon, *Governor Reagan,* p. 82.

His audience: Ibid., pp. 208–9.

While acknowledging: Ibid.

When asked by Robert Stripling: Ibid.

two-week stand: Morris, *Dutch,* p. 295.

"It's a long way": Ibid.

Within weeks Reagan began: Eliot, *Reagan,* p. 275.

first and only continuing host: Thomas W. Evans, *The Education of Ronald Reagan: The General Electric Years and the Untold Story of His Conversion to Conservatism* (New York: Columbia University Press, 2006), p. 3.

Airing on Sundays: Eliot, *Reagan,* p. 276.

James Dean: Evans, *The Education of Ronald Reagan,* p. 57.

Natalie Wood: Suzanne Finstad, *Natasha: The Biography of Natalie Wood* (New York: Three Rivers Press, 2001), p. 158.

Lee Marvin: Robert J. Lentz, *Lee Marvin: His Films and Career* (Jefferson, NC: McFarland & Company, 2006), p. 194.

Sammy Davis, Jr.: Gary Fishgall, *Gonna Do Great Things: The Life of Sammy Davis, Jr.* (New York: Scribner, 2003), pp. 123–24.

Over the eight years it ran: Encyclopedia of Television: A–C (volume 1), Horace Newcomb, ed. (London: Routledge, 2004), p. 968.

Bill Clinton: Newsweek, June 21, 2004.

Traveling to hundreds of cities and towns: Morris, *Dutch,* p. 305.

"I am seen by more people": Ibid., pp. 304–5.

As of 1958 he was one: Ibid., p. 305.

at least a quarter of a million of them: Reagan, *An American Life,* p. 128.

the relationship ended abruptly in 1962: Eliot, *Reagan,* p. 325.

In 1964 Ronald Reagan emerged: Ibid., p. 112.

What brought him this: Ibid., pp. 123–25.

the Goldwater campaign paid to have it nationally televised: Eliot, *Reagan,* pp. 333–34.

"a rendezvous with destiny": Reagan speech, October 27, 1964.

It was a speech he'd been polishing: Eliot, *Reagan,* p. 333.

When Reagan ran: Cannon, *Governor Reagan,* p. 160.

To denigrate Reagan's profession: Ibid., p. 116.

a televised campaign ad: Ibid., p. 151.

"As a politician": Reagan, *My Father At 100,* p. 24.

"The man who has *the job":* Cannon, *Governor Reagan,* p. 149.

that July night in 1980: Reagan Speech, Republican National Convention, July 17, 1980.

Chapter Eight: The Rise of Tip O'Neill

"All politics is local": Tip credited his father for the famous motto. Author John A. Farrell said it was a familiar phrase in Massachusetts during the younger O'Neill's upbringing. However, there's been speculation tying the motto to Finley Peter Dunne's "Mr. Dooley." His biographer Edward J. Bander has said this is not the case.

When he was tapped: Author interview with Tom Foley.

His father, Thomas: Farrell, *Tip O'Neill,* p. 35.

He was only nine months old: Ibid., p. 49
Young O'Neill remembered: Ibid.
O'Neill found warmth: Ibid., p. 42.
Tip's own lifelong moniker: Ibid., p. 13.
Here's Tip's own version: MOH, pp. 6–7.
A year later: Farrell, p. 51.
spoke out forcefully for workplace: https://
www.osha.gov/oas/
trianglefactoryfireaccount.html.
Unlike his brother William: Farrell, p. 35
While he was still a senior: Ibid., p. 64.
Two maxims he heard: Ibid., p. 65.
According to Thomas Sr.: Ibid.
what Tip should have done: Ibid.
The second lesson: MOH, p. 26.
"Tom, let me tell you something": Ibid.
In 1934 Tip was given: MOH, p. 3.
A year after she'd gone to work: Jean Edward
Smith, *FDR* (New York: Random House,
2007), p. xv.
Now, Tip, thanks to: MOH, p. 3.
Tip felt honor-bound: Farrell, p. 80.
"Tom was never much of a": People, August
18, 1980.
In 1941, Tip married: Farrell, p. 83.
He'd timed the wedding to occur: Farrell, p.
84.
Resuming their honeymoon: Ibid.
"Through the chairs": Hedrick Smith inter-
view with Tip O'Neill.

"worked your way up through the vineyards": MOH, p. 73.

A wild card suddenly appeared: Ibid.

"I had never lived very much": Miller Center, Presidential Recordings Program, JFK, dictabelt 39.

He, like Tip, was: MOH, p. 73.

"By the time I met Jack Kennedy": Ibid.

"dirtiest campaign you ever saw": MOH, p. 84.

Tip soon became: Farrell, p. 144.

To make up for his regular: Farrell, p. 146.

rooming with another freshman: Farrell, p. 140.

"Incidentally, I'm absolutely convinced": MOH, p. 147.

"I never want to see": Jimmy Breslin, *How The Good Guys Finally Won* (New York: The Viking Press, 1975), p. 68.

"Some fellas like women": Farrell, p. 496.

The only problem with him: MOH, p. 157.

One week he passed on word: Ibid., p. 158.

O'Neill, agreeing that this was fair: Ibid.

However, with his stance: MOH, pp. 189–206, Farrell, pp. 217–26.

"Take the gavel": New York Times, February 6, 2000.

Grabbing the microphone: Farrell, p. 287.

Putting down the future: Ibid., p. 290.

"You haven't got an enemy": Ibid., p. 322.

It had all begun: Ibid., pp. 346–47.

On August 8, 1974: Ibid., p. 380.

"Jerry, isn't this": MOH, pp. 266–67.

"Although I thought the pardon": MOH, p. 268.

Two years later: Farrell, p. 408.

I was in the room: Author interview with Tom Foley.

Chapter Nine: Hero

"The happy ending is our national belief": Mary McCarthy.

"Well I expect that smiling": TPO, April 7, 1981.

"Tip was in Pago Pago": Farrell, *Tip O'Neill,* p. 555.

"I'm having more luck": RR, April 22, 1981.

"Because of the attempted": TPO, April 28, 1981.

"The warmth of your words": Reagan speech to joint session of Congress, April 28, 1981.

"This is only the first skirmish": TPO, May 1, 1981.

"I was overjoyed to see": TPO, Remarks on the President's Speech, April 28, 1981.

"It is unfortunate in the": Ibid.

"I have been saying all": TPO, April 29, 1981.

"We stroked and we stroked": Farrell, *Tip*

O'Neill, p. 551.

recalls getting an urgent: Author conversation with Hedrick Smith.

"Tenderhearted and sentimental": Reagan, *My Father at 100,* p. 9.

"More meetings with": RR, May 6, 1981.

"to have someone explain": TPO, May 1, 1981.

"This was the big day": RR, May 7, 1981.

"I'm getting the shit": Farrell, *Tip O'Neill,* p. 558.

"I'm not talking": TPO, May 13, 1981.

Chapter Ten: Fighting Season

"Courage for some sudden act": Anthony Eden on Winston Churchill.

"At that moment": Time, May 18, 1981.

"I've always suspected": Reagan speech at Notre Dame, May 17, 1981.

"Now, today I hear": Ibid.

"For too long government": Ibid.

"I'm opposed to the": ABC, *Issues and Answers,* June 7, 1981.

"his lifestyle": Ibid.

"Consequently, he doesn't": Ibid.

Steven V. Roberts: New York Times, June 9, 1981.

"Tip O'Neill says you don't": Presidential press conference, June 16, 1981.

"Tip O'Neill has said": Ibid.

"And I know very much": Ibid.

"Let it go, Tom": This was his longtime friend and senior aide, Leo Diehl.

He'd had his political heroes: Farrell, p. 80.

"I would never accuse a president": Ibid., p. 574.

"Well, I'd have to say": Washington Post, June 17, 1981.

Reagan phoned the Speaker: Farrell, p. 574.

"Old buddy," the Speaker replied: Ibid.

"Politiburo of the Welfare State": HS, *Power Game*, p. 522.

"Hogarthian embodiment of the superstate": David Stockman, *The Triumph of Politics: Why the Reagan Revolution Failed* (New York: Public Affairs, 2013), p. 129.

The president, out of patience: Farrell, p. 559.

"Did you ever hear of the separation of powers?": Ibid.

"I was a Democrat myself": HS, *Power Game*, p. 515.

That night, in his diary: RR, June 18, 1981.

"Tip O'Neill is getting rough": RR, June 23, 1981.

In an extraordinary step: Farrell, p. 560; Associated Press, June 26, 1981.

But Reagan's big victory: Farrell, pp. 559–60.

It meant that three million seniors: United Press International, June 25, 1981.

On July 7, 1981, President Ronald Reagan: RR, July 7, 1981.

"the best thing he'd done since he was inaugurated": TPO, July 8, 1981.

Chapter Eleven: Battlefield Promotion

"I still believe that": Ted Sorensen, *Counselor* (New York: HarperCollins, 2008), p. 531.

"House Speaker Thomas": Washington Post, July 9, 1981.

here's how Tip: HS interview with O'Neill, Library of Congress, pp. 69–70.

"The interesting factor": HS interview with O'Neill, Library of Congress, p. 15.

"Six-thirty a": RR, July 22, 1981.

"This on top of the budget": Ibid., July 29, 1981.

"Is Tip O'Neill ready": New York Times Magazine, August 16, 1981.

"What I had to get used": MOH, p. 351.

David Rogers, an astute: Boston Globe, July 31, 1981.

"I sure as hell hope": Farrell, *Tip O'Neill,* p. 561.

Chapter Twelve: Turning

"Learned the Air Controllers": RR, August 2, 1981.

"The strike was called": Ibid., August 3, 1981.

Future Federal Reserve: The Reagan Legacy, Remarks of Alan Greenspan, Ronald Reagan Library, April 9, 2003.

"If these numbers were out": Richard Darman, *Who's in Control? Polar Politics and the Sensible Center* (New York: Simon & Schuster, 1996), p. 94.

"I'm withdrawing Soc. Security": RR, September 23, 1981.

"I'm encouraged that between us": Ibid., August 5, 1981.

"It's hard to describe": Ibid., October 6, 1981.

"We haven't obstructed": TPO, August 4, 1981.

"They got their cuts": Ibid., September 9, 1981.

Look what they get for it: Ibid., October 1, 1981.

Jakie Bloom was: MOH, p. 312.

"The Education of": Atlantic, December 1, 1981.

"If true": RR, November 11, 1981.

"Dave, in his heart": TPO, November 12, 1981.

"I think he's going to remain": *Washington Post,* November 8, 1981.

"Tip, if I had a": Farrell, *Tip O'Neill,* p. 621.

"Reagan," Deaver said: Ibid.

"Tip was an old-fashioned pol": Reagan, *An American Life,* p. 250.

His son Ron believed: Author conversation with Ron Reagan.

Chapter Thirteen: Summit

"Welcome, Mr. President": Chris Matthews, *Hardball: How Politics Is Played, Told by One Who Knows the Game* (New York: Summit Books, 1988), p. 37.

"I wonder if I'll ever get": RR, January 26, 1982.

"I've made a mil. speeches": Ibid.

"There has been some talk": TPO, January 28, 1982.

"Met with bi-partisan": RR, February 8, 1982.

"There is unrest among": Ibid., February 11, 1982.

"Tomorrow we begin": CJM.

"President hit hard": Ibid.

"I was the lone voice": TPO, January 25, 1982.

"He thought that Baker was": Author conver-

sation with Rosemary O'Neill.

"I think we should not": CJM.

"I called Tip O'Neill": RR, April 20, 1982.

"I'm slipping badly": Ibid., April 2, 1982.

Reagan began making: Ibid., April 3, 1982.

"Toby Moffett": CJM.

"After 45 years in": Washington Post, April 22, 1982.

"The D's are playing games": RR, April 26, 1982.

"I've read that crap": Reeves, *President Reagan*, p. 121.

"You can get me to": Farrell, *Tip O'Neill*, p. 588.

"I wasn't any more": TPO, April 29, 1982.

Within days after our: New York Times, April 29, 1982.

For Mike Deaver: Author conversation with Carolyn Deaver.

Chapter Fourteen: Partners

"The future of this economy is now in the hands of Tip O'Neill": Reeves, *President Reagan*, p. 122.

"I don't think he": TPO, May 25, 1982.

"We would go in and want": Author interview with Max Friedersdorf.

"It may be easier": United Press International, May 4, 1982.

"an aging prizefighter": Wall Street Journal, June 18, 1982.

"When I see him": United Press International, June 27, 1982.

"World's Record Apple Pie": New York Times, July 2, 1982.

"It's time for the doubters to eat humble pie": Ibid.

"As the Senator spoke": Ibid.

"people's crusade": Washington Post, July 20, 1982.

"It's like the saloon keeper": Associated Press, July 20, 1982.

"sneak attack": New York Times, July 20, 1982.

"Wake up, Mr. President!": United Press International, August 4, 1982.

"More than 200 members": Associated Press, August 4, 1982.

"Every time I ask": TPO, August 13, 1982.

"tax bill": RR, June 22, July 19, August 2, and August 4, 1982.

"I want him to use that smiling countenance": TPO, July 29, 1982.

"Senator Dole has shown": Ibid., August 3, 1982.

"The Republicans are not for": Ibid., July 28, 1982.

"Met with Jack Kemp": RR, August 4, 1982.

"There is a rumor": Ibid., August 10, 1982.

"Some of the people": TPO, August 17, 1982.

"The tax bill will not repeal": Ibid., August 18, 1982.

"Congress cannot with one vote": Ibid., August 18, 1982.

"Interesting photo opportunity": RR, August 18, 1982.

"Nancy wasn't alone": Ibid., August 19, 1982.

"Did you hear that the Irish": Farrell, *Tip O'Neill,* p. 589.

"bipartisanship can be fun": Washington Post, August 24, 1982.

"It happened last Thursday": Ibid.

"You are here because of Reagan": Ibid.

"If he could put aside": Ibid.

Chapter Fifteen: Tip at the Top

twelve seats: TPO, statement from November 2, and attached Democratic Policy Committee one-sheet from October 26, 1982.

"political tactic": Ibid., September 9, 1982.

"The president would rather": Ibid.

"The politics of the veto": Ibid., Letter from Democratic Leadership, September 8, 1982.

"prize bull": New York Times, September 10, 1982.

"billion-dollar ballot box bailout bill": Ibid., September 17, 1982.

"Voters across America": Reagan Remarks and a Question-and-Answer Session With Reporters Following the House of Representatives Vote on the Proposed Constitutional Amendment for a Balanced Federal Budget, October 1, 1982.

"stonewalling": Ibid.

"boosted the stock": Washington Post, October 2, 1982.

"Somebody told me": Reagan Remarks, Rally for Texas Republican Candidates in Irving, Texas, October 11, 1982.

"In Washington, the nine heavenly bodies": United Press International, October 29, 1982.

"Your heart would die for them": Farrell, *Tip O'Neill,* p. 594.

"tell them that Tip O'Neill": Ibid.

Franklin Roosevelt: Reagan Radio Address to the Nation on the Economy, October 16, 1982.

"fear": Reagan Radio Address to the Nation on Economic and Budget Issues, October 23, 1982.

"Democrats took the offensive": Washington Post, October 24, 1982.

REAGAN AND O'NEILL EXCHANGE

CHARGES: *New York Times,* October 24, 1982.

"Not long ago": Associated Press, October 29, 1982.

GOP fund-raising letter: TPO Press Collection.

"big, fat and out of control": Farrell, *Tip O'Neill,* p. 595.

pin a REPEAL O'NEILL *campaign button: Washington Post,* November 4, 1982.

"I wouldn't know him from a cord of wood": Farrell, *Tip O'Neill,* p. 595.

"For a while there": Interview with Robert Mrazek, originally for *Hardball* book.

"We don't want anyone to eat crow": TPO, November 3, 1982.

"They are an odd couple": New York Times, November 28, 1982.

Chapter Sixteen: Deal

"If we are truly": U.S. News & World Report, December 27, 1982.

"The old-age trust fund": Washington Post, November 7, 1982.

"Administration sources have suggested": Ibid., January 3, 1983.

Back in December: TPO, December 7, 1982.

"Reagan's Faithful Allies": New York Times, January 3, 1983.

"Are we going to let this commission die": Farrell, *Tip O'Neill,* p. 601.

"He didn't make a move that": Conversation with Jack Lew.

"the same old political football": *New York Times,* January 6, 1983.

"I'm not going to make choices": Ibid., January 16, 1983.

"Reagan's wariness of Social Security": Ibid.

"We weren't going to put our head": Jack Beatty, ed., *Pols: Great Writers on American Politicians from Bryan to Reagan* (New York: Public Affairs, 2004), p. 445.

"It is my understanding": Reagan statement on receiving the recommendations of the National Commission on Social Security Reform, January 15, 1983.

"acceptable to the president": TPO, January 15, 1983.

"S.S. team came by": RR, January 15, 1983.

"It was very helpful to have": *New York Times,* January 19, 2010.

"More than any other event": Robert Ball, "Restoring Financial Stability to Social Security," www.ssa.gov/history/50rb.html.

"all together": RR, January 17, 1983.

"we in government": Reagan Address Before a Joint Session of the Congress on the State of the Union, January 25, 1983.

"And here all the time": Ibid.

"But you understand": Reagan Remarks and a Question-and-Answer Session With Reporters on Domestic and Foreign Policy Issues, February 4, 1983.

"Oh, you've sold out": Ibid.

"He spoke of creating jobs": TPO, January 26, 1983.

"I will probably kick myself": Washington Post, January 27, 1983.

"On the same day": Newsweek, February 7, 1983.

"Well, I said": Ibid.

"God damn it, Tip": Farrell, *Tip O'Neill,* pp. 599–600.

"Tip & I": RR, January 31, 1983.

"the toughest going-over": Farrell, *Tip O'Neill,* pp. 599–600.

"just two Irishmen plotting": Time, February 21, 1983.

"Whether this means a ray of hope": TPO, January 31, 1983.

"We stand ready": Ibid., February 8, 1983.

"I understand he's getting married": Ibid., February 10, 1983.

"When I met with President Reagan": Ibid.

Chapter Seventeen: Lebanon and Grenada

"What I am": Reagan address to British Parliament, June 8, 1982.

It had actually been: Arthur Vandenberg speech to the Senate, January 10, 1945.

"Why are we there?": Farrell, *Tip O'Neill,* p. 612.

Two days later: Cannon, *President Reagan,* p. 356.

"If he asks my views": TPO, July 13, 1982.

As Tip O'Neill put it: Ibid., September 12, 1983.

"That country is coming apart": Author witnessed Rep. Foley's remark.

"If it were for six months": TPO, September 20, 1983.

"I believe the president": Washington Post, September 29, 1983.

It was Democratic congressman: Ibid.

"He was grateful": TPO, September 29, 1983.

"I was doing my duty": Ibid.

"The important thing": New York Times, October 13, 1983.

"I've OK'd an outright": RR, October 21, 1983.

On Sunday: Ibid., Saturday, October 22– Sunday, October 23.

The FBI described: Cannon, *President Reagan,* p. 386.

"He spoke of an agreement": MOH, p. 363.

"Phoned Tip & Howard": RR, October 24, 1983.

Author interview with Ken Duberstein.

"I am bitterly disappointed": TPO, October 25, 1983.

"The resolution would be": TPO, October 26, 1983.

"The people of America": Ibid.

"I will have plenty": Ibid.

"The question I asked": Ibid., October 28, 1983.

"He broke international": Ibid.

"Nobody wants to cut": Ibid.

"Today I feel even more": MOH, pp. 366–67.

The Speaker was: New York Times, November 1, 1983.

"Dropped in for a minute": RR, January 25, 1984.

"We took up the business": Ibid., January 26, 1984.

"I gave a little lecture": Ibid., January 27, 1984.

"Campaign time is coming": Ibid.

"One night, at a social": MOH, p. 364.

"Aiding and abetting": New York Times, February 3, 1984.

"He may be ready to": Wall Street Journal, February 16, 1984.

"The deaths lie on him": New York Times, April 6, 1984.

Chapter Eighteen: Victory and Survival

"I don't need you": Farrell, p. 507.

In February 1984: New York Times, February 29, 1984.

"See what happens": TPO, March 1, 1984.

"My wife said to me": Ibid.

Nevertheless he called: MOH, p. 372.

His son Michael: Dutch, p. 318.

In March 1984: New Republic, March 26, 1984.

"We threw up a partition": Matthews, *Hardball,* p. 170.

"I think it will go": TPO, March 14, 1984.

"We have the Boston Marathon": Ibid., February 29, 1984.

"Well, he still calls me": Ibid., January 30, 1984.

"On St. Patrick's Day": Ibid., February 22, 1984.

"I must not be too bright": Letter to President Reagan from Jerry Granat, April 9, 1984.

"You challenged their": Time, May 28, 1984.

"I was expressing": Ibid.

As Billy Pitts would: Farrell, *Tip O'Neill,* p. 635.

Not content to stop there: Washington Post, May 6, 1984.

"Whether or not Mr. O'Neill": Washington Post, June 21, 1985.

"Sure I have a candidate": *Time,* June 4, 1984.

"Sure she's pushy": Matthews, *Hardball,* p. 72.

"She has a lot of political": Associated Press, May 4, 1984.

"I was sitting in the broadcast": *MOH,* p. 359.

Worse was the: *Wall Street Journal,* October 9, 1984.

"If the point of this": Ibid.

"I never realized how easy": Cannon, *President Reagan,* p. 480.

"Well, the debate took place": RR, October 6–7, 1984.

"Another disastrous performance": Reagan, *An American Life,* p. 328.

"I want you to know": Reagan-Mondale debate, October 21, 1984.

when away from the Capitol: *MOH,* p. 359.

"Well 49 states": RR, November 7, 1984.

the usual crew: Farrell, p. 652.

The public inaugural was moved back a day because January 20 happened to fall on a Sunday in 1985.

"In my fifty years in public": Morris, *Dutch,* p. 512.

Chapter Nineteen: Mikhail Gorbachev

"long twilight struggle": John F. Kennedy, Inaugural Address, January 20, 1961.

"that, through misunderstanding": Reagan, *My Father at 100*, p. 207.

"What's so good about a peace": Weekly Standard, June 25, 2012.

"Address to the Nation on National Security": Reagan Address to the Nation on Defense and National Security, March 23, 1983.

"I've become more and more": Ibid.

Back in the spring of 1983: Time, May 16, 1983.

"an answer to arms control": Ibid.

"evil empire": Reagan Address to the National Association of Evangelicals, March 8, 1983.

"He says he is very curious": RR, January 5, 1982.

"I was right not to go": Ibid., November 16, 1982.

"Geo. Shultz sneaked": Ibid., February 15, 1983.

"There is possibility": Ibid., May 13, 1983.

"Expressed a desire": Ibid., August 7, 1983.

"George S. & I met and discussed": Ibid., February 22, 1984.

"gut feeling": Ibid., February 22, March 1, and June 14, 1984.

"He confirmed my": Ibid., March 5, 1984.

"evidence of not being well": Ibid., June 26, 1984.

"I was not and never have been": New York Times, April 24, 2006.

"restricted area": Newsweek, April 8, 1985.

The House voted to authorize: Los Angeles Times, March 28, 1985.

"But right down to the wire": RR, March 28, 1985.

"In thirty-two years": TPO, March 27, 1985.

"If the president": Ibid., March 26, 1985.

"Just wanted a last": RR, April 3, 1985.

"a particularly credible messenger": Farrell, *Tip O'Neill,* p. 662.

"I'm going to tell him": Associated Press, April 8, 1985.

"We have a mutual friend": Ibid., November 12, 1985.

"I'm part of the opposition": Newsweek, April 22, 1985.

"We're trying to understand what the position": Ibid.

"There's a big difference": Ibid.

"I remember when I went in": Congressional Record, November 13, 1985.

"New York lawyer": Los Angeles Times, April 11, 1985.

"master of words": Newsweek, April 22, 1985.

"had a flair": Associated Press, November 12, 1985.

"I think it augurs": Ibid., April 8, 1985.

"The president will be able": Ibid., November 12, 1985.

"It was hard to be impressed": MOH, pp. 294–95.

"I'll never forget the ride into Moscow": Ibid.

"We need to clear the decks": TPO, November 12, 1985.

"When President Reagan meets": Ibid., November 13, 1985.

"I don't want to send the president": Newsweek, November 25, 1985.

"where I hope to get Gorbachev": RR, November 17, 1985.

"He had to know we": Reagan, *An American Life,* p. 14.

"gold rubles": Farrell, *Tip O'Neill,* p. 663.

"It's not convincing": Cannon, *President Reagan,* p. 674.

"That evening it was our turn": Reagan, *An American Life,* p. 639.

"In an unusual procedure": TPO, November 21, 1985.

"I expect a full report": Ibid.

"You can't imagine": Address Before a Joint Session of the Congress Following the Soviet–United States Summit Meeting in Geneva, November 21, 1985.

"good listener": Ibid.
"I haven't gotten": RR, November 21, 1985.
"The gallery were full": Ibid.
"heartbreaking": Farrell, *Tip O'Neill,* p. 664.
"This": Morris, *Dutch,* p. 599.

Chapter Twenty: Hurrah!

raised Protestant by his Scots-English: Cannon, *Governor Reagan,* p. 14; Eliot, *Reagan,* p. 14; Reagan, *An American Life,* p. 22.
"I knew I was Irish": MOH, p. 7.
NO IRISH NEED APPLY: Ibid., p. 9.
O'Neill had loyally supported: Farrell, *Tip O'Neill,* p. 510.
Dubbed the "Four Horsemen": Edward M. Kennedy Institute.
"part of our blood": Associated Press, June 2, 1984.
"I'm proud that": Reagan speech in Dublin, June 4, 1984.
"All sides should have": Ibid.
"When he was in America": Reagan, Address Before a Joint Session of the Irish National Parliament, June 4, 1984.
The following month: Farrell, *Tip O'Neill,* p. 623.
personal letter from Tip: The White House, Memorandum of Conversation, December

28, 1984.

The president followed through: Farrell, *Tip O'Neill,* pp. 623–624.

On November 15: Ibid., p. 624.

"His feeling changed": Author conversation with Tom O'Neill.

The State of the Union address was postponed: Reagan, *An American Life,* p. 403.

"We've grown used to wonders": Reagan televised address, January 28, 1986.

"I know it is hard to understand": Ibid.

"As I listened to him": MOH, p. 363.

He then called: Author conversation with Peggy Noonan.

Chapter Twenty-One: Common Ground

"There is no limit": Cannon, *President Reagan,* p. 154.

Tip O'Neill made no: MOH, pp. 371–72.

"Still, after half a": Ibid., p. 372.

in 1935: Farrell, *Tip O'Neill,* p. 64.

His retirement season climaxed: Ibid., p. 674.

on the evening of March: Associated Press, March 17, 1986.

Washington Hilton: Washington Post, March 18, 1986.

honor him: Associated Press, March 17, 1986.

proceeds of which would: Ibid., March 18, 1986.

the 2,200 gathered: Ibid.

president Gerald Ford: Washington Post, March 18, 1986.

Irish prime minister: Ibid.

Senator Edward M. Kennedy: Ibid.

Bob Hope: Ibid.

"centerpiece": Thomas P. O'Neill III, *New York Times,* October 5, 2012.

There he stood in the ballroom: Associated Press, March 17, 1986.

"But to be honest, I've": Reagan speech, March 17, 1986.

"I have traveled": Washington Post, March 18, 1986.

"Mr. President": United Press International, March 18, 1986.

"You're a beautiful individual": Associated Press, March 17, 1986.

to Venezuela, Brazil, and: Ibid.

from early 1985 on: Author conversation with Hedrick Smith.

to make his mark: Farrell, *Tip O'Neill,* p. 659.

The measure he advanced: Ibid.

with Reagan's blessing: Ibid.

reducing the number: Baker, *Work Hard,* p. 232.

15 and 28 percent: Ibid.

it raised the rate: New York Times, June 8, 1989.

"the whole system": Cannon, *President Reagan,* p. 499.

For several nervous days: Baker, *Work Hard,* pp. 226–28.

A vote late in 1985: Farrell, *Tip O'Neill,* p. 660.

"voted to humiliate": Baker, *Work Hard,* p. 229.

The Speaker agreed: Farrell, *Tip O'Neill,* p. 660.

The night that: Ibid.

agreed-upon deadline: Baker, *Work Hard,* p. 229.

"Four frustrating hours": Ibid., p. 231.

"Three times he called": Farrell, *Tip O'Neill,* p. 660.

"an excellent speech": Baker, *Work Hard,* p. 231.

by seventy Republicans: Farrell, *Tip O'Neill,* p. 660.

to be his major second-term: Baker, *Work Hard,* p. 217.

"as beloved a leader": MOH, p. 330.

"the worst": Ibid., p. 360.

"out of touch": Ibid., p. 331.

"tremendous powers of": Ibid., p. 341.

"agreeable man": Ibid., p. 360.

"pretty good friendship": Ibid., p. 333.

"After the vote": Ibid., p. 374.

Chapter Twenty-Two: Last Battle

Back in the 1980s: Chris Matthews, *The New Republic,* March 2, 1987.

son of Irish: New York Times, November 6, 2011.

"a touchstone of his career": Ibid., November 6, 2001.

"We bought it": Cannon, *President Reagan,* p. 296.

Two months later: Ibid., p. 330.

"There is a totalitarian government": New York Times, July 1, 1984.

"If Congress says you can't": Cannon, *President Reagan,* p. 332.

"It is possible": Tayacan, *Psychological Operations in Guerrilla Warfare,* translated and published by the Congressional Research Service, October 15, 1984.

According to a White House: New York Times, October 19, 1984.

"It is nothing short of outrageous": Ibid.

"The president of the United States": Reeves, *President Reagan,* p. 253.

"I saw that picture and I'm told": MOH, p. 368.

"Tip has engineered a partisan campaign": RR, April 24, 1985.

President Daniel Ortega now made a startling

gesture: Reeves,*President Reagan,* p. 255.

"When that happened it was only a matter": MOH, p. 368.

"He is not going to be happy": New York Times, June 13, 1985.

"We send money and material now": Ronald Reagan speech, March 5, 1986.

"If we don't want to see": Ibid.

Time *described how: Time,* March 17, 1986.

"You can appreciate how hard I'm working": Farrell, *Tip O'Neill,* p. 671.

"dark day for freedom": Newsweek, March 31, 1986.

Chief of Staff Don Regan was the one: MOH, pp. 368–69.

"to participate in open dialogue": Associated Press, June 23, 1986.

"There's no question about it": United Press International, June 24, 1986.

"Tip refused to let me speak": RR, June 23, 1986.

noontime broadcast: National Journal, June 28, 1986.

"NSC Briefing": RR, December 5, 1985.

"I had a feeling": Donald Regan, *For the Record* (New York: Harcourt, 1988), pp. 41–43.

Chapter Twenty-Three: Legacy

"Let us endeavor": Shapiro, *The Yale Book of Quotations,* p. 777.

though the fallout: New York Times, December 2, 1986.

Geneva in 1985: Reeves, *President Reagan,* p. 280.

Reykjavik in 1986: Ibid., p. 340.

Washington in 1987: Ibid., p. 435.

Moscow in 1988: Ibid., p. 448.

Within a year of Reagan's leaving office: Cannon, *President Reagan,* p. xii.

for almost three decades: "Brutal Divide: LIFE at the Birth of the Berlin Wall," http://life.time.com/history/berlin-wall-photos-early-days-of-the-cold-war/#1.

"Not with a bang but a whimper": Shapiro, *The Yale Book of Quotations,* p. 237.

in 1987: Reagan speech, West Berlin, June 12, 1987.

"We welcome change": Ibid.

"for we believe": Ibid.

in late 1986: The Harris Survey (ISSN: 0273-1037), November 24, 1986.

"I was almost": MOH, p. 374.

Tip for thirty-four: Ibid., p. 3.

man's father, still in: New York Times, December 8, 1993.

"Reagan took Congress": MOH, p. 341.

St. John's High School: Ibid., p. 20.

"Chris, it goes away": Author conversation with Tip O'Neill.

He died in January 1994: Farrell, *Tip O'Neill,* pp. 689–90.

Reagan began his fade: Cannon, *President Reagan,* p. xiv.

handwritten letter: Ibid.

Alzheimer's disease: Ibid., p. xv.

"I only wish there was some way": Morris, *Dutch,* p. 666.

George Washington and Pierre L'Enfant: Washington Diary, June 28, 1791.

PHOTO CREDITS

Chris Matthews: 18, 42, 94, 454

Courtesy Ronald Reagan Library: 56, 118, 218, 492

Associated Press: 78, 190, 334, 362, 412 (bottom), 522, 550, 574

Getty Images: 132, 242, 266, 292, 536

Box 4, Folder 1, Thomas P. O'Neill, Jr. Congressional Papers (CA2009-01), John J. Burns Library, Boston College: 158

White House Photo: 388

Stuart Franklin/Magnum Photos: 412 (top)

ABOUT THE AUTHOR

Chris Matthews is the host of MSNBC's *Hardball.* His most recent bestseller is *Jack Kennedy: Elusive Hero,* which spent three months on the *New York Times* bestseller list. He is also the author of *Hardball; Kennedy and Nixon; Now, Let Me Tell You What I Really Think;* and *American: Beyond Our Grandest Notions.*